Uncomfortable Wars Revisited

International and Security Affairs Series

Edwin G. Corr, General Editor

Uncomfortable Wars Revisited

John T. Fishel and
Max G. Manwaring

Foreword and Afterword
by Edwin G. Corr

University of Oklahoma Press : Norman

Library of Congress Cataloging-in-Publication Data

Fishel, John T.
   Uncomfortable wars revisited / John T. Fishel and Max G. Manwaring;
foreword and afterword by Edwin G. Corr.
       p.   cm. — (International and security affairs series; v. 2)
   Includes bibliographical references and index.
   ISBN 0–8061–3711–8 (alk. paper)
      1. Low-intensity conflicts (Military science). 2. National security—United
States. 3. Security, International. 4. Strategy. 5. United States—Foreign rela-
tions—2001–. 6. United States—Military policy. 7. World politics—21st century.
8. Uncomfortable wars. I. Manwaring, Max G. II. Title. III. Series.

   U240.F58 2006
   355.02'18—dc22
                                                                    2005053899

Uncomfortable Wars Revisted is Volume 2 in the International and Security Affairs
Series.

1 2 3 4 5 6 7 8 9 10

CONTENTS

FOREWORD

EDWIN G. CORR

This highly significant book is a synthesis of the most important body of thought and literature on national security strategy, policy, and implementation that has emerged over the past two decades to guide the United States in its conduct of foreign policy and war in an increasingly dangerous and changed world. The Manwaring Paradigm, or the SWORD Model, as it is most often called in this volume, has gained acceptance among leading thinkers on national security—both practitioners and academics—in the United States. The paradigm is the basis for a number of scholarly books and articles. It has become a part of the core curriculum at military universities, schools, and training institutions of the U.S. armed forces and national security community. The paradigm and the suppositions derived from it have been incorporated into U.S. Army and U.S. Air Force doctrine in field manuals and texts.[1] In a very real sense this paradigm—originally set forth by Max Manwaring and subsequently elaborated and refined by him, John Fishel, a core group of intellectually close professional colleagues and practitioners, and a number of other contributors—is increasingly assuming the role in national security thinking and action today that George Kennan's policy of containment played throughout the half-century of the cold war.

Though already initially articulated in documents of the Small Wars Operations Research Directorate (SWORD) of the U.S. Southern

Command, the Manwaring Paradigm formally made its debut to the academic community and public in a book edited by Max Manwaring entitled *Uncomfortable Wars: Toward a New Paradigm of Low Intensity Conflict* (1991). In the foreword to that volume I described it as one "that should become a landmark and standard study in America's efforts to cope successfully with what is now officially termed 'low intensity conflict'" (p. xi). In *Uncomfortable Wars Revisited,* Manwaring and Fishel extend, sharpen, refine, and improve the founding concepts of the Manwaring Paradigm. They further demonstrate its validity as an over-arching framework for analyzing and conducting national security in the disorderly, threatening world of the twenty-first century.

Low-intensity conflict in the earlier book clearly included intrastate wars, terrorism, narcotics control, and international crime. In subsequent articles and books written or edited by Manwaring, Fishel, and other members of the core group that have elaborated on and refined the Manwaring Paradigm, its precepts have been applied productively to peacekeeping, peace enforcing, and homeland defense. It has proven applicable and effective for all types of conflicts other than major wars, as well as for the occupation periods of all modern wars. The paradigm is particularly relevant to our current occupation of Iraq and the global war against terrorism. Kimbra Fishel, an academic who is married to John Fishel, uses the SWORD Model to analyze and prescribe actions to counter nonstate actors (Al Qaeda and other globally affiliated terrorist groups) that threaten the continuance of the predominant world system that has been based on states since the Treaty of Westphalia of 1648.[2]

This book is thus an integrated, coherent, and concentrated presentation of the important body of study and thought that increasingly guides, and should guide, U.S. foreign policy and national security strategy. Twenty years of testing, revising, refining, and elaborating the Manwaring Paradigm make this book more enlightening and valuable than the 1991 pioneering presentation. It will be cited for many years to come as the embodiment of national security thinking of this period.

The term "uncomfortable wars" may have first appeared in print in 1986 in an article by General John Galvin, based on his Kermit Roosevelt Lecture in the United Kingdom earlier the same year.[3] Galvin called for "a new paradigm that addresses all the dimensions of the conflicts that may be ahead; and for changes in the preparation of military officers that would enable them to adapt to the changed nature of warfare." He also emphasized the societal dimensions of contemporary conflict and the "triangular nature of conflict that involves the government and its armed forces, the enemy and the people." At the time General Galvin gave these lectures, he was serving as the commander of the U.S. Southern Command (he later was commander of the U.S. European Command and of the North Atlantic Treaty Organization).

Heeding General Galvin's call for a new paradigm, Max Manwaring responded by drawing upon the theoretical work and research he and a team had been conducting under the auspices of the U.S. Army at the Army War College and at the Southern Command. Manwaring recruited practitioners John Fishel, General Galvin, General Fred F. Woerner, Wm. J. Olson, Court Prisk, and myself to write chapters for *Uncomfortable Wars: Toward a New Paradigm of Low Intensity Development.*

The development of the Manwaring Paradigm, referred to in the *New York Times* as "the Max Factors," had its roots in the United States' consistent and growing entanglement in intrastate wars and low-intensity conflicts during much of the cold war. The top U.S. government and armed forces leadership and the American public were less preoccupied with and gave less priority, attention, resources, and thought to our participation in low-intensity conflict and terrorism than they did to the potential nuclear war with the United Soviet Socialist Republic. Yet, as I wrote in the conclusion (p. 127) to Manwaring's edited volume approximately fifteen years ago,

> America's principal defense priority during the last forty years has been the management of low probability, high intensity nuclear conflict with a primary focus on Europe. Yet, ironically, nearly all the armed conflicts during that time have taken place in the Third World and have been classified as low intensity. With the exception of the tragic Vietnam experience—and in large part because of it—the United States has been slow to come to grips with this problem. We have been slow to adapt our thinking, organization, and resource allocations to high probability, low intensity conflict where our military's role is usually relatively

small and indirect, and where extraordinary support is required
for civilian authorities in their development efforts.

The Gulf War of 1991, the Afghanistan War, and the invasion of Iraq
belie the view expressed above that the United States' role in contemporary conflicts is likely to be somewhat limited militarily (in terms of
numbers and costs), but they emphatically demonstrate the need for the
U.S. government to be involved in counterinsurgency, governance, and
peacekeeping activities. Moreover, given the impacting budgetary and
human costs, it seems likely that the United States will again commit
large numbers of U.S. forces for direct combat, only very reluctantly, only
when vital U.S. interests are clearly and imminently threatened, and, if
possible, only with strong international support.

The above quotation, written a decade and a half ago, is not to
imply that military and civilian practitioners remain oblivious to the
type of conflicts and hostilities that characterize the current situation.
Ideally the military role is typically minor and indirect, and support
for civilian authorities and their development efforts is crucial. However,
the American opinion formers and the public, along with the government and military establishment, bear a part of the responsibility for
the delay in adapting attitudes, laws, and institutions that may be
more effective at coping with the increasing incidence and persistence
of various types of low-intensity conflict.

After the fall of the Berlin Wall and the subsequent dissolution of the
Soviet Union, the brief euphoria caused by premature visions of a "new
world order" was abandoned in the wake of the eruption throughout
many parts of the developing world of intrastate wars, terrorism,
criminal violence, regional wars, and failing states. As I wrote in my
introduction (p. xiii) to another volume edited by Manwaring, entitled
Gray Area Phenomena: Confronting the New World Disorder (1993),

> Within a few short years the nature of the international system
> and the verities that shaped U.S. national purpose have undergone
> fundamental changes. The United States emerged a victor from
> the Cold War, but. . . . The rules are more complex, and identifying
> purpose is more perplexing. Many new challenges at home and

abroad now emerge demanding immediate attention and action at a time when what we should do is unclear and when resources for programs are more constrained than ever. We will be engaged for some years to come in sorting through the current bewildering world disorder in search of an organizing paradigm to assist us in clarifying our purposes and courses of action.

The Manwaring Paradigm has been proposed as a basis for an improved strategy and theory of engagement for the United States and for weak governments of the developing world. It addresses threats to the stability of nations by nonstate actors and nongovernmental processes as well as half-political, half-criminal powers. Two Gulf Wars later, the nation is menaced by and engaged in asymmetric warfare around the world and on U.S. soil with terrorists and insurgents of Al Qaeda, at war with guerrillas in Afghanistan and Iraq, and confronted by intrastate wars in failing states and by growing international criminal networks. The adoption of a sound national security paradigm and strategy is urgent. The good news is that the intellectual work begun two decades ago to research and articulate a new approach to our national security efforts was prescient and productive. The effort has resulted in a viable and effective overarching paradigm to guide the actions of the United States in a security arena much changed from that of the twentieth century.

Those of us who were charged with directing and coping with U.S. efforts in low-intensity conflicts during the cold war period gave them constant thought and maximum effort. General Maxwell Thurman, the vice chief of staff of the U.S. Army from 1984 to 1986, was preoccupied with U.S. involvement in conflicts around the world, particularly in Latin America. Exercising proactive leadership, he charged the Strategic Studies Institute (SSI) of the Army War College at Carlisle, Pennsylvania, with the task of studying the "correlates of success in counterinsurgency." Manwaring, who had recently arrived as a professor at the college, used quantitative methods derived from political science to conceive the original model. He began gathering data by interviewing practitioners for the model's testing. Manwaring was recalled to active duty in 1986 as a U.S. Army colonel and was assigned to the newly established SWORD as the deputy director under Colonel Robert Herrick, who had worked with Manwaring on the model at Carlisle, to continue the research.[4]

SWORD produced a series of papers. Manwaring wrote a research report ("A Model for the Analysis of Insurgencies," 1987) that served as the theoretical basis for the 1991 *Uncomfortable Wars*. The second published book based on the paradigm was *Low-Intensity Conflict: Old Threats in a New World* (1992), which I co-edited with Stephen Sloan, a fellow professor in the political science department at the University of Oklahoma, where I held the Henry Bellmon Chair for eight years. That volume demonstrated the paradigm's universality by extending its application to cases outside of Latin America. Later the same year, Manwaring and Fishel published the theoretical and methodological underpinning of the paradigm as an article entitled "Insurgency and Counter-Insurgency: Toward a New Analytical Approach," in the London-based journal *Small Wars and Insurgencies*. Other important books and articles followed (see Selected Bibliography). Particularly useful were *Managing Contemporary Conflict: Confronting the New World Disorder* (1996), edited by Manwaring and Olson, and *"The Savage Wars of Peace": Toward a New Paradigm of Peace Operations* (1998), edited by Fishel. These volumes plowed new security territory and demonstrated the immense value of the Manwaring Paradigm both analytically and operationally. The books, articles, and thinking of many of the dedicated and talented practitioners and scholars who have contributed to the development of the paradigm and its application gained such acceptance and stature in the national security community within the decade that Ernie Evans wrote an article ("Our Savage Wars of Peace," 2000) calling this school of thought and its literature to the attention of the academic community.

A unique, continuous, and symbiotic dialogue among practitioners (many of whom were scholars) and academics was needed and perhaps inescapable. A 1988 report (*Supporting U.S. Strategy for Third World Conflict*) prepared under the leadership of General Paul Gorman pointed out the turmoil and hostility of the Third World: in more than thirty wars and about twice as many guerrilla conflicts, over sixteen million people had been killed in developing countries during the previous four decades. Similarly, the *Economist* outlined twenty-five "big wars" going on in the Third World in March 1988.[5]

The study's foundation was reinforced by Manwaring and Fishel's constant consultations with the works of classical thinkers on war and politics and their examination of conflicts throughout history. A review of the U.S. Marine Corps *Small Wars Manual* (1940; reprinted in 1987) had considerable impact. Almost seventy cases of intrastate wars and terrorism were examined and seventy-two questions posed to participants in these cases, both in the course of the development of the Manwaring Paradigm and for this book. A few cases were salient and had more impact than others—not statistically but conceptually, in terms of "lessons learned." Particularly influential in shaping thought were the British success in Malaya, the U.S. experience in supporting the Philippines against the Huks, the Italians' defeat of the Red Brigades, and, of course, the French and United States debacles in Vietnam.

Latin America provided several salient examples. Because of the Southern Command's responsibilities for U.S. security in the western hemisphere, the SWORD research team paid attention to, had experience in, and engaged in dialogue with U.S. civilian officials and Latin American military and civilian officials. Insurgencies, terrorism, and narco-terrorism plagued the hemisphere. General Galvin and his successor, General Woerner (for whom Manwaring and Fishel worked at SOUTHCOM), and I were strong backers of the SWORD research and were in dialogue on how to deal with insurgents and terrorists.

I served in Southeast Asia during the Vietnam War and also in Colombia, where violence and insurgency have thrived since the 1950s. I was the U.S. ambassador in Peru (where the Shining Path guerrillas dynamited my embassy and residence), in Bolivia (where narcotics traffickers dynamited my residence and made attempts on my life), and in El Salvador (where a bloody civil war was in process). The situation in El Salvador and the extent of U.S. involvement there made it of particular interest in the development of the paradigm.

I first met Max Manwaring in El Salvador, while he was revising the initial model. He visited that troubled nation for work related to SWORD (and also for research on his prize-winning book, co-edited with Court

Prisk, *El Salvador at War: An Oral History,* 1988). My exchange on this subject with John Fishel also began in El Salvador. He visited there on several occasions, accompanying the U.S. southern commander and other senior officers advising the Salvadoran armed forces. Although SWORD Model terminology differs from the words we were employing in El Salvador, the concepts, key dimensions, goals, and actions advocated by the U.S. government and by important Salvadoran leaders were in essence very close to the seven key dimensions of the SWORD Model.

This began with the Salvadoran de facto government established after the coup of young democratically inspired military officers and was evident in the Alvaro Magana interim government that enacted reforms called for by the young officers and by Salvadoran Christian Democrats. Similarities to the seven dimensions are very clear in the leadership of Christian Democrat President José Napoleón Duarte, who had the vital support of Minister of Defense Eugenio Vides Casanova and his vice minister, Renaldo Lopez Nuila. This was manifested in many policies and statements of the Salvadoran government and especially so in my frequent conversations with President Duarte, who placed tremendous emphasis on democratization for the Salvadoran government to achieve legitimacy. It is equally apparent in U.S. documents, such as the *Report of the National Bipartisan Commission on Central America* (January 1984) and my statement of objectives to the embassy country team (senior U.S. officials) shortly after my arrival in San Salvador to assume my duties.

Another example of the closeness of the El Salvador experience that was to emerge in SWORD research is the 1983 *First Woerner Report* written by Brigadier General Woerner, then commander of SOUTH-COM's 193rd Infantry Brigade, recommending a Salvadoran campaign plan to achieve greater unity of effort. Major General Marc Cisneros, serving under General Woerner, who was then the U.S. southern commander, prepared the 1988 *Second Woerner Report.* It likewise stressed the need for unity of effort. Both of these reports were based on extensive conversations between visiting SOUTHCOM teams with Salvadoran and embassy officials. Both reports were requested by and approved by the U.S. ambassador.

I do not intend to suggest that the paradigm consciously patterned the El Salvador experience or that U.S. actions in El Salvador from 1981 until 1994 were based on the Manwaring Paradigm. The United States' deep involvement in the Salvadoran civil war began in 1981, prior to commencement of work on the paradigm at Carlisle. Examination of the Manwaring and Fishel article on the analytical approach in *Small Wars and Insurgencies* shows that interviews on the initial forty-three cases studied were conducted in 1985 and 1986. The 1987 Manwaring article is the first public formal iteration of the SWORD Model. The development of the SWORD Model and the conduct of the war in El Salvador were distinct in their direction and conduct. However, ambassadorial interest in the Manwaring Paradigm, the U.S. southern commanders' and SWORD researchers' deep involvement with the U.S. embassy in El Salvador, and the strategy and actions of the Salvadoran leaders during the civil war there seem to have engendered a positive interaction that was mutually beneficial for success in the war and in the development of the paradigm.

Manwaring and Fishel (as well as other contributors to the development of the SWORD Model) have not relied solely on recent conflicts in their endeavors to create this new paradigm. Rather, they repeatedly return to the fundamentals: the teachings of great classical theorists and recognized modern thinkers on war, conflict, and politics. They constantly revisit Sun Tzu's ancient classic, *The Art of War,* and the more recent definitive work by Carl von Clausewitz, *On War.* The maxims and still-perceptive advice by Sun Tzu and Clausewitz appear throughout the text. This advice forms a foundation for the sound, social science–based and real world–tested national security paradigm of two of our era's most gifted thinkers and dedicated public servants. Manwaring and Fishel are the George Kennans of the post–cold war era.

The genius of Kennan's theory of engagement, expressed in his famous Mr. "X" article, was that it combined the realism of power politics with the pragmatism of American idealism. Like containment theory, the legitimate governance theory embodied in the Manwaring Paradigm is also a pragmatic foundation for national and international stability and well-being in the international security arena. Perhaps the greatest threat to U.S. national security is the danger that many Americans do not easily change their thinking to coincide with changes in the world. Fortunately, the Manwaring Paradigm helps us to cope with different sets of rules and threats that became paramount after the lid covering them was lifted by the end of the cold war. The top leadership of our country needs to endorse the Manwaring Paradigm in a manner similar to that of President Harry S. Truman and his contemporaries when they adopted the policy of containment.

Manwaring, Fishel, and their colleagues have made a tremendous contribution to making the world a safer and better place for mankind. They merit our gratitude.

PREFACE

This book follows several previous works aimed at revitalizing strategic thinking on "uncomfortable" contemporary conflicts, that is, conflicts other than major wars. The main theme is that conflict—regardless of level of discomfort—must fit into an overall foreign policy structure that identifies supportable ends, effective ways, adequate means, and clear purposes. In addition, decision makers charged with policy and asset management must also take into consideration the empirical experience of the relatively recent past, which clarifies the actions that make the difference between winning and losing an "uncomfortable war."

In this book we identify the essential concepts that can help operationalize foreign and defense policy structure and the associated empirical concepts. Although the United States and its global partners face many new problems in an increasingly challenging setting, success in the contemporary global security environment will be constructed on the same fundamental components as those developed in the past. These dimensions of success—or failure—include a sound theory of engagement; the development and use of appropriate civil and military instruments of national and international power to support the theory of engagement; and the promulgation of a management structure that will ensure an effective unity of effort.

By coming to grips with the lessons of success and failure that should have been learned over the past several years, decision makers and their staffs can develop the conceptual, operational, and organizational instruments necessary to win a contemporary conflict. These empirical lessons can also liberate decision, policy, and opinion makers from the intellectual vise of previous (and often limited) experience so that the decision to engage both purpose and power in a contemporary conflict is competent at the outset and supported in its conduct.

These lessons, and the dimensions that inform them, are not new or radical. However, several aspects that support these lessons are new or given new emphasis in this book: the specific combination of variables considered to be the most powerful indicators of success; the inter-dependence of these variables; the importance of the legitimacy dimension; the use of these variables as objective measures of effectiveness at the macro level for winning or losing in the contemporary conflict arena; reference to the interdisciplinary field—and theory—of international relations as much as or more than revolutionary theory in comparative politics; and the empirical development of the conceptual framework, which warrants confidence that the findings are universal and explain much of the reality of the contemporary strategic-political security environment.

The authors wish to thank the people whose knowledge, experience, analytical powers, wisdom, and many hours of work over a period of nearly twenty years made this book possible. Clearly, it is impossible to name every person individually. However, a few "guiding lights" must be acknowledged. They include Colonel Robert M. Herrick, U.S. Army (retired), the director of SWORD; the late General Maxwell R. Thurman, whose question began the research; and Ambassador Edwin G. Corr, whose constant prodding finally convinced us that we needed to put this book together. We also want to thank the many scholars and practitioners who joined us in previous books. In particular, we both want to express our thanks to Kimbra Fishel, whose insights have proven invaluable to this, as well as the works on which she directly collaborated. In this context, we respectfully dedicate this volume to Generals John R. Galvin and Fred F. Woerner Jr., U.S. Army (retired), who have been thoughtful strategists and constant inspirations and supporters of a new paradigm for the successful conduct of "uncomfortable wars."

Finally, neither this book nor the individual chapters in it should be construed as reflecting the official position of the U.S. government or the Department of Defense. We alone are responsible for any errors of fact or judgment.

UNCOMFORTABLE WARS REVISITED

CHAPTER 1

Introduction to the
SWORD Model

In 1957, Lieutenant General James M. Gavin resigned from the U.S. Army as a protest regarding the lack of official interest in preparing to deal with small wars (e.g., internal wars, limited wars, terrorist wars, insurgency wars, low-intensity conflict, or what we will hereafter call "uncomfortable wars"). After that, several authors, including Morton Halperin (1962), Harry Eckstein (1964), and B. H. Liddell Hart (1967), articulated the logic set forth by Gavin. The Vietnam disaster seriously curtailed the development of the understanding of this kind of small-scale contingency-type conflict. Not until the early 1980s and the publication of Harry Summers' pioneering analysis of the Vietnam conflict did the process begin again. Nevertheless, General John R. Galvin and Samuel Sarkesian affirmed that governmental and scholarly resistance to "uncomfortable wars" persisted.[1]

The vice chief of staff of the U.S. Army, General Maxwell Thurman, understood that to escape the intellectual vise imposed by one's own limited experience, one first had to examine the process by which a government in power resists, defeats, or succumbs to an organized violent internal adversary. As a result, in 1984 General Thurman mandated the empirical examination of a large sample of uncomfortable wars that would accomplish three goals: allow the testing of competing theoretical approaches to internal conflicts; determine the extent to which the outcome of such conflicts is predictable; and generate a new paradigm, which came to be known as the SWORD Model (developed by the Southern Command's Small Wars Operations Research Directorate, or SWORD), to improve prospects for success in future different but similar conflict situations.[2] The results of part of that mandated research were first published as an article by Max Manwaring and John Fishel in 1992 (see chapter 5 for details on the research process).[3]

Since then, the Vietnam syndrome, associated polemics, and resistance to dealing with uncomfortable wars have not gone away.[4] Indeed, the United States is still essentially at the point where it was when General Gavin resigned in 1957. To quote a retired general officer who shall remain unnamed, "As a nation we don't understand the contemporary international security arena, and as a government we are not prepared to deal with it."[5]

These lessons in asymmetry and the related challenges to the United States are not being lost on the new political actors emerging into the contemporary multipolar global security arena. Ironically, strategies being developed to protect or further the interests of a number of new players on the international scene are inspired by the dual idea of evading and frustrating superior conventional military force within the global chaos. The better a power such as the United States becomes at the operational (i.e., attrition) level of conventional war, the more a potential adversary turns to asymmetric solutions.[6] One need look no further than the war in Iraq at the time this book was written, following the "end of major combat operations."

Today, well over half the countries in the world are faced with one variation or another of asymmetric uncomfortable wars. Thus, the purpose of this book is to draw from the lessons of history to better prepare today's civilian, military, and opinion leaders—and voters—for the unconventional and asymmetric warfare challenges that increasingly face the United States and the rest of the global community. In this connection, Ralph Peters warns us that in current and future conflicts, "Wise competitors . . . will seek to shift the playing field away from conventional military confrontations toward unconventional forms of assault. . . . Only the foolish will fight fair.[7]

To help leaders, scholars, and citizens come to grips analytically with the most salient strategic lessons and rules that dominate contemporary conflict, in the text that follows we have chosen to summarize the lessons derived from the SWORD Model, omitting any kind of detailed discussion of ongoing conflict situations—no matter how salient. We do this so that the reader will not lose sight of the proverbial forest and concentrate, for example, on individual Iraqi and Afghanistani trees. Developing the broad strategic vision necessary to maximize opportunities and minimize risks in the current and future global chaos will lead to winning the war—not just the battles.

RETHINKING PROBLEM AND RESPONSE

As Colonel Harry Summers (U.S. Army, retired) paraphrased General Douglas MacArthur's guidance to the army in 1935, the quintessential strategic lesson to be learned from any conflict is to "bring to light those fundamental principles, and their combinations and applications, which, in the past, have been productive of success."[8] As a consequence, these strategic-level lessons provide a short list of primary, intermediate, and advanced rules for playing in the contemporary global security arena.

Perhaps the most crucial element in applying these rules is to avoid the pitfalls of unidimensional and short-term thinking. In "loss" situations it is clear that broad strategic concerns have played little part in the debates as to what to do with the billions of dollars and thousands of lives allocated to a given conflict situation. In the recent past, the United States has faced security problems on an ad hoc case-by-case, situation-by-situation, and crisis-control basis. The tendency has been to rely on hard military power, sophisticated technology, and luck. In the long term, such narrow approaches have yielded less-than-satisfactory results. In those loss situations the United States has been known to "declare victory and come home" only to see the problem that brought on the American involvement in the first place remain unresolved—and worsen.

Hard Military Power

Victory in any kind of war—including uncomfortable wars—is not simply the sum of the battles won over the course of a conflict. Rather, it is the product of connecting and weighting the political, economic, informational, and military instruments of national power within the context of strategic appraisals, strategic vision, and strategic objectives. Sun Tzu warned that "in war, numbers alone confer no advantage. Do not advance relying on sheer military power."[9] The promulgation of such a concept requires a somewhat different approach to modern conflict than that generally used by the United States and other Western powers over the past several years.

The American experience in Vietnam and Somalia, the French experience in Indochina and Algeria, and the Dutch experience in Indonesia provide five examples of this unidimensional approach to conflict. The data over time and throughout the world demonstrate that the more intense and voluminous the military actions of the intervening Western power, the more likely the incumbent government is to lose to the adversary. This seems contrary to the popular wisdom of escalating the level of a given conflict to the point where victory is assured, which is predicated on the idea that the enemy military force is the primary center of gravity: a 5 to 1, or a 10 to 1, or a 100 to 1 ratio of superiority will be required to win. What appears to have happened in several of the cases noted above is that the Western intervening powers did not generally commit their own forces unless their surrogate (ally) was losing. They then committed forces piecemeal (i.e., in gradually escalating numbers) in response to a deteriorating situation. The more they did militarily, the worse things got.[10] In the other cases of Western loss—Somalia, for example—the intervening Western power de-escalated before victory had been achieved. In other words, it "declared victory and went home" (and turned the problem over to an inferior international [United Nations] force).

Sophisticated Technology

In the recent past, the United States has tended to rely heavily on relatively sophisticated technology, such as precision munitions and laser designators, to subdue an adversary. As one example, efforts against the Taliban and Al Qaeda in Afghanistan come immediately to mind. Clausewitz's translator, Michael Howard, reminds us that an adequate response must be essentially a strategic political-economic-social-psychological-security effort. These additional controlling dimensions take into account the "forgotten" social-moral aspect of war and stress that "if this part of a conflict is not conducted with skill, no amount of operational military or police expertise, technical advantage, or outside support can possibly help."[11]

Indeed, strictly military actions appear to be much less important than supporting economic and political actions. Evidence indicates that a strong strategy by a targeted government to attain or enhance its moral legitimacy is the single most effective thing it can do for its own survival.[12] Because of the superior conventional power and technology available to a targeted government, an illegal attacker is at a disadvantage in attempting to overtly or directly challenge it. Thus, the assault is generally indirect and centers on a regime's moral right to govern—or ability and willingness to govern. As General Sir Robert Thompson argued, the outcome of uncomfortable wars such as those in Malaya and the Philippines would be determined by the relative ability of the violent opposition and the government to shift the "hearts and minds"—and support—of the people in their respective favor.[13] This is not to deny the importance of effective military action but rather to point out that military and police action alone cannot determine the outcome of the conflict. As we are seeing in Afghanistan, unless the new government can consolidate and enhance its legitimacy, there is great danger that both the Taliban and Al Qaeda will return and reestablish a terrorist sanctuary.

Luck

In our interviews for the SWORD project and subsequently, hundreds of respondents explained their loss or defeat as a result of "bad luck." The argument was that "luck is an agile spirit that jumps both ways in double quick time. All that matters is that luck should run good on the last throw."[14] A frequent explanation for the French defeat in Algeria, the British loss of Aden, and the American embarrassment in Vietnam was that luck simply ran bad on the last throw.[15]

This is not a recent issue. In his fourteenth-century discussions on *fortuna* (i.e., luck), Niccolò Machiavelli pointed out that Julius Caesar's successful campaigns in Gaul and elsewhere were not the result of letting fortuna go its own unencumbered way. Caesar and his officers worked hard, consistently, and prudently to force luck to jump in Rome's favor at every opportunity.[16] Likewise, in 1066, William the Conqueror took full advantage of the technological and tactical superiority that the stirrup provided his Norman cavalry as a type of weapons "launching platform." Despite this advantage over the English infantry at the Battle of Hastings, William had no numerical superiority, invading England with only a 1 to 1 ratio at best. Many participants and subsequent writers thus attributed William's success against King Harold of England to his good luck.[17] Not so. William managed the problem very carefully and deliberately. Probably the most important weapon he employed in his invasion of England was legitimacy. William's ascendancy to the English throne was a holy endeavor, blessed by the pope. Moreover, the pope excommunicated Harold for having reneged on a solemn oath to allow Duke William of Normandy to become king of England. The papal edict that condemned Harold to hell forever threatened all his followers with the same fate if the English crown was not surrendered to the pope's choice. At the same time, William could offer land and booty to his supporters, and the church would offer absolution for any sin to anyone involved in William's holy cause. The only appeal was to God himself through a trial by ordeal that would declare His judgment: the Battle of Hastings was that trial. The result was a foregone conclusion. Everyone, including Harold, knew that he was guilty as charged. The outstanding valor, initiative, and aggressiveness demonstrated by Harold and his followers in defeating a Scandinavian invasion force in the north only a few weeks previously were not evident at Hastings. William's superior moral power and the concomitant undermining of Harold's legitimacy (as well as the superior tactics and technology of cavalry and stirrups) were the crucial factors in the Norman invasion of England—not luck.[18]

THE PRIMARY RULES THAT SHOULD
HAVE BEEN LEARNED FROM VIETNAM

If the lessons from Vietnam teach anything, they teach the need to go back to basics. Sun Tzu argued, "War is of vital importance to the State; the province of life or death; the road to survival or ruin. It is mandatory that it be thoroughly studied."[19] Carl von Clausewitz, who arguably made the most detailed study of warfare in modern times, defined the most fundamental step in undertaking a war: "The first, the supreme, the most far reaching act of judgment that the statesman and commander have to make is to establish . . . the kind of war on which they are embarking; neither mistaking it for, nor trying to turn it into, something that is alien to its nature."[20] Determining the nature of the conflict is thus "the first of all strategic questions and the most comprehensive."[21]

It does not stand on its own, however. Five highly interrelated and reinforcing strategic-level lessons, all of which should have been learned from the American experience in Vietnam, are particularly germane to the conduct of the asymmetric wars that characterize our current geo-political situation. To create a strategy of success, decision makers need to carefully examine and define the nature of a given conflict; fully understand the strategic environment within which the conflict is taking place; determine the primary centers of gravity within that strategic environment that must be attacked and those that must be defended; appreciate the "centrality of rectitude" (i.e., moral legitimacy) in pursuing a given strategy or in supporting a given government; and examine these lessons as a strategic whole. This last lesson takes us back to where we began and is the foundational basis for ultimate success.

Understanding the Nature of the Conflict

The most fundamental principle that American leadership ignored in Vietnam was the need to understand the kind of conflict they were getting the nation into. Then, as the war continued, both civilian and military leaders tried to turn that uncomfortable war into something that it was not. As a consequence, the failure to correctly define the nature of the conflict provided an erroneous guiding basis to the subsequent conduct of the war. That, in turn, sealed the unsuccessful outcome of the war even as U.S. troops began arriving in Vietnam. The final result was the exhaustion of the American army against a secondary guerrilla force—and the ultimate failure of the military to support the national policy of containment of communist expansion.[22]

In the tradition of the American way of war, civilian and military leaders thought that "kicking ass" and destroying the enemy military force was the goal of policy. Military violence was the principal tool.[23] At the same time, because a "limited war" such as that in Vietnam implied a low-effort task unworthy of serious concern, it was something to be conducted with complaisance. The Vietnam conflict thus became a traditional war of attrition—a Second World War, if you will—"writ small."[24] However, in that limited war of attrition, 58,000 Americans and 3.6 million Vietnamese died. In terms of total populations, 3.6 million Vietnamese are proportionally equivalent to 27 million Americans.

Former secretary of defense Robert McNamara observed that "there are some people to whom life is not the same as to us, . . . we'd better understand that and write it down."[25] That is perhaps true, but in the strategic context of the uncomfortable Vietnam conflict, relative regard for life was not a simple cultural issue. General Vo Nguyen Giap explained unequivocally that the Vietnamese took those awful casualties because they were involved in a national war of liberation and that the people participated enthusiastically in the resistance and consented "to make every sacrifice for its victory."[26]

Many American military officers and civilian officials complained that the war in Vietnam had been "won" militarily but "lost" politically, as if these dimensions of the conflict were not completely interdependent. In becoming involved in a modern guerrilla conflict—whether relatively straightforward such as that in Chechnya or more complex such as the Colombian crisis—an actor is likely to be involved in a set of simultaneously waged political-psychological wars within a general conflict. In those terms, a state will not be engaged only in a military war. Rather, as Michael Howard points out, operational and technical military factors are subordinate to the "forgotten" political-social-psychological-moral dimensions of contemporary conflict. If the struggle is not conducted with skill and based on a realistic understanding of the situation and people in question, defeat is inevitable.[27] The clearest example of this result is found in France's war in Algeria in the 1950s and 1960s, in which the French achieved nearly total tactical and operational victory yet lost the war: Algeria became independent.

Thus, it is imperative that senior decision makers, policy makers, and their staffs correctly identify the nature of the conflict in which they are involved; determine the central strategic problem and the primary political objective associated with it; prioritize other objectives; and link policy, strategy, force structure and equipment, and coordinated political-economic-psychological-moral-military campaign plans to solving that central strategic problem. This linkage encompasses Clausewitz's "forgotten dimensions of strategy" and the indirect approach to conflict indicated by Sun Tzu.[28] The skillful strategist will seek more effective ways to "render the enemy powerless" than to merely attack his main military force.[29] It follows that a political-social-psychological-moral-military effort would be a potent combination of ways to control a conflict such as that experienced against the Vietcong guerrillas in Vietnam. Such a conceptual exercise may be difficult, but it is crucial, given the obvious alternative.

Understanding the Strategic Environment

Another reason for the American defeat in Vietnam was that U.S. leadership paid little or no attention to the strategic environment within which the conflict was taking place. Once the nature of the conflict is defined, the next step in the process is the full consideration of the strategic situation—and the most important threats implicit and explicit in it. That becomes the conceptual foundation from which to develop a strategic vision for the successful pursuit of the conflict. The primary consequence of ignoring the strategic environment in Vietnam was complete frustration on the part of the leadership and troops involved in the guerrilla war for national liberation (as well as the American public at home).[30]

U.S. and South Vietnamese forces would conduct series after series of highly effective military operations that devastated the main Vietcong infrastructure and continually forced them and their North Vietnamese allies to withdraw from the immediate battlefield. Yet, despite enduring series after series of what is traditionally considered defeat, the insurgents and their allies kept coming back. They returned from different directions, always refreshed, resupplied, and rededicated. Eventually, of course, they prevailed.[31]

American leaders could not understand the tenacity and the persistence of the Vietcong guerrillas or how the enemy could keep coming back, defeat after defeat. As a consequence, analysts argue that the U.S. leadership did not understand three crucial things within the context of the strategic environment. They did not completely understand the enemy and his structure, they did not really know their allies, and they ignored the geopolitical aspects of the general security situation.[32]

Understanding the Enemy Sociopolitical Situation

American leaders did not analyze the sociopolitical situation in Vietnam and did not understand the implications of the fact that the guerrilla war in which they were involved was only the latest in a long series of wars of national liberation against foreign invaders. Again, U.S. leadership was thinking in terms of a conventional war of attrition—like World War II—whereas Vietnamese guerrilla roots and mentality were located in struggles against the Chinese, against French colonialism, against the Japanese during World War II, against the French again from the end of the Japanese occupation to the French defeat at Dien Bien Phu in 1954, and finally, against American "neocolonialism." As a result, the North Vietnamese and their South Vietnamese guerrilla allies were involved in a total war for independence. The will to overcome the foreign invaders had been inculcated into generations of highly nationalistic patriots for well over a hundred years.[33] General Giap summed up the sociopolitical situation in the following terms: "The guiding principle of the people's war was long-term resistance and self-reliance that inspired in the people and the army a completely revolutionary spirit which instilled into the whole people the will to overcome all difficulties, to endure all privations, the spirit of a long resistance, of resistance to the end."[34]

Understanding the Guerrilla Structure and Threat

Most Americans thought they were fighting a limited war of attrition against a traditional enemy—albeit an enemy dressed in black pajamas. However, the threat that the South Vietnamese government and the United States had to deal with was not a limited or a traditional one. Rather, the Vietcong were developing a clandestine internal political structure to take control of the national territory and the people in it.[35]

At the strategic level, the Vietcong focused their primary (and indirect) attack on the legitimacy of the corrupt and American-dominated South Vietnamese government. Aside from spectacular actions such as the Tet Offensive and shows of force to keep South Vietnamese and U.S. forces off-balance and frustrated, the main military effort was that of "armed propaganda." Operationally, the guerrillas expanded political, military, and support components and—using terrorist "armed propaganda" tactics—consolidated their position with the "masses" throughout the country. The purpose was to convince the people that the Vietcong were the real power in the country and that the incumbent regime in Saigon was unwilling and unable to perform its fundamental security and service functions. Tactically, the guerrillas generally operated in relatively small units with political, psychological, and military objectives—in that order. "Armed propaganda" was conducted not to "win" in a conventional sense but to violently intimidate and control the population, further discredit the South Vietnamese government and the Americans; and give the country and the world the impression that the Vietcong were more powerful than they really were. American leadership generally ignored the internal support structure that was being built while the main forces in their black pajamas were attacking U.S. and South Vietnamese forces from "all different directions."[36] Instead, the United States and its allies (beginning with the battle of the Ia Drang in 1965, through the siege of Ke Son and the Tet Offensive in

1968, until the spring offensive of 1972) focused on regular regiments of the North Vietnamese Army (NVA) and Vietcong main force units while ignoring the real war that was going on all around them.

KNOWING YOUR ALLY AND THE ASSOCIATED THREAT

At the same time, American leadership did not take the trouble to really get to know their allies. To be sure, some great friendships were generated between many U.S. and South Vietnamese military and between some American and South Vietnamese civilians. Nevertheless, American civilian and military leadership did not understand that the struggle between Vietcong challengers and the incumbent South Vietnamese government was a struggle over the moral right to govern. American leaders did not fully appreciate the psychological-political fact that the Vietcong focus was not so much on soldiers and politicians as on social classes and groups. Guerrilla attacks on the South Vietnamese government were generally indirect and relied on societal grievances such as political and economic injustice, racial and religious discrimination, and debilitating internal corruption and unwelcome foreign domination.[37]

This was the essential nature of the threat posed by the revolutionary guerrillas of Vietnam; it is typical of wars for liberation. A counterinsurgency effort that does not respond to legitimate internal sociopolitical concerns and deals only with enemy military capabilities is ultimately destined to fail. In Clausewitzian terms, the military instrument for success in war depends on the other two elements of his "remarkable trinity"—that is, military success depends on the perceived justice of the government's political objectives and the resultant popular passions.[38] The war in Vietnam is a case in point.

THE GEOSTRATEGIC ENVIRONMENT
AND THE ASSOCIATED THREAT

The thread that allows an insurgency to develop, grow, and succeed is adequate freedom of action over time and space. Guerrillas maintain their freedom of action and movement through the establishment and maintenance of remote base areas, sanctuaries, and supply routes.

At the same time, they establish and maintain supporting political-economic-military infrastructure within the general population.[39]

The Ho Chi Minh Trail provides a good example of how the United States failed to deal effectively with one geographical element in the strategic environment, which was also one of North Vietnam's most effective geostrategic weapons. The trail became a network of roads from North Vietnam through "neutral" Laos and Cambodia into South Vietnam. General Maxwell Taylor has stated that as early as 1961, he informed President John F. Kennedy that the Vietcong could not be beaten as long as infiltration by means of the Ho Chi Minh Trail remained unchecked.[40] Anthony Joes explains this point:

> The failure both to close the Trail and to adopt an alternative strategy that would have neutralized its effects also meant that Hanoi could fight on interior lines, a tremendous advantage. It meant that the enemy was free to invade South Vietnam continuously: The NVA's (North Vietnam Army's) colossal 1972 Easter (Tet) Offensive would have been quite impossible without the Laotian springboard. It meant that when hard pressed by allied forces, the enemy could simply retreat into Laos or Cambodia. Thus the policies of the Johnson administration made a lasting, or even a temporary, American military victory impossible. And that fact, in turn, meant that attrition . . . would take longer than key segments of the American public would accept.[41]

American leadership considered the war in Vietnam a "unique" problem, to be dealt with on an ad hoc, piecemeal, and operational basis as each separate crisis or issue arose.[42] Worse, the assumptions upon which U.S.—and, thus, South Vietnamese—actions were based were not well informed, were erroneous, or were ignored. As a consequence of not understanding the enemy, not knowing the entirety of the South Vietnamese situation, and not dealing effectively with the reality of the geostrategic situation outside and within the boundaries of Vietnam—as well as not responding appropriately to the threats within that strategic environment—the uncomfortable counterguerrilla war could not be won.

Centers of Gravity

Another fundamental principle that U.S. leaders found too difficult to address in Vietnam was that of attacking centers of gravity.[43] From both a theoretical and a practical standpoint, the successful conduct of a war requires accurate determination of and aggressive attacks on the primary sources of an adversary's physical, psychological, and moral strength. These are the hubs of "all power and movement on which everything depends."[44] As a result, centers of gravity provide the basic architecture from which to develop a viable ends, ways, and means strategy.

Beyond attacking the traditional enemy military formations or some of their support structure, American leadership found that in Vietnam it was easier to deal with tactical and operational-level "nodes of vulnerability."[45] As a war of attrition dictates, an unconscionable number of people were injured and killed, but the sources of Vietcong and North Vietnamese strength remained virtually unscathed.

The major implication of this situation is that the primary centers of gravity defined in the guiding strategic vision constitute a possible set of simultaneously waged political-psychological-social-moral-military wars within a general conflict. In becoming involved in a war such as that in Vietnam, centers of gravity may change as the situation changes, and the so-called wars-within-the-war will also change.[46]

Summers provides some illustrations of the dynamism of the centers of gravity in the later part of the Vietnam conflict. After the Paris Accords of 1973, "one of the first questions [the North Vietnamese] asked was whether the center of gravity had shifted from the U.S.–South Vietnamese alliance to new centers of gravity—the destruction of the South Vietnamese armed forces and the capture of Saigon."[47] Once the North Vietnamese determined that the alliance was indeed irrelevant, preparations were begun that led to the defeat in detail of the South Vietnamese army, the fall of Saigon, and the unconditional capitulation of the South Vietnamese government and the final unification of the country. Here the center of gravity changed three times—from the "community of interest" of the United States and South Vietnam, to the classical enemy military force, to the capital city.

An important additional implication here is the fact that centers of gravity must be attacked—and defended. It is as necessary for an attacker to take measures to defend his own centers of gravity as it is for him to deal with his opponent's centers of gravity. Again, and in this context, U.S. leadership failed to defend American public opinion against the full-scale "propaganda war" that was conducted by North Vietnam and its allies throughout the world. American leadership failed to understand that the "streets of Peoria" and the "halls of Congress" were decisive in determining the outcome of the war thousands of miles away in Vietnam.

Senior leadership must remember that each facet of conflict has its corresponding threat and center of gravity. The basic problem is to constantly reevaluate the principal threat and the proper order of priority for the others. The secondary problem is to develop the capability to apply long-term political, moral, psychological, and economic (as well as military) resources against the various centers of gravity that a guerrilla or other type of uncomfortable war generates. Shrinking from these inevitable requirements for success in contemporary conflict only prolongs the struggle. And as Sun Tzu prophetically wrote, "there has never been a protracted war from which a country has benefited."[48]

The Centrality of Rectitude and Moral Legitimacy

Another crucial principle that emerged out of the war in Vietnam is that of rectitude or moral legitimacy. The counterguerrilla strategy against the Vietcong had no chance of success without U.S. leaders' coming to terms with the fact that the conflict was conducted in an essentially political-moral context. This umbrella concept focuses on the moral right of the South Vietnamese government to govern and demonstrates that legitimacy constituted the central strategic problem: it was the hub of all power and movement around which everything revolved. Popular perceptions of right and wrong, poverty, lack of upward mobility, and corruption threatened the right—and the ability—of the South Vietnamese regime to conduct the business of the state. These popular perceptions were key to the outcome of the conflict.[49]

One of the primary objectives of the Vietcong was to destroy and take control of the South Vietnamese government. By transforming the emphasis of the war from the level of military violence to the level of a struggle for moral legitimacy, the guerrillas could strive for "total" objectives—the overthrow of the government—instead of simply attempting to obtain leverage and influence for "limited" political, economic, or territorial objectives in the traditional sense. Thus, the use of indirect moral force permitted the Vietcong to engage in a secret and internal war—striking at the government's right to govern—while appearing to the people to pursue altruistic purposes. In these terms, this war was not an extension of politics; this war *was* politics. It was a zero-sum game in which there could be only one winner. It was also, despite the perceptions held by U.S. leadership at the time, a total war.[50]

To counter this type of sociopolitical challenge, the government must first recognize what is happening and then be willing to acknowledge that its civil support is fragile and its control over the populace contested. General John R. Galvin argues that to establish its moral legitimacy, a disputed government must address contentious, long-ignored, but popular issues tied to key facets of national life—sociopolitical, economic, educational, juridical—as well as engaging the guerrillas on the battlefield.

The resulting burden on the military institution is large. Not only must it subdue an armed adversary while attempting to provide security to the civilian population, it must also avoid inadvertently furthering the insurgents' cause. If, for example, the military's actions in killing fifty guerrillas cause two hundred previously uncommitted citizens to join the insurgent cause, the use of force will have been counterproductive.[51]

It follows that every policy, every program, and every action taken by a government—and its external allies—involved in an internal war scenario must contribute positively and directly to developing, maintaining, and enhancing the ability and willingness of that regime to control its territory and govern its people in that territory with rectitude. This course of action provides an umbrella of moral legitimacy. This lesson will be crucial for vulnerable governments that wish to retain their ability to govern in the coming decades.[52]

Indigenous and foreign allied leadership must realize that the highest priority must be to strengthen and legitimize the state. Thus, critical points about moral legitimacy must be understood at three different levels. First, regime legitimacy is the primary target of the insurgents. Second, the regime and its allies must protect and enhance moral legitimacy as the primary means by which that regime might survive. Third, a besieged government looking abroad for support against an internal foe—or to deny support to that adversary—must understand that rectitude and legitimacy is a double-edged moral sword that will either assist or constrain foreign willingness and ability to become effectively involved.

Again, the words of Sun Tzu are particularly apt: "Those who excel in war first cultivate their own humanity and justice and maintain their laws and institutions. By these means they make their governments invincible."[53]

Looking at the Strategic Whole

The fact that the U.S. armed forces were never defeated on the Vietnam battlefield obscures another important fact of that war: American tactical and operational successes tend to dim the strategic defeat. The problems and lessons of Vietnam must be examined as a strategic whole, within the framework of the combination of fundamental principles that in the past have been the basis of success. Success in any one component of grand strategy cannot generate overall success; indeed, success only becomes a viable *possibility* when all the components of a strategy form a logical conceptual framework, architecture, or strategic paradigm within which judgments, comparisons, and data may be given meaning.

This reality takes us back to the question of how the United States could have won all the battles in Vietnam but lost the war. The answer is that American leadership failed to apply all five fundamental principles of military theory and grand strategy in the conflict:

- The assessment of the nature of the conflict was incorrect.
- The strategic environment within which the war was taking place was misunderstood or ignored.
- The primary centers of gravity were not carefully and continually assessed, prioritized, and considered in nonmilitary (e.g., sociopolitical) terms.
- There was no appreciation of the centrality of rectitude and moral legitimacy in supporting the counterguerrilla effort.
- These fundamental principles were not brought together and put into a strategic paradigm through which to understand and conduct the war.

The central unifying theme of these lessons is decisive. If a country such as the United States desires efficiency and effectiveness in a matter as crucial as war, the civil-military leadership must concern itself with two critical points: the instruments of national power must be organized, trained, and equipped within prescribed budgetary considerations; and those actions must be preceded by clear, holistic, and logical policy direction as well as the establishment of structure, roles, missions, and strategy that will ensure the achievement of the political ends established in that policy. This fundamental "rule" is as valid for current and future conflict as it has been in the past.

THE INTERMEDIATE RULES DERIVED FROM OTHER POST–WORLD WAR II "UNCOMFORTABLE WARS"

In the mid 1980s, practitioners and academics deemed it important to begin to face the so-called Vietnam syndrome and try to understand the variables that make the difference between winning and losing uncomfortable guerrilla wars. The intent was to improve prospects for success in contemporary and future uncomfortable conflict situations and to do a better job of protecting and advancing U.S. national interests in the developing global instability. One such effort was initiated in 1984 by the vice chief of staff of the U.S. Army, General Maxwell Thurman. He mandated the empirical examination of all cases of insurgencies faced by Western powers and their allies in the postwar period that would allow the testing of competing theoretical approaches (i.e., strategic paradigms) to internal guerrilla conflicts, determine the extent to which the success or fail outcome of such conflicts is predictable, and generate a new paradigm to improve prospects for success in future similar situations.[54] This mandate resulted in an initial list of sixty-nine internal wars, of which forty-three met the insurgency criteria. The remaining twenty-six cases were examined in later research as the application of the new paradigm was expanded beyond insurgency.

The results of part of the mandated research were published in 1992.[55] The research suggested that even though every conflict is situation specific, it is not unique: analytical commonalities apply at the strategic and high operational levels. Indeed, the SWORD Model as finally conceived comprises seven dimensions (derived from the statistical process known as factor analysis), each composed of multiple independent variables, that determine the success or failure of an internal war. The resultant paradigm has power and virtue in part because of the symmetry of its application, both for a besieged government and its allies, and for a violent internal challenger and its allies. That is to say, no successful strategy—on either side of the conflict spectrum—has been formulated over the past fifty years that has not explicitly or implicitly taken into account all of the following strategic dimensions, or "wars within the war": (1) the legitimacy "war" to attack or defend the moral right of an incumbent regime to exist; (2) the more traditional police-military "shooting war" between belligerents; (3) and (4) "wars" to isolate belligerents from their internal and external support, respectively; (5) the closely related "war to stay the course"—that is, the effort to provide consistent and long-term support to a host government; (6) intelligence and information "wars"; and (7) "wars" to unify multidimensional, multilateral, and multiorganizational elements into a single effective effort. The application of these dynamic dimensions in a successful strategy assumes that a realistic strategic vision and policy are based on the fundamental principles discussed in the "strategic lessons of Vietnam" section above.

The Legitimacy "War"

As noted above, the data show that the moral right of a regime to govern is the most important single dimension in an uncomfortable internal war. Thus, a politically strong and morally legitimate government is vital to any winning strategy. The rectitude and legitimacy of the incumbent regime is the primary target—the primary center of gravity—as far as the internal adversary is concerned. In that connection, the interaction between an allied outside power and the incumbent government, especially with regard to the publicly perceived level of the "Americanization" of a conflict, is critical to success. A counterinsurgency campaign that fails to understand the lack of rectitude and morally legitimate governance problems and responds only to "enemy" military forces is very likely to fail.

As an example, leaders on both sides recognized early in the conflict in El Salvador that this dimension would be key to success or failure for the insurgents and the government. Speaking for the insurgents, Guillermo M. Ungo identified the legitimacy of the regime as the primary center of gravity in that situation.[56] President José Napoleón Duarte understood the problem and countered with a nationalistic program designed to preempt the efforts of the Farabundo Martí National Liberation Front (FMLN) guerrillas. His argument was simple: "If the Christian Democrats demonstrate in El Salvador that a democratic system can bring about structural [structure] changes peacefully, the polarized choice between domination by the rightist oligarchy and violent revolution by the Left will no longer be valid."[57]

The Shooting "War"

Experience affirms that military force should not be applied ad hoc in response to either political or military failure, or in an attempt to "try something that might work." If military force must be inserted into a nationalistic milieu, it should be done overwhelmingly at the outset. Nevertheless, the data indicate that the best possible use of "foreign" military personnel in an internal conflict is one variation or another on the "train the trainer" role. Accordingly, the "outside" forces that might be brought into most counterguerrilla/terrorist situations do not necessarily need the skills required for success against combined-arms armies on the north German plain or in the Middle Eastern desert. What they do need is a high degree of professionalism, the ability to insert themselves unobtrusively into a nationalistic environment, and the will to help build and equip an indigenous military force capable of achieving political and psychological as well as police-military objectives. Above all, that security organization must have the mentality to engage internal adversaries without alienating the citizenry.[58]

Successful examples of this type of effort include U.S. military Mobile Training Teams (MTTs) training the first Cazador ("Hunter") units of the Venezuelan Army into superior organizations during 1961–1964 and the Bolivian Ranger units that destroyed Ernesto "Che" Guevara's guerrilla organization in Bolivia in 1968. This approach did not require many "foreign" troops; they were in relatively little physical danger; and they kept a low political profile.[59]

The "Wars" to Isolate the Guerrillas/Terrorists

The objective here is for a belligerent to isolate his opponent politically, psychologically, and militarily from his primary sources of support and sanctuaries—whoever and wherever they may be. To ignore this dimension of internal conflict as too difficult and too dangerous in its domestic and foreign political-military ramifications is to deny the possibility of ultimate success.[60]

This dimension is clearly demonstrated in nearly all the cases examined, but the classic example of this type of war is Greece during the period 1946–1949. In this case, the Greek insurgent forces received logistical and other support from Greece's Communist neighbors— Albania, Bulgaria, and Yugoslavia. This support included food, clothing, arms, ammunition, training, transit areas, replacement centers, field hospitals, and supply depots. Countermeasures undertaken to control those borders by the Greek government and the army failed to have any significant effect on reducing the offensive capabilities of the guerrillas.

The Greek National Army was capable only of pushing its insurgent enemies from one area to another. In the north, the insurgents would move into adjacent Communist territory and subsequently reappear in another part of Greece. However, in the spring of 1949, the Yugoslavian and other frontiers were closed to the Communist guerrillas as a result of negotiations and political decisions made in London, Moscow, and Belgrade. Denial of the various external supporting facilities to the insurgents quickly brought the insurgency under control.[61]

A more recent example of the isolation of belligerents from internal sources of support is found in the Italian "counterterrorism" case during the late 1970s and the early 1980s. The Red Brigades and the other 297 leftist groups claiming responsibility for various terrorist and insurgent acts were isolated from the rest of the Italian community as a result of the effects of the legitimacy war, the intelligence and information wars, and the paramilitary shooting war. As the "terrorists" withdrew more and more into their own compartmentalized secret organizational structure, isolation from the rest of the world became more and more complete. That separation from the outside world further restricted access to the internal Italian political reality, the capability to recruit new members, and the ability to organize significant actions.[62]

The "War" to Stay the Course

All support to a besieged government or, conversely, to a supported violent internal guerrilla challenger must be consistent to be effective. Examination of the post–World War II conflict spectrum clearly indicates that when military, economic, or political aid to a client was withdrawn by an ally or coalition of allies during a conflict (or when any of this support was provided inconsistently), the possibilities for success in the general war were minimal. The data indicate that when aid was provided consistently over the long term, chances for success in an internal war were considerably enhanced. An important center of gravity thus lies in the "community of interest" of the supporting ally (or allies) and the supported government or insurgent/terrorist organization; what happens politically and psychologically in capitals of the world thousands of miles from a "war zone" may be more decisive than any series of military engagements in that zone.[63]

A host of cases (including the Algerian war, 1954–1962; the Vietnamese reunification, 1954–1973; the war in El Salvador, 1980–1989; the Afghan war, 1979–1989; the recent situation in the former Yugoslavia) provide examples of this phenomenon. Nevertheless, in most of the cases in which the British were involved, they managed to create the perception that they were "there to stay" until the conflict was clearly under control. This was the situation in Malaya (1948–1960) and Oman (1965–1975), to mention two examples. Such was not the case in Aden, however. In 1966 Britain announced its intention to withdraw its security forces on the date when that country was to become independent in 1967. To the insurgents this meant that the British would pull out of Aden regardless of the ability of the new government to deal with the ongoing insurgency. As a result, the intended government never really had a chance.[64]

The Intelligence and Information Wars

Individual men and women lead, plan, execute, and support a given conflict. As a result, a major concern in an internal war must be individuals. The intelligence apparatus must be in place, or created, that can locate, isolate, and neutralize an opposing belligerent's organizational and leadership structure. The data demonstrate clearly that the best police, paramilitary, or military forces are of little consequence without appropriate and timely intelligence. Likewise, willing support to the state on the part of a majority of the populace—motivated by legal, democratic, and honest informational actions on the part of the government—is directly related to the synergism and effectiveness of a counterguerrilla war. In the final analysis, however, gaining legitimate long-term military and political power depends on winning the proverbial "hearts and minds" of a people.[65]

The key role of effective—or ineffective—intelligence is clearly demonstrated in the Cuban and Nicaraguan insurgencies of 1956–1959 and 1979, respectively. In these classic cases, the intelligence organizations of the regimes of Fulgencio Batista and Anastasio Somoza continued a "business as usual" attitude during the insurgencies. That is, priority targets tended to be the personal enemies and legitimate internal political opposition of the two dictators. Because of the misdirected effort and lack of concern for any kind of rectitude involving citizens, innocent or not, the real motives of the Cuban and Nicaraguan dictators came into focus. Consequently, the sacrifices necessary to press a fight against insurgents who promised serious reform were not readily forthcoming from either citizen or soldier—and the key element of moral legitimacy was totally subverted.[66]

A good example of an information "war" against a violent internal enemy is, again, found in the Italian case. In that situation, the state and the media embarked on a strong countersubversive public diplomacy campaign. The objective was to expose and exploit the fact that the various left-wing, right-wing, and separatist, pacifist, and other subversive groups operating in Italy during the late 1970s and the early 1980s were not organizations of the masses. Rather, they were self-appointed elites whose goals were not what the people wanted or needed, but instead what the insurgent leaderships wanted or needed. The antisubversive information "war" demonstrated that for the Red Brigades and their allies, those Italians who were not fellow ideological "true believers" were not really people. The thousands of victims killed, maimed, or abducted by the would-be insurgents were not looked at as human beings deserving of some personal dignity but were considered "tools of the system," "pigs," and "watch dogs." As the government and media exposed this fact, counterinsurgent intelligence was willingly provided.[67]

The "War" for Unity of Effort

This dimension of uncomfortable wars involves overcoming parochial bureaucratic interests, fighting "turf battles," overcoming cultural obstacles, and ensuring that all efforts are centered on the ultimate goal—success. That is to say, the necessary organization at the highest levels must exist to coordinate and implement an effective unity of political-diplomatic, social-economic, psychological-moral, and security-stability efforts against those who would violently depose a government. Again, this principle applies equally to an organization that threatens an incumbent regime. In any case, the ability to accomplish these aims in a manner acceptable to the populace is key and equates once again to legitimacy. Without an organization that can establish, enforce, and continually refine a holistic plan and generate consistent national and international support, authority is fragmented and ineffective in resolving the myriad problems endemic to survival in contemporary conflict—and thus, failure ensues.[68]

Ambassador Robert Komer has pointed out that unity of effort was a major deficiency in the Vietnam War.[69] This was also the case for the United States at the Bay of Pigs (Cuba) in 1961; for the British at Aden in 1967; and for the Spanish in the western Sahara in 1975–1976. Other analysts have observed that the "strategic ambiguity" of past United Nations (UN) and current North Atlantic Treaty Organization (NATO) efforts in the former Yugoslavia is also a result of a lack of national and international unity of effort. On the positive side of the unity of effort dimension (with the exception of the 1968 fiasco in Aden), British counterinsurgency experiences seem to dominate, perhaps because of that nation's tendency to appoint an overall coordinator of military and civil activities, with general direction and support by a committee of the cabinet.[70]

SOME ISSUES AHEAD

Even though prudent armies must prepare for high-risk, low-probability conventional war, there is a high probability that the president and Congress of the United States will continue to require military participation in small uncomfortable wars well into the future.[71] The harsh realities of the new world disorder are caused by myriad destabilizers. The causes include (among others) increasing poverty, human starvation, widespread disease, and lack of political and socioeconomic justice. The consequences are seen in such forms as terrorism (both international and domestic), social violence, criminal anarchy, refugee flows, illegal drug trafficking and organized crime, extreme nationalism, irredentism,

religious fundamentalism, insurgency, ethnic cleansing, and environmental devastation. The horrific events of September 11, 2001, brought
home to the people of the United States just how vulnerable this country
is to terrorist attack, while Palestinian terrorist attacks on Israeli civilians
should be a constant reminder of our own vulnerability.

The Problem

These destabilizing conditions tend to be exploited by militant nationalists, militant reformers, militant religious fundamentalists, ideologues,
civil and military bureaucrats, terrorists, insurgents, warlords, and rogue
states working to achieve their own narrow purposes. As a result, the
interdependent global community is experiencing "wars of national
debilitations, a steady run of uncivil wars sundering fragile but functioning nation states and gnawing at the well-being of stable nations."[72]
The threats to national and international stability will be gravely
complicated by "1,000 other snakes with a cause"[73]—and the will to
resort to illegal and asymmetric measures to achieve their nefarious
objectives. In this security environment, military and police forces have
little choice but to rethink security as it applies to the uncomfortable
menaces that many governments have tended to wish away.

The Challenge

Uncomfortable wars will likely have new names, new motives, and new
levels of violence. Nevertheless, whether they are called "teapot wars,"[74]
"camouflaged wars,"[75] "unrestricted wars,"[76] or something else, future
internal as well as external wars can be identified by the lowest common
denominator: motive. And as a corollary, whether they are considered
"spiritual" insurgencies, "commercial"[77] insurgencies, or anything else,
small wars are the organized application of violent or nonmilitary coercion or threatened coercion intended to resist, oppose, or overthrow an
existing government and to bring about political change.[78] It is daunting,
and sometimes overwhelming, to think of the implications for guerrillas,

terrorists, and other self-appointed saviors, who might employ nuclear, chemical, biological, electronic, and informational weapons to attain their objectives. The point remains, however, that whatever it is called, whatever rationale justifies it, whatever means it uses, guerrilla war is widely perceived as an effective way of achieving power and influence.

In this context, every guerrilla war will be unique. It will reflect the history, geography, and culture of the society in which it occurs. Yet analytical commonalities—and strategic-level principles—will continue to be relevant. Ian Beckett is eloquent when he states, "The past of guerrilla warfare and insurgency represents both the shadow of things that have been and of those that will be."[79] The challenge, then, is to adapt those ever-present strategic-level principles to the situation at hand and pursue the contest holistically and with vigor.

The Reality

Although present and future uncomfortable internal conflicts may have different trappings, the hard-learned lessons of the past must be remembered. The continuing relevance of relatively recent experience can be seen in the analytical commonalities that define threat and dictate response, as derived from the SWORD Model.[80]

Moral legitimacy remains the most important single principle of the post–World War II era. It can be seen in the Kurdish problem in Iraq, Iran, Turkey, and Russia from at least 1961 to the present; Sierra Leone since 1991; the Islamic Salvation Front in Algeria since 1992; and Chechnya since 1999, to name a few examples.

Appropriate use of military force is still a key element in determining the success or failure of counterguerrilla wars. The irrelevance of heavy Russian military equipment and conventional training, illustrative of inappropriate use of force, can be seen in the Peruvian effort against the Sendero Luminoso ("Shining Path") and in the Ethiopian case.

The logical need to isolate belligerents from sources of support is obvious in any number of contemporary cases. Two examples would include Colombia and Chechnya. In Colombia, the alliance formed with narco-traffickers is providing generous financial assistance in return for protection of narcotics operations. In Chechnya—and earlier in Afghanistan—the war against Russian domination would be impossible without substantial outside aid from state and nonstate political actors.

The need to "stay the course" remains constant. Without outside aid and internal support, the Irish Republican Army could not function effectively in Northern Ireland. Likewise, the Middle Eastern Kurds would be unable to carry on their wars for national liberation.

Intelligence and information also remain vital to the success or failure of contemporary guerrilla/terrorist war. Participants and observers argue, for example, that the failure of the stability operations in Somalia was due in large part to a failure of the United States and the UN to develop adequate and timely human intelligence about militia groups in that country. In contrast, information campaigns have been an unquestioned key to the success of the Zapatista insurgency in Mexico.

Unity of effort is the last principle that will be noted here. Suffice it to say that the many problems of the UN operation in the Congo (UNOC), the UN operation in Somalia (UNOSOM II), the UN operations in the former Yugoslavia, and the NATO operation in Kosovo stem from a lack of unity of effort among the various contingents making up the specific force.

The Task

Steve Metz and others have identified two characteristics of asymmetric guerrilla threats that are particularly important: defense planners today cannot know precisely what sort of threats will emerge and what types will prove effective; and the effectiveness of asymmetric threats that have an impact will sooner or later decline as an enemy adjusts.[81] These characteristics are both seen clearly in the events of September 11 and its aftermath. The task for the United States is to make the required adjustments sooner rather than later. This demands a willingness to seriously examine our own experience and that of others—dispassionately and honestly. It requires that we fully recognize, apply, and adapt the principles articulated in the SWORD Model, for, as the research shows, this paradigm generally applies to most, if not all, forms of modern conflict. Moreover, it is already well established in U.S. joint and army doctrine.[82] However, the applicability of the model does not mean that decision makers and leaders should follow it slavishly; for, as one observer of army doctrine put it, "Doctrine is not dogma."[83]

◆ ◆ ◆

The value of the ideas or rules derived from the experiences of the past lies in their utility as a conceptual framework within which data from specific situations might be placed and understood. If American and other leaders consider these ideas not as a template but with serious intent, they may be able to translate battlefield courage, logistical superiority, and tactical victories into strategic successes in the current and future security arena.

PART I

The Inescapable World in Which We Live

CHAPTER 2

THE REALITY OF THE CONTEMPORARY GLOBAL SECURITY ENVIRONMENT

Terrorism versus Globalism

Since the end of the cold war, and especially since September 11, 2001, the nature of the global security system and the verities that shaped U.S. purposes, policies, and priorities have undergone fundamental changes. Cold war concepts of security and deterrence are no longer completely relevant. On the positive side of this change, the United States finds itself in a new global security environment that involves the economic integration of free markets, technologies, and countries to a degree of engagement and prosperity never before witnessed. On the negative side of globalization, the nation finds itself in a security environment characterized by unstable peace and chaos caused by myriad political instabilities and destabilizers, some of which would reject modernity and revert back to the questionable glories of the twelfth century.

Thus it is that global political violence clashes with global economic integration. More often than not, the causes and consequences of the resultant instabilities tend to be exploited by such destabilizers as rogue states, substate and transnational political actors, insurgents, illegal drug traffickers, organized criminals, warlords, militant fundamentalists, ethnic cleansers, and a thousand other "snakes with a cause" and the will to conduct terrorist and other asymmetric warfare. The intent is to impose self-determined desires for change on a society, nation-state, or other perceived symbols of power in the global community.

The solution to the problem is not to simply destroy small bands of terrorist fanatics and the governments that support them. Additional measures, as the research for the SWORD Model indicates, are called for. Once a terrorist group is brought under control or neutralized, multidimensional political-economic-security national development or reconstruction efforts must be taken to preclude the seeds that created that organization in the first place from germinating again. In these conditions, exacerbated by the terrorist attacks on New York and Washington, D.C., on September 11, 2001, and by the devastating U.S.-led responses in Afghanistan and Iraq, the United States has little choice but to reexamine and rethink national and global stability and security as well as how to achieve a peaceful and prosperous tomorrow.

THE CURRENT PICTURE

If the appropriate magic could be conjured and one could look down through the familiar artificial political lines and colors of a current world map into the twenty-first-century strategic reality, one could see the details of a complex new global security environment.[1] That milieu would contain several types of ambiguous and uncomfortable wars and their aftermath. Several snapshots within the larger picture would reveal an asymmetrical terrorist concept of conflict and war.

Perhaps the most obvious example would be the 26 ongoing high-intensity wars, 78 low-intensity conflicts, and 178 small-scale internal wars overlapping with the others. This picture would also show unspeakable human destruction and misery—and related refugee flows—accumulating over the past ten years. During the period since the Persian Gulf War, anywhere from 80 million to 210 million people have lost their hopes, their property, and their lives. The resultant political alienation, sufficiently reinforced by economic and social deprivation, tends to direct the survivors and their advocates toward conflict and the tactics of despair, which include but are not limited to terrorism. This disillusionment and willingness to resort to violent strategies (far too often accompanied by terrorist tactics) can be seen in places such as Afghanistan, Sierra Leone, and Rwanda. Add to this kind of instability the efforts of such transnational terrorist organizations as Al Qaeda to overthrow the current international system and its leading member, the United States—as evidenced by the attacks on the USS *Cole*, Khobar Towers, U.S. embassies in Kenya and Tanzania, the Pentagon, and the World Trade Center—and one finds an extraordinarily chaotic world.

Another series of snapshots would yield a view of a vicious downward spiral that manifests itself in diminished levels of popular and institutional acceptance of and support for weak and ineffectual governments and generates further disorder, violent internal conflicts, and mushrooming demands by various groups for political autonomy. These governance issues further translate into the constant subtle and not-so-subtle struggles for power that dominate life throughout much of the world today. This, in turn, leads to the slow but sure destruction of the state, the government, and the society and hundreds of thousands of innocents.[2] Finally, the results of these dynamics can be seen not so much in the proliferation of a host of new countries but in an explosion of weak, incompetent, misguided, insensitive, or corrupt governments throughout the world.

Looking further down through the familiar and troubling world map in this hypothetical view of our current global security environment, one can discern a number of examples of "fuzzy nationalism" that cannot be shown on two-dimensional space. Nationalist discontent, often accompanied by religious militancy, appears to be growing and dividing in an amoeba-like manner as weak and incompetent governments fail to provide political, economic, and social justice; a sense of identity; and basic security for all their peoples. In turn, these injustices fuel regional and global conflict and related terrorist activities. One example of such regional conflict arising from discongruity between cultural identity and the vagaries of state boundaries is the ethnic Kurds, who live in four different countries: Iran, Iraq, Russia, and Turkey. Another example involves the mixed cultures of the peoples who live in the Balkans.

Similarly, one can see a checkerboarding of emerging city-states, shanty-states, amorphous warlord-controlled regions, criminal anarchist–controlled regions, and an unsteady run of uncivil wars sundering fragile but functioning nation-states and gnawing at the well-being of stable nations.[3] These destabilizing situations tend to be exploited by militant

nationalists, militant reformers, militant religious fundamentalists, ideologues, civil and military bureaucrats, insurgents, criminals, warlords,
and other stateless political actors with an extremist political agenda
and the will to resort to extreme violence to achieve their ends. Again,
this is a phenomenon that ranges around the world.

An even deeper look into this theoretical vision of asymmetric battlefields and ambiguous internal wars reveals the human suffering created
by weak and insensitive governance that spawns disease, poverty, crime,
violence, and regional, national, and global instability. Ultimately, this
instability, along with the destabilizers noted above, leads to a crisis of
governance and a downward spiral into failing and failed state status.[4]
This crisis is the consequence of some of the victims and their advocates attempting to mobilize support for serious reform or to wage a
sustained conflict against a perceived power symbol deemed responsible
for whatever instability that is being perpetrated. Snapshots taken
around the world capture this state of affairs, from Haiti to Colombia,
Indonesia, and Zimbabwe, among others.

With another adjustment of focus into the context of contemporary
terrorism and the global security environment, one can see a psychological state of mind in individuals who have no understanding that
hard work leads to its just reward and where life inside a group or gang,
sharing a muddy bunker or a cold safe-house, constitutes an improvement in physical and emotional security. The emotions of these individuals include hatred for those with more or better of anything and
contempt for those outside their own small brotherhood.[5] As examples,
Italian Red Brigadists, Irish Republican Army and Ulster Nationalists,
and French and Spanish Basque militants are documented as thinking of
outsiders as not really people but subhuman or even not worthy of life.[6]

Thus, as these few snapshots illustrate, armed nonstate groups all
over the world are challenging the nation-state's physical and moral
right to govern. This almost chronic political chaos can be seen propagating its respective forms of instability and violence in large parts of
Africa, Eastern Europe, the Middle East, Asia, Latin America—indeed,
in most places around the globe. In many of these cases, governments
are waging war on their citizens, are fighting to survive assaults from
their citizens, or have become mere factions among other competing

political factions claiming the right to govern all or part of a destabilized national territory. In other cases, the concept of the state is being challenged by groups that, while operating from the territory of a state, seek to organize the world based on prior universalist structures.

The primary implication of the complex and ambiguous situations described above is that winning the military struggle against Osama bin Laden and his Taliban protectors, to name only one example, will not end the threat of terrorism against the United States or anyone else in the global community. This is because the Taliban, Osama bin Laden, and Al Qaeda are not isolated cases but a single component of the entire global security problem, which is a manifestation of a complex and potentially durable phenomenon arising from the issues of human motivation and weak governance.[7]

A corollary to that implication is the need to move away from cold war–era responses to perceived threats. When what mattered most in U.S. national security policy were military bases, preserving access to sea lines of communication, choke-points, and raw materials (and denying those assets to the Soviet Union and its surrogates), the United States could generally ignore internal conditions in other countries. But since the United States also is now interested in the need for nonhostile dispositions toward the country, the nonproliferation of weapons of mass destruction (WMD), the capacity of other countries to buy American-made products, the continued development of democratic and free-market institutions, and human rights—as well as cooperation on shared problems such as illegal drugs, the environment, and the victims of natural and man-made disasters—then the United States and its allies must concern themselves with the internal conditions that spawn subnational, national, regional, and global instability.[8]

TERRORISM AND GOVERNANCE

The terrorist attacks on New York City and Washington, D.C., on September 11, 2001, reminded Americans of realities long understood in Europe, the Middle East, Asia, and Latin America. That is, terrorism is a very practical, calculated, and cynical form of warfare for the weak to use against the strong. It is a generalized political-psychological asymmetric substitute for conventional war.[9]

Contemporary terrorism is a lineal descendent of the type of low-intensity conflict seen in the Third World over the past fifty years. It is popular in part because the sorts of rural and urban insurgencies that had some success during the cold war are no longer as expedient as they once were. Additionally, as the means of causing mass destruction become less expensive and more available, the angry, the frustrated, and the weak rely on more asymmetric forms of violence to impose their own vision of justice on peoples, countries, and the global community.[10]

Those who argue that instability and conflict—and the employment of terrorism as a tactic or strategy in conflict—is the result of poverty, injustice, corruption, overpopulation, and misery may well be right. Evidence demonstrates, however, that those problems tend to be used to divert attention away from local governance issues to somebody or something else.[11] In any event, it is naïve to think that instability and conflict will disappear until the deeper human and political realities that produce poverty and misery are confronted.

More specifically, terrorism and its associated asymmetry emerge when fragments of a marginalized self-appointed elite are frustrated to the point of violence by what they perceive as injustice, repression, or inequity. We must remember that it is individual men and women—such as government leaders, civil and military bureaucrats, and transnational corporate leaders—who are ultimately responsible for confronting political, economic, and social injustice. And it is individual men and women—the so-called terrorists—who react violently when a government or other symbol of power is perceived to be unable or unwilling to deal effectively with a given injustice. These individual men and women are prepared to kill and to destroy, and perhaps to die in the process, to achieve their self-determined objectives.[12]

However, an overt or direct challenge puts an illegal attacker at a disadvantage owing to the generally superior conventional power of a targeted government. Thus, the assault is frequently indirect, focusing on weak or ineffective governance or a regime's legitimacy. The ultimate outcome of such a confrontation is thus primarily determined not by the skillful manipulation of violence in the many military battles or police engagements that might take place but by the relative ability of the violent opposition and the government to gain the support of a people or part of a society. Thus, effective political-psychological persuasion coupled with political-psychological-military coercion on the part of the internal attacker can lead to a general weakening of the state. The weakening of an incumbent regime is achieved in direct proportion to the deterioration of its perceived legitimacy.

As a consequence, the intent of an illegal violent attacker is to create (through persuasion and coercion) the popular perception that a governing regime is not providing or cannot provide the necessary balance among political freedom, economic and social development, and physical security that results in peace, stability, and well-being of the peoples of a polity. Additionally, a population must be convinced that the violent internal opposition's proposed political philosophy—even if it is as seemingly irrational as extreme militant reformism, tribalism, or warlordism—represents a relatively better alternative.

In these terms, terrorism undermines the people's faith in the existing political system, the state's ability to sustain a healthy economy, and the government's capability to provide a lawful environment for basic personal security. Terrorism also challenges the integrity of the country's political institutions and creates increasing levels of instability. The objective is to destroy the political equilibrium of the state and facilitate the taking of political power to install the alternative system. As an example, the fact that Islam is a nonviolent religion practiced by millions throughout the world should not blind one to the fact that militant Islamist factions violently seek political power to impose alternative social-economic-political codes.[13]

"Perception" is the operative term in this process. Many legitimate governments face internal and external terrorist threats not because of any lack of legitimacy but because of their unwillingness to submit to the dictates of a given nonstate political actor. In addition, a targeted government or symbol of power may be nothing more than a convenient scapegoat.[14]

This scapegoating is evident in the current wave of international terrorism, in which militant Islamist elements such as Al Qaeda, Hamas, and Hezbollah attack Israel, Saudi Arabia, and the United States when their underlying objective is to overturn the current international system. These terrorist movements are clearly revolutionary in the sense of classical realism.[15] But the focus of their attack is on the legitimacy of the states that make up the system, as a surrogate for the system itself, with all of its institutions.

The perception of moral incorrectness or malfeasance also arises from the reality of governments being unwilling or unable to provide basic services (to maintain decent roads, education, health, and other public services) for all segments of the population, or to provide basic personal security and functional legal systems that protect civil rights and a sense of societal equity. Illegitimate governance is also apparent when disparate ethnic, religious, or other political groups in a society insist on establishing separate identities and the government reacts with thuggish brutality.[16] These governance issues are both causes and consequences of terrorism.[17]

THE MORE COMPLEX THREAT SITUATION

In the context of disillusioned individuals violently reacting to perceived root causes of poverty, misery, and general injustice suffered as a result of the policies pursued by their governments and the global community, there is not one single type of terrorism. There are many. The terrorist phenomenon threatens more than airports, railroad stations, malls, and buildings of administrative governance such as the World Trade Center, the Pentagon, and the Oklahoma City federal building. Terrorists also threaten the stability and existence of governments, international organizations, transnational corporations, and the entire world order.

Internal Wars

Terrorist attacks against all of these targets often result in some form of internal war. These small internal wars (or low-intensity conflicts, guerrilla wars, small-scale contingencies) will likely have different names, different motives, and different levels of terrorist violence, but they are simply new manifestations of an old problem.[18] Regardless of whether these organizers of violence are called criminal anarchists, insurgents, guerrillas, or terrorists, they will likely use terror as a tactic or a strategy to achieve their ultimate objective of change or destruction.

Sooner or later, the spillover effects of international, national, regional, intranational, and transnational terrorist destabilization efforts and the resultant internal conflicts place demands on the global community—if not to solve the underlying problems or control the violence, at least to harbor the living victims.[19] It is in this context that individual nations such as the United States and international organizations such as the United Nations (UN), the North Atlantic Treaty Organization (NATO), other regional organizations, and nongovernmental organizations are increasingly being called on to respond to a given conflict or its aftermath.[20]

At the same time, the international community is increasingly expected to provide the leverage to ensure that legitimate governance, once regained, is given to responsible, uncorrupted, and competent political leadership that can and will aggressively address the governance root causes that created a given crisis in the first place. The main threat to Afghanistan or any other country that might be purged of terrorists is a return to the anarchy of the past and the possible creation or revival of some form of internal conflict.[21]

Multidimensional Threats

The threats in contemporary conflict come in other forms, both direct and indirect. A very visible direct challenge to the state may be manifested in public violence against officials and institutions that are somehow defined by the terrorists as "bad." An indirect threat usually comes in some form of progressive political and psychological discrediting of public institutions. The intent is to psychologically erode the basic public support that must underlie the legitimate functioning of the state. Moreover, a specific challenge to the state may be both direct and indirect.

As an example, the direct consequence of the 1985 Colombian terrorist attack on the national Supreme Court and the assassination of eleven of its justices caused that key institution to function even more slowly and less effectively than usual. This inefficiency led to a further discrediting of the court, to the inability to guarantee civil rights and personal liberties, and, indirectly, to the substantial weakening of the state. In turn, the internal violence and dislocation of people exacerbated by the weakening of the Colombian state spilled over to that country's neighbors and began to create regional instability.[22]

Threat and Response

It may be helpful to think of instability as a third-level threat to national or regional security. Root causes that generate political, economic, and social injustices may be considered a second-level threat to security and stability. The unwillingness or inability of a regime to develop long-term, multidimensional, and morally acceptable reforms to alleviate societal injustice (sooner rather than later) to enhance national well-being should be understood as the most fundamental first-level threat.

At the same time, another threat emerges at a fourth level; it is both a cause and an effect of instability and violence. That is, once a violent internal foe—such as Sendero Luminoso insurgents, Somalian or Southeast Asian warlords, ethnic cleansers, Sierra Leone's armed pillagers, or militant fundamentalists—becomes firmly established, first-level reform and development efforts aimed at second-level root causes become insufficient to control or neutralize a third-level (e.g., terrorist) threat. That third-level violent internal force, regardless of whether it is sincerely attempting to achieve specific political objectives or merely hoping to gain some visceral satisfaction, can be defeated only by a superior organization, a holistic and unified strategy designed to promulgate deeper and more fundamental reforms, and carefully applied deadly force.[23]

Some additional considerations that help to define the contemporary threat and to dictate response focus on the issue of ambiguity. In many situations, the definitions of "enemy" and "victory" become elusive and the use of power to achieve some form of success becomes problematic. Underlying these ambiguous issues is the fact that most contemporary conflict tends to be an intrastate affair, pitting one part or several parts of one society against another. Thus, virtually no rules of traditional warfare apply. There is normally no formal declaration or termination of conflict, no easily identifiable enemy military formations to attack and destroy, no specific territory to take and hold, no single credible government or political actor with which to deal, no international legal niceties such as mutually recognized national borders and Geneva Conventions to help control the situation, and no guarantee that any agreement between or among contending authorities will be honored.

Unfortunately, the tendencies noted here for intrastate conflict have spilled over into the global environment. Thus, international terrorists, epitomized by Al Qaeda, operate under the same lack of rules, complicated further by the issue of sanctuary granted by states that "harbor terrorists." The new century, therefore, marks a new age of unconventional conflict in which only the foolish will fight fair.[24]

Because of the pervasiveness of instability, violence, and terrorist strategies, the United States and the West—as the primary recipients of most of the benefits of global stability and economic integration—have practical reasons to do their utmost to protect and enhance stability and state-based governance. In the interests of national and global security, the United States and its Western allies have the responsibility to understand and implement the strategies that bring prosperity and peace to the rest of the world—before even more people become immigrants, refugees, or pensioners of the West.[25] Yet an enforced peace can provide only the beginning environment from which to start political reconciliation, economic reconstruction, and moral legitimization processes.

TOWARD A NEW STABILITY EQUATION

The fulfillment of a holistic legitimate governance and stability imperative consists of three principal short- and long-term programs that are necessary to free and protect a people from lawlessness, instability, and violence, as well as the aftermath of violence. These programs constitute a basis for a realistic and pragmatic approach focused on the circular relationship of legitimate governance to security, the relationship of security and stability to development, and the relationship between development and political competence. The intent is to build viable institutions that respond to the needs of a society and strengthen governance. The three corollary elements of a strategic stability equation are a military and intelligence capability to provide an acceptable level of internal and external security; the economic ability to generate long-term socioeconomic capability-building; and the political capability to develop a type of political and corporate governance over the long term to which the governed peoples can relate and which they support.[26]

The Relationship of Legitimate Governance to Security

Probably the most fundamental societal requirement regarding governance is that of security. It begins with the provision of personal security to individual members of the society and extends to protection of the collectivity from aggressive internal (including criminal) and external enemies and perhaps, from repressive internal (i.e., local and regional) governments. Personal security is the primary basis upon which any form of societal allegiance to the state is built. Until and unless a population feels that its government deals with the personal security problem and other fundamental issues of social justice fairly and effectively, the potential for internal or external factors to destabilize and subvert a regime is considerable.

The military-police part of the strategic stability equation is generally well understood. Clearly, the military and police forces involved in a national reconstruction, stability, peace, or counterterrorist operation must be capable (as noted above) of establishing individual and collective security. At the strategic level, that entails establishing order and the rule of law and ensuring freedom from intimidation and violence; isolating terrorists, insurgents, and criminal organizations from all sources of internal and external support; and sustaining life, relieving suffering, and helping to regenerate the economy.[27]

The intelligence function makes the military element viable. Logically, the best trained, best equipped, and most mobile forces responsible for the achievement of the above objectives cannot do so without precisely identifying the leadership of the illegal organization and where it is located. That requires an intelligence capability several steps beyond the usual, involving the establishment of unified national and operational intelligence capabilities that include the collection, fusion, and analysis of all sources of information; the active support of intelligence operations as a dominant element of strategy, operations, and tactics; and an effective interrogation capability at the operational and tactical levels, as well as the strategic level, to take full advantage of human intelligence sources.

The Relationship of Security and Stability to Development

The international security dialogue is focusing on internal development and national reconstruction. That requirement equates to a holistic capability-building effort. Until solutions to development problems are addressed on a coherent and long-term basis, no self-sustaining national development will be possible. National development thus provides the capability for the nation-state to develop the political and economic strength to provide internal order and progress.

In the past, socioeconomic development has been emphasized, under the assumption that security and political development would follow. That has generally not happened, because the causal relationships are more tenuous and far less direct than previously thought. Indeed, some evidence suggests that security and political development may, in fact, lead socioeconomic development. Coherent long-term, multilevel, and multilateral measures must be designed both to create and strengthen human and physical infrastructure and also to generate the technical, professional, and ethical bases through which competent and legitimate leadership can effectively provide individual and collective well-being.

The Relationship between Development and Political Competence

Appropriate responses to the problems of terrorism relate to the issue of legitimacy (as discussed in chapter 1), which a governing entity must have before it can effectively manage, coordinate, and sustain political, economic, and social development. This capability implies the political competence to develop responsible governance and a resultant national and international purpose and resolve, supported by the people, as well as the competence to legitimize and strengthen national political, economic, and security institutions. The degree to which this objective is achieved will define, more than anything else, progress toward viable stability and peace.[28]

Because of the various systemic and other problems noted above, outside political help is usually needed if a threatened government is to deal with a given stability threat. Ultimately, however, targeted entities must reform and strengthen themselves. What an outside power or coalition of powers can do is to facilitate the establishment of a temporary level of security that might allow the carefully guided, unified, and monitored development of the underpinnings of technical, professional, and ethical competence that are necessary for long-term success in achieving a civil society and a sustainable peace (see chapter 3). Such long-term facilitating policies, organizations, and programs would, of course, be situation and culture specific. However, several general points are critical for any facilitator to consider. First, the facilitator should create a small multinational organization with a long-term mandate to generate enforceable goals, help institutionalize processes for capability development, provide evaluation, and develop strategies to ensure the global investment in effective multilateralism. Second, the facilitator should also promulgate self-help legislation and programs to develop competent professional leaders, fight corruption, and support people who are resisting violent solutions to internal destabilization problems. And finally, the facilitator must ensure that all programs directly support the vision of legitimate governance and civil society and that they are applied at all levels.

The Ultimate Aim

The days of delineating a successful international security and stability end-state as simple short-term self-protection, limited adherence to human rights and the election of civilian political leaders, or material compassion for a humanitarian problem are numbered. More and more, the American people expect U.S. efforts, especially if these efforts involve the expenditure of large amounts of tax dollars or the expenditure of American lives, to make the world—and the United States—a better place in the long term.

Thus, the main element of U.S. foreign policy, military management, and public diplomacy in the current international security environment must go beyond the notion of democratic enlargement to that of a selective, long-term, patient but firm and vigilant pursuit of responsible and competent (i.e., legitimate) governance. This is not simple or naïve idealism. The concept of legitimate governance is a marriage of Wilsonian idealism and realpolitik that provides a pragmatic foundation for national and global stability and well-being.[29]

POLITICAL-MILITARY IMPLICATIONS FOR PLAYING IN THE NEW GLOBAL SECURITY ARENA

In today's complex global security environment, the problem of preparing only for a specific type of operation to respond to some form of terrorism or other type of aggression is moot—the situation may change, and the type of operation may become irrelevant. Thus, as noted earlier, an enforced peace is only the beginning. If a legitimate civil government (that deals effectively with the root causes that brought on the conflict in the first place) does not ensue, the intervening power faces the unhappy prospects of declaring victory, going home, and waiting for the inevitable relapse into the status quo *ante,* or risking taking part in what will prove little more than a static and sterile military occupation.

As a consequence, time-honored concepts of national security and the classical military means to attain it, while necessary, are no longer sufficient in fighting a terrorist foe. At a minimum, three critical areas for interagency civil-military exploration and development exist: understanding and dealing with the political complexity of stability and counterterrorist operations; addressing and resolving the problem of ad hoc arrangements in strategic planning and coordination; and developing a more mature stability and counterterrorism doctrine.

Political Complexity

The political complexity of contemporary stability and counterterrorist operations stems from the fact that internal conflicts are often carefully plotted by the antagonists and engage many national and international civilian and military organizations and nongovernmental organizations in addition to the people who are the ultimate center of gravity in the conflict. Responses to direct and indirect threats must therefore be primarily political, psychological, and moral rather than what is typically thought of as conventional military force (see chapter 4). Moreover, to avoid introducing strategic ambiguity and increasing the probability of mission failure, responses must be well organized, highly collegial, and conducted with considerable political skill.

Until appropriate long-term political-psychological responses to direct and indirect terrorist threats become reality and until realistic political-psychological responses to multiagency and multilateral coordination and cooperation problems in the contemporary global security environment become habitual, the United States and the rest of the international community face unattractive alternatives. The time, treasure, and blood expended over the short term, as in Somalia, will likely have accomplished very little.[30]

Strategic Planning and Coordination

In this regard, hard-learned lessons from the not-too-distant past are relevant and instructive. As an example, ad hoc problem solving and the convoluted strategic planning and coordination situation that developed in the early Bosnian experience arose from a systemic disconnect between NATO operational and U.S. planning and implementing processes.

Additionally, the United States was not at that time prepared to work collegially between and among the U.S. civil-military representation, coalition partners, international organizations, and nongovernmental organizations.[31] Independent uncoordinated planning produced operational and tactical confusion and required additional improvisations.[32]

Such a convoluted situation reduces the credibility and effectiveness of any kind of operation. For multiagency, multiorganizational, and multilateral operations to achieve any measure of effectiveness, logic and good management practices call for organizational mechanisms to achieve a unity of effort (see chapter 4).

Creating that unity of effort requires, first, that the primary parties be in general agreement with regard to both the objectives of a political vision and the associated set of operations. Such an agreement regarding a strategic or operational endgame, while a necessary condition for unity of effort, is not sufficient. Additionally, an executive-level management structure must be created to ensure continuous cooperative planning and execution of policy among and between the relevant U.S. civilian agencies and armed forces so that all civil-military action directly contributes to the achievement of the political end-state. Improved coordination within the operational theater and between the regional military commander and the multiple U.S. government agencies in Washington is also crucial. Moreover, coalition military, international organization, and nongovernmental organization processes must be integrated with U.S. political-military planning and implementing processes. Above all, however, educational as well as organizational solutions must be crafted.

The Need for More Mature Doctrine

The need for more mature doctrine is made clear when every civil and military organization involved in multilateral situations (such as those in the former Yugoslavia or Somalia) operates under its own procedures or doctrine. To compound this problem, extant doctrine is generally designed to provide conventional military solutions to traditional military problems. No standardized doctrine for all levels in such operations exists, even within the long-standing and mature NATO alliance. Moreover, there is little or no doctrinal recognition of the fact that responses to terrorist threats or to terrorist-made disasters are primarily political and psychological in nature and may be multinational as well. In that context, we are operating with very old doctrine and legalities that need to be changed and brought up to speed as soon as possible. Joint doctrine (within two or more branches of the U.S. armed forces) is good, interagency doctrine is sporadic, and coalition doctrine, except for the NATO alliance, is virtually nonexistent.[33]

Difficult as unity of effort may be to accomplish from an ethnocentric perspective, the doctrinal problem of bringing likely civil-military and international partners together on a level playing field must be dealt with quickly and completely. Relevant doctrine at the conceptual level for providing standardized direction and guidance for multilateral efforts must accomplish several aims:

- recognize the real locus of power (e.g., the civil population) in a given operational area;
- deal with the civilian and military resources and time the stages needed to plan for and implement a successful conclusion to a given mission;
- ensure early and continuous coordination in the assessment and plan-development processes to establish mission responsibilities, to foster supported and supporting relationships and limits, and to avoid unilateral ad hoc reactions to contingencies;
- permit the various cooperating political-military actors to plan, coordinate, and integrate their activities at specified stages of the implementing process;
- and ensure that conditions are established to allow a host nation to develop or renew its political solvency and legitimacy, so that a given mandate for peace and stability may in fact be fulfilled.[34]

Implementing the extraordinary challenges explicit and implicit in the new global security environment will not be easy. Indeed, the entire U.S. civil and military interagency community will be required to use its analytical and educational resources to flesh out concepts and doctrine that reflect the continuities and new dimensions of terrorism. Additionally, the interagency community will have to use its collective ability to engage and help likely coalition counterparts understand and develop these concepts and doctrine for themselves. Difficult as these requirements may be, they are far less demanding and costly in political, monetary, and military terms than allowing the business-as-usual and crisis management approaches to work at cross-purposes with the reality of globalization and the necessity for global stability.

THE CHALLENGE, THREAT, AND MAIN TASK FOR NOW AND THE FUTURE

A multipolar world in which one or a hundred actors are exerting differing types and levels of power within a set of cross-cutting coalitions and alliances is extremely volatile and dangerous. The security and stability of the global community is threatened, and the benefits of globalism could be denied to all. Thus, it is incumbent on the United States and the rest of the international community to understand and cope with the threats imposed by diverse state and nonstate actors engaged in the destabilizing and devastating political violence that is called terrorism.

The challenge is to come to terms with the fact that contemporary security, at whatever level, is at its base a holistic political-diplomatic, social-economic, psychological-moral, and military-police effort. Thus, the fundamental mind-set must be changed from a singular military approach to a multidimensional, multiorganizational (and, at times, multinational) paradigm.

The ultimate threat is that unless and until leaders at the highest levels recognize what is happening strategically, reorient their thinking and actions appropriately, and are able to educate and lead their various constituencies into the realities of the post–cold war world, it is only a matter of time before the destabilizing problems associated with global integration on the one hand and global terrorism on the other will mortally consume one vitally important actor or another. By then, it will probably be too late to exert decisive influence on the situation, and political-military chaos, criminal anarchy, and uncivil wars will continue to spread throughout the world. In the meantime, territory, infrastructure, security, stability, peace, and prosperity will be quietly and slowly destroyed, and hundreds of thousands of innocents will continue to die.

The main task in the search for security now and for the future is to construct stability and well-being on the same strategic pillars that supported success and effectiveness in the past. The first pillar of success is a conceptual requirement: develop a realistic game plan, strategic vision, philosophy, or theory of engagement to deal with terrorists and terrorism, and the human and physical disasters they create. The second pillar is an organizational requirement: the creation of planning and management structures to establish as complete a unity of effort as possible to plan and implement the philosophy. The third is an organizational and operational requirement. Organizationally, it involves developing and implementing the appropriate combination of political, economic, informational, moral, and coercive instruments of national and international power to pursue the multidimensional requirements of the contemporary global security environment. Operationally, it involves learning to understand friends as well as adversaries and assessing potential adversaries culturally, so as to better influence their thought and behavior. (Note that in the case of adversaries, current and potential, the proper conclusion is to "better defeat" them.) The entire effort involves training and educating leaders at all levels to carry out a twenty-first-century game plan.

CHAPTER 3

THE CENTRAL POLITICAL CHALLENGE IN THE GLOBAL SECURITY ENVIRONMENT

Governance and Legitimacy

The contemporary global security environment requires a new approach that recognizes the fact that legitimate governance is the central strategic problem facing the global community. In these terms, instability and violence are the general consequences of unreformed political, social, and economic institutions and concomitant misguided, insensitive, incompetent, and corrupt (i.e., illegitimate) governance. As a consequence, it is imperative to establish, enhance, and maintain the specific internal security, socioeconomic, and political conditions that have proven to lead to sustainable peace, sustainable development, and legitimate civil societies.

With the end of the cold war, many new challenges at home and abroad demand attention and action at a time when what should be done remains unclear. The confusion in the current environment stems in part from the quixotic hope that the disappearance of the Soviet Union would automatically move the world from war to peace. It did not. Instead, the world changed in unexpected ways, and the promise of a peace dividend degenerated into a "new world disorder." The contemporary chaotic strategic environment reflects a lack of legitimate governance in many parts of the world—and the instability and ambiguous threats that thrive under those conditions. This new world disorder and the chaos associated with it are thus the product of a radically changed global security environment and the lack of a central strategy to deal with it.

What Samuel Huntington called a "clash of civilizations" and the political chaos that dominate the world today can be seen propagating their respective forms of instability in various parts of Africa, the former Yugoslavia, the Middle East, Asia, and much of the rest of the global community.[1] Hard evidence over time and throughout the world, however, shows that destabilizers and instabilities related to the clash of nationalities and political disorder are the general consequences of misguided, corrupt, insensitive, and incompetent governance.[2] Thus, governance is the central strategic problem of the contemporary unstable global security environment.

The general threat to the United States and the rest of the global community is the widespread violent challenge to incumbent governments' moral right to govern. It can be direct, as in the case of the highly organized and politicized terrorism experienced in Italy during the late 1970s and early 1980s, or it can be indirect, as in the case of roving bands of government-controlled thugs operating in contemporary Zimbabwe.[3] In any case, the basis of this challenge is the growing perception that many governing regimes (and their legal opposition) do not or cannot provide the necessary balance among political freedom, economic and social development, and physical security that results in peace, stability, and well-being. In that context a challenger's proposed explicit or implicit alternative political structure or philosophy—even if it is as extreme as that of warlordism, jihad, or archaeo-Trotskyite groupescules—represents a different (and purportedly better) way of attaining that balance. As a result, an incumbent government and its legal and illegal opposition stress or "spin" the positive popular perception of its own moral legitimacy. That is the primary means by which it might survive.[4]

These dynamics produce a vicious downward spiral manifested in decreased popular and institutional acceptance of and support for the incumbent regime. Such struggles have brought about the destruction of the government, the society, and—as in the case of Rwanda in the 1990s—hundreds of thousands of innocent people.[5] The consequences of these dynamics are evident not only in the proliferation of new countries but also in an explosion of weak, incompetent, and corrupt governments throughout the world.

A LEGITIMATE GOVERNANCE
STRATEGY OF ENGAGEMENT

To ensure that America's and the world's embrace of democracy and free-market economies—following the victory over communism—is sustained and enhanced, the United States must move forward to a "legitimate governance" strategy of engagement. Legitimate governance is more than de facto or de jure legitimacy. Legitimate governance concerns the manner of governing rather than the fact of international recognition that a given legal entity represents a nation-state, or the fact that a given regime claims to represent a nation-state. Legitimate governance is defined as governance that derives its just powers from the governed and generates a viable political competence that can and will effectively manage, coordinate, and sustain security, as well as political, economic, and social development.[6] Legitimate governance is inherently stable because it has the political competence and societal support to adequately manage internal problems, change, and conflict that affect individual and collective well-being.[7]

The Essential Architecture for Legitimate Governance

For a fragile or vulnerable government, the highest priority must be to legitimize and strengthen the state. The data show that five conditional indicators of legitimate governance must be implemented by political actors facing the nontraditional and traditional threats and internal violence inherent in the current global chaos. These variables are not new in discussions dealing with the idea of legitimacy. Rather, they reflect traditional theoretical concepts closely associated with the classical political-philosophical notion of legitimacy. In general terms they represent consent of the governed and moral rectitude on the part of the governors.[8]

These key indicators and measures of legitimate governance are not exhaustive, but they provide the basic architecture for the common actions necessary to constructively assist embattled governments (e.g., fragile democracies) in their struggle to survive and develop. As such, these indicators constitute a strong coherent conceptual framework on which to construct policy, strategy, and operational efforts. The degree to which a political actor effectively manages a balanced mix of these five variables enables the strengthening, stabilizing, and legitimizing of a governing regime.[9]

The five proven variables that define the legitimizing and strengthening of the state and reflect the classical concept of legitimacy are (1) free, fair, and frequent selection of leaders; (2) the level of participation in or support for the political process; (3) the perceived level of corruption; (4) the level or rate of political, economic, and social development (i.e., the degree to which the government meets the expectations of delivery of necessary government services); and (5) the level of regime acceptance by major social institutions.[10]

Selection of Leaders

The first indicator of legitimate governance—free, fair (i.e., honest and transparent), and frequent selection of leaders—is associated with the philosophical concept of popular consent. In this context the free and fair election or selection of leaders means the absence of corruption of the process and that the process must be culturally understood and accepted by the people involved. This universal requirement for the popular consent to the selection of leaders is a strong indicator—and measure—of governmental moral legitimacy.

As an example, the turning point in the Hukbalahap insurgency in the Philippines was the decision by Minister of Defense Ramon Magsaysay to have the Filipino military guarantee the honesty of the 1951 elections.[11] Similarly, the 1963 elections in Venezuela, the 1975 elections in Portugal, and the elections of 1982, 1984, 1985, 1988, and 1989 in El Salvador were key factors in discrediting the claim of these countries' Communist parties and insurgent factions that peaceful democratic change was not possible.[12]

Individual Participation

Uncoerced popular participation in or support for the political process is another key to a foundation of moral legitimacy for any given method of governance. Although the periodic free and fair selection or election of leaders is an important element in defining legitimacy and democracy, it should not be considered sufficient in itself. Participation or acceptance subsumes the subsequent manifest support of the results of the electoral process and the government by the governed.

In El Salvador, for example, despite serious threats from the insurgents, over 80 percent of the people voted in the elections noted above. People such as the provisional president in 1982, Alvaro Magana, voted for the first time at age fifty-five—not because no previous elections had been conducted but because up to that time the people had seen no point in voting. Those elections of the 1980s generated the popular support and momentum for a system that peacefully brought about serious political, economic, and social changes.[13] Similarly, during the height of the terrorist threat in Italy during the late 1970s and early 1980s, popular support generated by a fair and transparent electoral process upheld the successful counterterrorist effort mandated by the normally fractious Italian parliament.[14]

The electoral process includes more than just open voting. It also demands the ability to organize and present alternative points of view and policies. It is, therefore, closely related to the development of interest groups—what has come to be called "civil society." Ironically, it was this very process that provoked the repression that brought about the civil war in El Salvador, just as it was the success of the process that ultimately produced the successful settlement of that war.[15]

Corruption

The level of corruption of the political, economic, social, and security organs of a nation-state is closely related to the degree of strength or weakness of the state governmental apparatus. Yet corruption, while it always relates to the use of public office for private gain, means perceived corruption. As such, it is both culturally and time dependent.

Nevertheless, corruption can be a major agent for destabilization. The corruption phenomenon has a crucial impact on a regime's ability to perform its functions fairly and equitably. Experience demonstrates that the necessity of meeting a specific client's desires and the intensity of the client's expectations and demands are factors that work against legitimate governance—and against any allegiance to the notion of the public good or consent of the governed. As such, the level of corruption is another important indicator and measure of stability and moral legitimacy.

The Bolivian situation of the late 1970s and early 1980s is instructive. Roberto Suarez Gomez was one of Bolivia's leading drug barons at that time. With his expanding wealth, Suarez became a factor in national politics and engineered his country's 189th coup d'etat. This "coca-*coup*" placed General Luis Garcia Meza in the presidency through a reported $1.3 million bribe. When Garcia Meza assumed office, he appointed a relative of Suarez as the minister of the interior, thereby giving him control of all counterdrug operations in Bolivia. Although the Garcia Meza regime lasted little more than one year, the fortune it generated for the Bolivian narco-elite was significant. One observer suggested the following: "Think of a preposterous figure, double it and know damn well that you've made a gross under-estimate."[16] Clearly, narco-corruption prevented any effective antidrug campaign in Bolivia. However, that corruption led to a collapse of the rule of law and a general weakening of government in direct proportion to its perceived legitimacy. Thus, under those conditions, the best-motivated and best-armed organization on the scene organized Bolivia's 190th coup and took control of that instability.[17]

Sustainable Development

The capability of the government to deliver the basic, essential public services—security, along with political, economic, and social development—is critical to legitimate governance because such services provide the basis for internal strengthening of the state and for demonstrating that the government is responsive to the needs of the people. Such a system is inherently "just" and stable. Any number of cases, mostly in the developed West, show that the level of a regime's ability to fairly and effectively allocate resources for personal security and sustainable development is another indicator and measure of stability and legitimate governance.

Perhaps one of the greatest ironies of the success of communist political warfare in Vietnam, Cambodia, and Laos was the delegitimization of its own cause elsewhere in Southeast Asia, especially in Thailand. The aftermath of that communist victory exposed for all to see that the communists could not live up to their promises for economic well-being, peace, equality, honesty in government, and justice. The communists instead brought economic disaster, more violence, injustice, corruption, and death. In that connection the communist victory in Indochina initiated a stream of hundreds of thousands of refugees who would rather face death in the South China Sea than live under the new communist governments in the region. Thus, it was the clear evidence of a lack of security, economic failure, and political repression in Southeast Asia that combined to make Thailand the "domino that did not fall."[18]

REGIME ACCEPTANCE BY MAJOR SOCIAL INSTITUTIONS

The problems of a society in transition and becoming more and more complex (i.e., modern) cannot be solved by a central government acting alone. This effort requires the cooperation of business and industry; urban and rural labor unions; educational, religious, and cultural institutions; local, regional, and national bureaucracies; and the security forces. As a consequence, active acceptance of and support for a government by the existing and nascent societal institutions of a nation-state are reinforcing requirements for stability, social peace, and legitimate governance.

The critical importance of institutional societal support for a governing regime is seen in the Argentine case. The Proceso de Reorganizacion Nacional that ruled Argentina from 1976 to 1983 was infamous for its brutality and systematic use of state terror in the "Dirty War." Despite the growing evidence of repression and morally reprehensible use of force against the insurgents—and anyone else who got in the way—it was not until the military and political defeat in the battle with the

British for the Falklands/Malvinas Islands that the major Argentine social institutions withdrew their support from the military government. With the loss of institutional support, especially that of the Roman Catholic Church, what was left of moral legitimacy was also lost, and the regime crashed.[19]

The Social Contract

All five indicators of legitimate governance focus on the moral right of a regime to govern. That moral right can be perceived as having been originally derived from the governed in the form of a "social contract." The social contract as described in traditional political theory is maintained through the continuing consent of the governed and through the continuing acceptance and support provided by a country's social institutions. That consent and support are dependent on governments providing or creating propitious conditions for the general well-being in a morally acceptable manner. If a regime breaks that contract for any reason, internal and external instability and violence will be the likely result.

TOWARD THE ULTIMATE POLITICAL OBJECTIVE

The realities generated by the Soviet and Eastern European revolutions of 1989 and the ending of the cold war reflect an extremely dangerous and volatile world. Problems of interdependence, multipolarity, and the proliferation of weapons of mass destruction and sophisticated nonlethal weapons are compounded by other factors, including the bureaucratic incompetence and corruption that compromise governments' ability to control national territory, provide meaningful internal development, and maintain basic legitimacy. These dynamics are manifested in a number of disparate activities characterized by instability and violence. Nevertheless, instability and violence are not the primary threats in the international security environment. The primary threat is the unwillingness or inability of governments to deal with the causes of instability.

Thus, intranational, national, and global security depend on a combination of internal and external political, economic, social, and security activities that provide the bases for a legitimacy strategy of engagement for sustainable development and peace and the creation of civil society. At the same time, the way in which the global community (or the United States, acting in the role of an international "consultant") confronts illegitimate governance and prevents or responds to its depredations sets the stage for how the rest of the tragedy will play out. In these terms, the United States must operationalize the legitimizing elements that lead to the achievement of the strategic objective and outline a "facilitator" role for American leadership in the contemporary global security environment.

Applying a Legitimacy Strategy of Engagement

A legitimacy model for engagement depicts the activities and efforts of the various political actors involved in an attempt to achieve sustainable stability, prosperity, and peace in a given part of the world. It portrays the allegiance of a people as the primary center of gravity. The balance of persuasive and coercive measures will determine success or failure in the achievement of a just civil society and a durable peace. Thus, the government and its external allies can coerce and persuade the populace into demonstrating supportive actions on their own behalf. The internal illegal opposition and its allies can do the same thing. In addition, the people and their institutions can coerce and persuade the government or opposition to change the conditions in society, to meet their demands, and to undertake the types of behavior and actions that they perceive to be legitimate. Thus, this model also depicts an interesting and dynamic competition for the allegiance of a people.

The essential foundational elements for achieving a just civil society and sustainable peace are postulated as clusters of related political, economic, social, and security activities that must be performed at the strategic or macro level. These broadly inclusive elements are establishing security, capability-building, and nurturing legitimate governance.

ESTABLISHING SECURITY

A fundamental societal requirement is for government to provide security—that is, "to insure domestic Tranquility, provide for the common defence."[20] Security encompasses personal security for all members of a society as well as corporate, institutional, and national security. The security problem posed by intranational or nonstate actors ends with the establishment of firm but fair control over the entire disputed territory.

Strategic planners must understand that once an illegal internal enemy—such as Peru's Sendero Luminoso, Sierra Leone's armed pillagers, Zimbabwe's governmental thugs, Southeast Asia's narcotics organizations, or Colombia's "Hobbesian Trinity" of insurgents, narco-barons, and paramilitary vigilante groups—becomes firmly established, reform and development efforts are insufficient to deal with the entire security problem. The illegal challenger organization will finally be defeated only by a superior organization and a political-military strategy designed to neutralize or eliminate it. The sum of the parts of a desired countereffort to deal with a major internal security threat requires not only a certain political competence to coordinate a wide-scale political-military security effort, but also the exertion of effective, discrete, and deadly force.[21] However, for ultimate effectiveness, the political and security forces must be able to deal with the illegal opposition on the basis of the rule of law.[22]

In addition to the need to establish and maintain the rule of law, personal and collective freedom from intimidation and violence includes two other elements. First, there is a need to politically, psychologically, economically, and militarily isolate warring political and criminal factions from all sources of internal and external support. Second, security requires sustaining life, relieving suffering, and regenerating a distressed economy.

CAPABILITY-BUILDING

The international security dialogue focuses on the problem of national economic development. Underdevelopment and the resultant individual and collective poverty are being recognized as among the world's most overwhelming threats. On the positive side of capability-building for sustainable development, the term implies the development of political competence that can and will manage the development of the national economy honestly and effectively. On the negative side of this problem, ignoring the political competence variable within the context of an economic development program implies all of the instabilities and threats associated with the corrosion of the fabric of society.

For example, authoritarian governments that are insensitive to social and political change—such as those of the former Soviet Union, Eastern Europe, and elsewhere in Africa, Asia, and Latin America—supported industrialization and economic growth policies and programs for over fifty years. These policies and programs produced environmental degradation, increased poverty, disease, backwardness, and social disintegration. Decision makers and policy makers appear to have done little more than watch, pontificate, and improve their personal perquisites while ecosystems, infrastructure, and stability were slowly destroyed, and tens of thousands of innocents were victimized. The status of East Germany (the German Democratic Republic) when it was reintegrated into the Bundesrepublik is only one case in point. The ongoing relative political instability in Indonesia is another.[23]

In the past, stimulation of the economy was expected to automatically lead to societal stability and political development over the long term. Somehow, stimulation of the economy was also expected to reduce economic disparities, improve equity, and restore justice. That has not happened. To generate a viable political competence that can and will manage, coordinate, and sustain security and economic and political development, three additional goals must be accomplished: perceived corruption must be significantly reduced, political consent must be fostered, and popularly accepted peaceful societal conflict resolution processes must be established and maintained. With these building blocks in place, legitimate civil society and sustainable peace become genuine possibilities.[24]

NURTURING LEGITIMATE GOVERNANCE

Finally, in nurturing a sustainable civil society and a durable internal peace, it is also necessary to develop aggressive unified political-diplomatic, social-economic, psychological-moral, and military-police engagement in society to deal effectively with the multidimensional root causes of the instability and violence. The intent is to eliminate the corruption and generate the societal acceptance and support that governing institutions need to adequately and fairly manage internal problems—and to guarantee individual and collective well-being.

Generally, this requires a concerted anticorruption and public diplomacy effort. No policy, no strategy, and no internal or foreign engagement can be sustained for any length of time without at least the tacit support of the people involved. Lessons learned from Malaya, Vietnam, and the former Yugoslavia demonstrate the absolute necessity of protecting one's own center of gravity while taking the offensive against that of an adversary. That requires capturing the proverbial hearts and minds of the peoples involved.

No group or force can legislate or decree these measures for itself. It must develop, sustain, and enhance them by its actions over time. Legitimization and internal stability derive from popular and institutional perceptions that authority is genuine and effective and uses morally correct means for reasonable and fair purposes. In most cases, developing the essential architecture for legitimate governance will involve a risky long-term attempt to change a failed or failing state's political culture. The intent would be to provide physical and structural security; serious political, economic, social, and judicial reforms; and rational ways and means of sustaining these ends. Indeed, the state in question need not be "failed or failing," as the cases of the newly independent East Timor and occupied Iraq demonstrate. The extent to which all the indicators of legitimate governance are applied will vary, depending on the situation. The evidence from over seventy wars of the late twentieth and early twenty-first centuries shows, however, that when all five variables are strong and dynamic, the probability of success is increased.[25] Conversely, when some of the indicators are weak or applied in an ad hoc, piecemeal, or unbalanced manner, the probability of failure is increased. The implication is clear—a decision that one or more of these indicators is "too hard" to accomplish will result in a final decision for failure.

Redirection of Policy

In this era of geopolitical change, the United States has the opportunity and responsibility to redirect policy from one that is essentially ad hoc crisis management (and vulnerable to the whim of television coverage and domestic polling) to one that is basically proactive and positive (and to which the American people can relate). By emphasizing a foundation of moral legitimacy, along with socioeconomic, security, and political competence factors, that strategy for engagement draws on the major historical currents of U.S. foreign policy to provide a new paradigm for strategic engagement.

The new strategy does two things. First, it provides a conceptual framework by which to cope successfully with the changed and transitional global security environment. Second, the adroit application of this paradigm can help make the world—and the United States with it—a better place. If the United States is to fulfill the promise that the end of the cold war offered, there is no choice but to meet the legitimate governance challenge of the new world disorder.

Coping with Chaos: A Role for the United States

In this time of change, the United States clearly cannot police the world and do all the things that all the various actors in the global community would like. Yet as the greatest beneficiary of global integration, the United States has the greatest interest in maintaining and enhancing the interdependent order. Nevertheless, such exercising of global leadership must be carefully thought-out and selective. The nation must be focused on the strategic problems and issues that are most relevant to American interests, and efforts and resources should be centered where they can make the most positive differences. The United States must also be willing to act unilaterally when direct national interests are most at risk, in alliance and partnership when interests are shared by others, and multilaterally when interests are more general. In any case, the nature of the response must depend on the type of threat and on what best serves long-term national interests.

Increasingly, the United States, the United Nations, and other international political actors are being called on to respond to injustices and instabilities generated by unreformed political leadership. In this connection the international community is expected to provide the leverage to ensure democratically elected, uncorrupted, responsible, and competent leadership. One might hypothesize that the most effective type of global role for the United States is that of strategic "facilitator" for the development of legitimate civil societies, rather than that of "policeman" or "social worker." The key to success is to carefully pick clients as well as fights. The idea would be for the United States to act more like an international consultant, helping clients reconcile what they can have with what they do have—"rather than playing the aging Santa Claus rapidly running out of toys for resentful pre-teens with guns."[26]

CRITICAL GUIDING POINTS

In the long term the people and government of a fragile, failing, or failed state must save themselves from themselves. In the short term, however, a vulnerable people or government will likely require outside help. Probably the best measure that can be taken by an outside power or coalition of powers is to help establish a temporary level of security that might allow the carefully guided development of the ethical and professional underpinnings necessary for the promulgation of a holistic strategy of governmental legitimization and strengthening.

Additional critical points are, first, that the host government and its internal allies—and its external "facilitator"—must be in general agreement on a strategic vision of the legitimate governance political objective (end). Second, these parties must be in general agreement on courses of action (ways) that are designed to contribute directly to the achievement of the mutually agreed-upon end-state. Third, these parties must be in general agreement on the economic, human, and other resources (means) necessary and available to support the mutually agreed-upon courses of action. Fourth, these requirements reflect a need for an organizational structure for improved coordination and cooperation between and among the host government and its internal and external allies. Finally, all of these facets require mutual cultural awareness and sensitivity. Otherwise, efforts may be irrelevant or even counterproductive.

HOLISTIC AND LONG-TERM "FACILITATOR" ORGANIZATIONS AND PROGRAMS

The necessary organizations and programs to promote and consolidate legitimate governance are, of course, situationally and culturally specific. However, multiple prescriptive and cautionary points for the facilitator to understand and apply have become evident through past experience.[27]

First, the facilitator (or facilitators) should create a small organization, preferably multinational in composition, with a long-term mandate to do several things: institutionalize the necessary consultation, planning, and implementation processes for sustainable political, economic, and social development; generate a rational, prioritized, and synchronized set of milestones for programs that will preclude piecemealing and "ad hockery"; provide evaluation; develop strategies to get relevant programs through the facilitator's, as well as the assisted country's, legislative and bureaucratic processes; and hold host country officials accountable and responsible for meeting standards, milestones, and objectives.

Second, the facilitator should promulgate programs and legislation designed to accomplish the following general aims: support (politically, economically, and militarily) those peoples who are resisting attempted subjugation by armed and violent internal factions, by outside forces, or by both; and provide and institutionalize long-term administrative, technical, and professional leader education and development programs to impart understanding, competence, and know-how. Both types of legislation should not be "giveaway" but should instead be concentrated on self-help and mutual assistance approaches within a given community. An example of such legislation and associated program would be the 1947 Truman Doctrine for economic and military aid to Greece and Turkey.

Third, the facilitator should also ensure that all programs directly support the mutually agreed-upon strategic vision of legitimate governance and that all are applied at the highest levels. Grassroots programs, by themselves—such as the improvement of the administration of justice—tend to make corrupt institutions more effective. Again, experience clearly shows that effective reform must begin at the top and consistently be supported from the top.[28]

Implementing the recommended extraordinary challenges of reform and regeneration will not be easy. It will, however, be far less demanding and costly in political, economic, social, and military terms than allowing the causes and consequences of a failing or failed state's illegitimate governance to continue, thereby generating crises that work to the detriment of all.

CHAPTER 4

STRATEGIC CLARITY

We live in a time in which a number of our basic assumptions about geopolitics and military power have been rendered obsolete. In just a few short years, the nature of the international system and the verities that shaped U.S. national purpose have undergone fundamental changes. The United States emerged a victor from the cold war, but success has undone more than one champion; and unlike winning a game, having won the cold war has only made the playing field more crowded. The intellectual and political coherence of policies that saw stability, security, and peace as indivisible—and thus provided a sound foundation on which to plan, to structure requirements, to build campaign plans and force structures, and to sell to the public the need for sacrifice through taxes and service—ended when the cold war ended. The playing field, rules, and participants are more complex, and identifying the objectives of the game is more perplexing. Many new challenges at home and abroad have emerged, demanding immediate attention and action at a time when what we should do is unclear and when resources for foreign-affairs programs are constrained.

Perhaps the greatest threat to U.S. national security is the danger that we Americans do not change our thinking to coincide with the changes in the world around us. America's principal defense priority for more than forty years was the management of low-probability, high-intensity nuclear conflict, with a primary focus on Europe. Ironically, however, the more than a hundred armed conflicts that took place during that time were classified as low intensity and took place outside Europe. During the cold war era, we Americans were slow to adapt our thinking, organization, and resource allocations to high-probability, low-intensity conflict, in which our military's role is usually relatively small and indirect and extraordinary political support is required for civilian authorities in their development efforts. As a result, the national security planning focus has been on the relatively unambiguous military high end of the conflict spectrum, while for some years U.S. civilian agencies and military forces have been increasingly engaged in operations at the highly political and ambiguous lower end of the conflict scale. World leadership now and in the future will depend on a different set of assumptions, assets, and resources than it did during the cold war era of superpower confrontations.

Considerable form and structure, institutional habits, and ways of thought remain. Indeed, some people now long for the "good old days" when the enemy was obvious and the terms of reference simple. It is daunting, and at times overwhelming, to think of the nuances of a complex multipolar and largely anarchic world. Nevertheless, like it or not, prepared for it or not, we must develop an organizing paradigm to assist us in generating strategic clarity out of the current bewildering global political chaos and ambiguity. To achieve the vision necessary to reach this end-state, we must first examine common strategic lessons learned from recent U.S. civil-military experience and analyze the most salient contemporary keys to planning and implementing strategic clarity—and achieving success.

RECENT U.S. CIVIL-MILITARY EXPERIENCE AND STRATEGIC AMBIGUITY

The lessons learned from such highly diverse U.S. experiences in the human emergencies encountered in Iraq, Afghanistan, Bosnia, Kosovo, Haiti, Somalia, and elsewhere in the global security environment are closely interrelated and focus on five common themes: (1) general considerations that help define threat and dictate response, (2) the political complexity of contemporary conflict, (3) the need to generate shared goals among and between the various players, (4) the need for an integrated strategic planning and implementation process, and (5) the need to provide more mature civil-military leadership preparation. The consistency of the lessons derived from these and other complex man-made and natural disasters over the past ten years and more is impressive and warrants confidence both that these lessons represent the major dimensions of effective contemporary conflict management efforts and that this experience is more than adequate to initiate the process of rethinking the problem and reshaping response.[1]

General Considerations That Help Define Threat and Dictate Response

When Americans think about national and global security, we tend to invent for ourselves a comfortable U.S.-centric vision: a situation with battlefields that are well understood, with an enemy who looks and acts more or less as we do, and a situation in which the fighting is done by uniformed military organizations—somewhere else. We must recognize, however, in protecting American interests and confronting and influencing an adversary today, that the situation has changed.

Above all, the world has seen and will continue to recognize a wide range of ambiguous and uncomfortable threats in the "gray area" between conventional war and peace. These threats and challenges are the consequences of root-cause pressures and problems perpetrated or exploited by a variety of internal and international nonstate political actors and manifested by transnational illegal drug trafficking, organized crime, corruption, terrorism, warlordism, insurgency, civil war, regional wars, Islamist terror, large-scale refugee flows, famine, and ethnic cleansing, among a host of other horrors. Delineating enemies and defining success in such a complex environment is problematic, and strategically planning for the use of military force to secure, maintain, and enhance vital interests becomes all the more difficult. Underlying these ambiguities is the fact that contemporary conflict is often an intrastate affair, pitting part of one society against another. Transnational terrorism—particularly the Islamist variety—only expands the range of phenomena that make up these threats (see chapter 2).

As a consequence, the terms "enemy," "power," and "victory" need to be redefined. The enemy is no longer a recognizable military formation or an industrial capability to wage a traditional war but instead has become violence and the causes of violence. Power is not simply combat firepower directed at a conventional enemy military entity or war-making capability but is instead multilevel and combined political, psychological, moral, informational, economic, societal, military, police, and civil bureaucratic activity that can be brought to bear appropriately on the causes as well as the perpetrators of violence. And "victory" is no longer the obvious and acknowledged destruction of military capability but instead is now perhaps more aptly referred to as "success" and may be defined—more and more, and perhaps with a bit of "spin control"—as the achievement of stability and a sustainable peace.

These ambiguities intrude on the "comfortable" vision of war in which the assumed center of gravity has been enemy military formations and the physical capability to conduct war. However, as Clausewitz observed, "in countries subject to domestic strife . . . and popular uprisings, the [center of gravity] is the personalities of the leaders and public opinion. It is against these that our energies should be directed."[2] Although he was not addressing transnational terrorism, his analysis is equally useful in this venue. Thus, in contemporary intranational conflict, the primary center of gravity has changed from a familiar military concept to an ambiguous and uncomfortable political-economic-psychological-security paradigm.

In these terms, conflict is no longer a simple military-to-military confrontation. Conflict now involves entire populations. Conflict now involves large numbers of national civilian and military agencies, other national civilian organizations, international organizations, nongovernmental organizations, and subnational indigenous actors involved in dealing in one way or another with complex threats to security, peace, and well-being. As a result, an almost unheard-of unity of effort is required to coordinate the multilateral, multidimensional, and multiorganizational paradigm necessary for successful engagement in the contemporary interdependent world.[3]

Finally, contemporary nontraditional "conflict" is not a kind of appendage—lesser or limited—to the traditional military paradigm. It is a great deal more. As long as opposition exists that is willing to risk all to violently take down one or more governments and establish its own, there is war. In this zero-sum game there can be only one winner; as a consequence, the war is total.[4]

This is a reality for now and into the future. The threat inherent in not taking the totality of contemporary conflict seriously is straight-forward. Unless thinking and actions are reoriented to deal with that fact, the problems of global stability and security will resolve them-selves—there won't be any.

The Political Complexity of Contemporary Conflict Situations

The political complexity of contemporary stability problems stems from the fact that intrastate conflicts are the result of careful political consideration and strong political motivation. Additionally, a large number of national and international civilian and military organiza-tions and nongovernmental organizations are engaged in a broad political, economic, informational, and security effort to bring peace and stability to specified peoples. Thus, contemporary conflict is not only political but also cultural. Understanding and working effectively in that complex environment depends on mind-set adjustments that will allow leaders and planners to be comfortable and at ease as part of a synergistic process.

The political complexity issue dominates contemporary conflict situations at two different levels—the type of conflict and the coopera-tion politically necessary to deal with it. First, in internal conflict, confrontation is transformed from the level of military violence aimed at limited objectives to the level of a political-psychological struggle for the proverbial hearts and minds of a people, who become the ultimate center of gravity. Within the context of a people being the ultimate center of gravity, antagonists can strive to achieve the Clausewitzian admonition to "dare to win all"—the complete political overthrow of a given government—instead of simply attempting to obtain leverage for limited territorial, economic, political, or social concessions in the more traditional sense. Thus, contemporary conflict is not an extension of politics; politics is an extension of conflict.[5]

In this environment, responses to direct and indirect threats must be primarily political and psychological. The blunt force of military formations supported by tanks and aircraft could be irrelevant or even counterproductive. The more subtle use of political, economic, psychological, and moral instruments of power—supported by public diplomacy, careful intelligence work, and surgical precision in "law-enforcement efforts"—within a society would be imperative.[6] At the second level of political dominance, that of leadership and cooperation, a mandate likely to be promulgated for military intervention in an intrastate instability situation such as that in the Balkans might read something like this:

> In cooperation with international organizations, national civilian agencies, nongovernmental organizations, and coalition partners, initiate a combined peace and stability operation to aggressively take control of a contested area, stop any escalation of violence, and impose an internationally acceptable level of law and order. In addition, be prepared to support relevant civil agencies in dealing with the political, economic, and social aftermath of the violence.

This kind of situation requires the greatest civil-military and military-military diplomacy, cooperation, and coordination. In such situations, responses must also be well organized, highly cooperative, carefully coordinated, and conducted with considerable political skill. Otherwise, "strategic ambiguity" is introduced; belligerents are given the opportunity to "play at the seams" of the operation and frustrate objectives; allies are allowed to pursue their own agendas; political, personnel, and monetary costs rise; and the probability of mission failure increases.[7] As an example, the ongoing tragedy in West Africa is a reminder that "trying to do good is not as much futile as exceptionally complicated. Succeeding is a product of shrewd planning, not wishful thinking."[8]

Generating Shared Goals

In the past, small-scale peace and stability operations tended to be unrealistically viewed as providing military solutions to military problems. Presently, the complex realities of these kinds of missions must be understood as a holistic process that relies on various civilian and military agencies and contingents working together in an integrated fashion to achieve a common political end. In the Balkans, for example, early U.S. military coordination during the assessment and plan-development phases did not involve key U.S. civilian organizations, international organizations, coalition partners, or nongovernmental organizations. Later, planning and implementing procedures broke down in the face of competing national interests and institutional agendas, as well as segregated planning and implementing processes. Moreover, in the absence of a single overarching political-military campaign plan, ad hoc reaction to changing conditions and "mission creep" became the norm. As a result, there was no strategic clarity, little if any unity of effort, and very limited effectiveness.[9]

A former supreme allied commander in Europe, General John R. Galvin (U.S. Army, retired), argues that continuous and cooperative planning among and between national and international civilian and military organizations, beginning with a strategic assessment of a given situation, can establish a mechanism for developing a common vision for ultimate political success (i.e., strategic clarity). After that is in place, shared goals and objectives, a broad understanding of what must be done or not done or changed, and a common understanding of possibilities and constraints will generate an overarching campaign plan that becomes the basis for developing subordinate plans that will make direct contributions to the achievement of a desired end-state. Thus, the roles and missions of the various national and international civilian and military elements evolve deliberately—rather than in response to "mission creep"—as the situation changes to accommodate progress toward the achievement of a mutually agreed-upon political vision. All of these integrative efforts ultimately ensure the conditions that will allow a host nation to develop or renew its political solvency and legitimacy—and that increase the likelihood that a given mandate for peace will, in fact, be achieved.[10]

The Need for Integrated Strategic Planning and Implementing Processes

Ad hoc problem solving and the resultant strategic ambiguity that has developed in diverse man-made and natural disasters—such as Bosnia, and Central America in the aftermath of Hurricane Mitch, respectively— is a consequence of a systemic disconnect between U.S. civilian and military, coalition partner, international, host nation, and nongovernmental organization planning and implementing processes. By definition, independent uncoordinated (called "stove-pipe") planning and implementation processes prevent unity of effort. They also sow confusion; require sometimes counterproductive "quick fixes" to command and control arrangements, mission limits, supported and supporting logistical and personnel mechanisms, rules of engagement, and status-of-forces agreements; contribute to the duplication and triplication of effort; and add significantly to the political, monetary, and personnel costs of a given civil-military operation.[11] The most recent case supporting this analysis is the "ad-hockery" accompanying the postconflict occupation and reconstruction of Iraq.

Given such a convoluted organizational and procedural situation, making any kind of operation credible or effective is extremely difficult. For contemporary civil-military operations to achieve any measure of effectiveness beyond "putting a lid on the situation," logic and good management call for integrating organizational mechanisms—and mind-set adjustments—designed to achieve a unity of effort. That is, political-diplomatic, social-economic, psychological-informational, and military-police efforts must be well coordinated and integrated to be effective against those illegal violent elements who would destroy a given failing or failed state. As difficult as this task may be in an ethnocentric cultural environment, the United States needs to reorient its thinking and actions to deal with the issues of leader judgment and unity of effort, or "there won't be any" solutions to the problems of global chaos.[12]

Civil-Military Leadership Development

At least at the outset, U.S. military and civilian leaders appear to have had some difficulty in rising to the challenge of operating cooperatively in complex conflict situations. The requirements of the contemporary global security environment take us beyond traditional peacekeeping responsibilities, beyond providing humanitarian assistance, beyond repelling simple aggression. The amorphous contemporary global security task is to create internal conditions within failing or failed states that can lead to peace and stability with justice.

Once the necessary internal conditions for peace and stability are established, "only sustained, cooperative work to deal with underlying economic, social, cultural, and humanitarian problems can place an enforced peace on durable foundations."[13] Otherwise, it will be only a matter of time before a relapse into instability and conflict occurs. Thus, civilian and military leaders at all levels must know how to make difficult decisions in ambiguous situations. They must understand the complete political-strategic nature of their tactical and operational actions. They must understand ways by which force can be employed to achieve political and psychological as well as military ends. They must understand the ways in which political-psychological considerations affect the use of force. They must understand how to communicate and deal with a diversity of organizations, peoples, and cultures. They must understand and deal with the local and global media. Finally, they must understand how to cooperatively plan and implement interagency, international organization, nongovernmental organization, and coalition military operations. As General Galvin stated, "Any denial of any of this is unthinkable."[14]

Validity of the Lessons

In sum, these are five sets of the most salient lessons from America's most recent conflicts: from Afghanistan to Iraq, from Bosnia to Central America, from Haiti to Lebanon, from Rwanda to Serbia, and from Vietnam to Zaire. The consistency of these lessons derived from recent experience inspires confidence that the lessons are valid. "If we can't learn from this experience, we are doomed to the status quo—and 'ad-hocking' it every time."[15]

KEYS TO PLANNING AND IMPLEMENTING STRATEGIC CLARITY

Two common denominators transcend the lessons noted above and have immediate implications for the U.S. military and other civilian agencies involved in dealing with contemporary complex conflict situations. The first common denominator, unity of effort, involves the political, coalitional, and multiorganizational partnership requirements that mandate doctrinal and organizational change for strategic clarity and greater effectiveness in conflict situations. This, in turn, depends on the second denominator: the professional civil-military leadership that will ensure not just unity of military command but unity of all civil-military effort.[16]

Unity of Effort

The United States is not the only political actor in the global security arena, and it is not the only player in more specific smaller-scale contingency operations. At the same time, the U.S. military is not the only participant in any kind of U.S. involvement in the international security environment. A bewildering array of U.S. civilian agencies, international organizations, and nongovernmental organizations, as well as coalition and host country government civilian and military organizations, respond to complex humanitarian emergencies and state collapse. For any degree of success in "going beyond declaring victory and going home" and actually providing the foundations of a sustainable and just peace, involvement must be understood to be a holistic process that relies on various U.S. and other civilian and military agencies and contingents working together in an integrated fashion. The creation of that unity of effort to gain ultimate success must be addressed at different levels.

First, at the highest level, the primary parties to a given conflict must be in general agreement with regard to the objectives of a political vision and the associated set of operations. Although such an agreement regarding a strategic or operational end-state is a necessary condition for unity of effort, however, it is not sufficient. Sufficiency and clarity are achieved by adding appropriate policy implementation and military management structure—and mind-set adjustments—at the following three additional levels.

The second level of effort requires an executive-level management structure that can and will ensure continuous cooperative planning and execution of policy among and between the relevant U.S. civilian and military agencies (i.e., vertical coordination). That structure must also ensure that all political-military action at the operational and tactical levels directly contributes to the achievement of the mutually agreed-upon strategic political end-state. This requirement reflects a need to improve coordination both within the operational theater and between the theater commander and Washington.

Third, steps must be taken to ensure clarity, unity, and effectiveness by integrating coalition military, international organization, and nongovernmental organization processes with U.S. political-military planning and implementing processes (i.e., horizontal coordination). Clearly, the political end-state is elusive and operations suffer when no strategic planning structure exists that is empowered to integrate the key multinational and multiorganizational civil-military elements of a given operation. Also, duplication of effort (an immediate consequence of the absence of such a strategic planning body) is costly in political, personnel, and financial terms.

At a base level, however, unity of effort requires education as well as organizational solutions. Even with an adequate planning and organizational structure, ambiguity, confusion, and tensions are likely to emerge. Only when and if the various civilian and military leaders involved in an operation can develop the judgment and empathy necessary to work cooperatively and collegially will they be able to plan and conduct operations that meet the needs of the host nation and also use the appropriate capabilities of the U.S. interagency community, international organizations, nongovernmental organizations, and coalition military forces. Unity of effort ultimately entails the type of professional civilian and military education and leader development that leads to effective diplomacy, as well as to professional competence.

Leader Development

Until civilian and military leaders learn to think and act strategically and cooperatively within the global security environment, the United States and the rest of the international community face unattractive alternatives. Either they can leave forces in place to maintain a de facto military occupation, as in Cyprus, or they can depart the scene with the sure knowledge that a given conflict will erupt again and again, as in Rwanda. At a minimum there are five educational and cultural imperatives to modify cold war and ethnocentric mind-sets and to develop the judgment needed to deal effectively with these complex contingencies.[17]

First, the study of the fundamental nature of conflict has always been the philosophical cornerstone for understanding conventional war. It is no less relevant to nontraditional conflict. Thus, as discussed previously, concepts such as "enemy," "war," and "victory" should be reconsidered and redefined for intrastate and other forms of asymmetric conflict. Moreover, nontraditional interests centering on national and international stability need to be reexamined and redefined. Finally, the application of all the instruments of national and international power—including the full integration of legitimate civil and military coalition partners—to achieve political ends has to be rethought and refined.

Second, civilian and military leaders at all levels must understand the strategic and political implications of tactical actions. They must also understand the ways in which force can be employed to achieve political ends and the ways in which political considerations affect the use of force. In addition, leaders at all levels need to understand "ambiguity" and be fully prepared to deal with it.

Third, U.S. civilian and military personnel are expected to be able to operate effectively and collegially in coalitions or multinational contingents. They must also acquire the ability to deal collegially with civilian populations and with local and global media. As a consequence, efforts that enhance interagency as well as international cultural awareness, such as civilian and military exchange programs, language training programs, and combined (multinational) exercises, should be revitalized and expanded.

Fourth, planners and negotiators who will operate at the strategic and high operational levels should be nurtured to function in coalitional decision-making and planning situations that can blend the U.S. deliberate planning process with concurrent multinational and multiorganizational practices.

Finally, education and training for contemporary man-made or natural emergencies must prepare military "peacekeepers" or "humanitarian relief providers" to be effective warfighters. The "savage wars of peace" have and will continue to put such forces into harm's way. Political actors in an intrastate conflict are likely to have at their disposal an awesome array of conventional and unconventional weaponry. For many societies, violence is a normal and accepted way of causing change or keeping things "the way they always have been." In either case, military peacekeepers and relief providers must—first and foremost—be good soldiers. Because of the environment in which they must work, these soldiers must also display political sensitivity, considerable restraint, and iron discipline.[18]

CONCLUSIONS

The lessons from a half-century of bitter experience suffered by governments involved in dealing with global instabilities and destabilizers show that a given international intervention often ends short of achieving the mandated peace. Too often, this is because short-, mid-, and long-term objectives are unclear, the endgame is undefined, consistent and appropriate support is not provided, and civil-military unity of purpose remains unachieved. Thus, it is imperative to develop leaders and organizational structures that can generate strategic clarity and make it work.

Even though every conflict situation differs in time, place, and circumstance, none is ever truly unique. Certain analytical commonalities can be ascertained in any contemporary conflict. The final outcome of a conflict such as those in the former Yugoslavia, in Afghanistan, and in Iraq is not determined primarily by the skillful manipulation of violence on the battlefield. Rather, control of the situation and its resolution are determined by the qualitative leader judgments and the synergistic processes established before, during, and after a conflict is politically recognized to have begun and ended. These are the essential components of strategic clarity. And strategic clarity is essential to success in the new millennium.

PART II

The Fundamental Keys for Rethinking Problem and Response

CHAPTER 5

A POPULACE-ORIENTED MODEL FOR REEXAMINING CONTEMPORARY THREAT AND RESPONSE

More than a decade ago we published an article entitled "Insurgency and Counter-Insurgency: Toward a New Theoretical Approach," in which we reported the results of some seven years of research on insurgencies, counterinsurgencies, and other conflicts that had taken place in the years since the end of the Second World War.[1] That research was codified in the SWORD Model, named after the Southern Command's Small Wars Operations Research Directorate, or SWORD. At the time, our cases of insurgencies (and counterinsurgencies) numbered forty-three, with the total cases of all types of conflict considered being sixty-nine. Since the article was published we have added many more cases, although we have not subjected them to the same quantitative analysis. We have, however, used qualitative tools that have tended to support our original conclusions.[2]

The research involved a modified Delphic technique that asked both practitioners and scholars what factors they felt had determined the outcome of the insurgency they had fought or studied. Out of this inductive research came seventy-two variables that the "experts" believed were determinative of the outcome of an insurgency. Insurgencies were then coded by won/lost outcome from the point of view of the counterinsurgency force, and the independent variables were subjected to factor analysis. This process yielded seven factors (or dimensions), which were then treated as the independent variables in determining outcomes with respect to the forty-three cases under investigation:[3]

1. Military actions of the intervening power
2. Support actions of the intervening power
3. Host government legitimacy
4. Host government military actions
5. Actions against subversion
6. Unity of effort
7. External support to the insurgent

Probit analysis was performed on all seven factors with respect to outcome, with particularly interesting results. Three dimensions (factors 1, 2, and 3) were individually statistically significant, at the 0.05 level or better, in explaining the outcomes of the conflicts. Factor 7 would have been significant at the lesser standard of 0.10. Together, however, the seven dimensions were statistically significant at the 0.001 level, with an R^2 value of 0.90.[4] In other words, the seven dimensions of the model in combination explained 90 percent of the variance in the outcome of the forty-three insurgencies studied. Put another way, the SWORD Model correctly explained (predicted after the fact) the outcome of 88 percent of the cases.

In only five cases did the model prove incorrect. Three were close calls: of these, two were given a probability of .48 of turning out the way they actually did, and the third was assigned a probability of over .40 of coming out the way it did (but was affected by an intervening variable). The two additional cases initially appeared to be serious errors on the part of the model (with only a .12 and .31 chance of predicting the actual outcome), but again, the actual outcome for each of these cases appears to have been due to intervening variables.[5]

The SWORD Model thus demonstrated its utility in explaining the outcomes of virtually the entire universe of insurgencies that took place in the forty years between 1945 and 1985 and involved a Western state as one of the antagonists. It clearly demonstrated that the seven dimensions involving the actions of the intervening power (both military and support), the perceived legitimacy of the host government and its opposite, the degree of support for the insurgents, host government military actions and operations targeted on the insurgents, and unity of effort tended to determine the outcome of these conflicts.

Subsequently, we, along with other colleagues, have examined many additional cases of insurgencies and other kinds of conflict and subjected them to qualitative analysis using the SWORD Model. In our most direct attempt to test the model against noninsurgency situations, we applied it to peace operations. That study applied the model to nine different peace operations ranging from traditional peacekeeping to peace enforcement.[6] The results were similar to those that we had previously reported: the model worked well to explain the outcomes. Some differences of detail became apparent, however.

As noted above, legitimacy was individually one of the statistically significant dimensions with respect to insurgency, and its importance was likewise confirmed with respect to peace operations. Whereas the other two statistically significant dimensions (military and support actions of the intervening power) did not appear to be individually quite as important in peace operations, unity of effort emerged as critical to the success of a peace operation.[7]

This discussion leads us to the point from which we began the argument in the previous chapters. The world has changed in significant ways since the end of the cold war, but many of the threats remain much the same. Although no peer competitor to the United States currently exists, many asymmetrical adversaries are challenging this country (as well as its friends and allies) in a manner similar to the insurgencies that have plagued the international system for the past half-century and more. As the SWORD Model shows, the central problem for any given state is legitimacy.

THE STRATEGIC OBJECTIVE:
A SUSTAINABLE PEACE—WITH JUSTICE

Given the essentially political-psychological-moral nature of the legitimate governance problem, the contemporary security environment requires a new populace-oriented paradigm. An "enforced" peace is only the beginning step in developing appropriate responses to the instability and violence that "are so hard to prevent, they must now get the attention they so urgently deserve."[8]

A Populace-Oriented Model

A populace-oriented extension of the SWORD Model for taking responsibility for intranational interventions and going beyond "declaring victory and coming home" depicts the activities and efforts of the various players involved (figure 1).[9] It portrays the allegiance of a population as the primary center of gravity. Persuasive and coercive measures will determine success or failure in the achievement of a just civil society and a durable peace. Thus, both the government and its external allies and the internal illegal opposition and its external allies can coerce and persuade the populace into actions on behalf of either side. Then, in addition, the people can coerce and persuade the government or opposition to change the conditions in society to meet their demands, and to undertake the types of behavior and actions that the citizenry perceives to be legitimate.

As indicated by the number 1 on figure 1, the primary goal of government and violent opposition forces is to undertake direct and indirect political, economic, social, psychological, and security programs and actions to shift popular support in their respective favor. These actions and programs can consist of armed propaganda (as used with great effect by the Vietcong) or the provision of social services (as Hamas does in the West Bank and Gaza, effectively replacing the Palestinian Authority in one of its critical governing roles). On the government side, this can take the form of effective civil defense programs such as the Rondas Campesinas supported and, in some cases, established by the Peruvian army in its war against Sendero Luminoso (Shining Path) during the 1980s and 1990s. In Clausewitzian terms, the people and their allegiance are the key center of gravity in any war of this nature.

The movement indicated by the number 2 in the figure focuses on development and other indirect activities designed to capture the "hearts

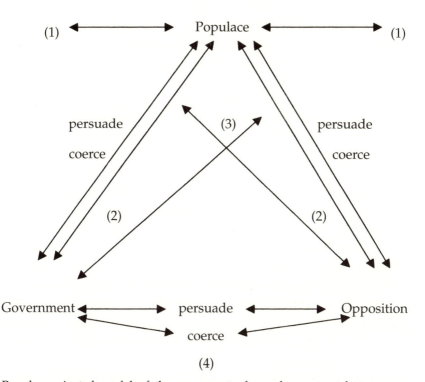

Populace-oriented model of the movement of popular support between an incumbent government and an illegal internal foe. (1) Overall goal: gain popular support. (2) Development and other activities designed to gain popular support. (3) Indirect activities designed to isolate government and opposition forces from the populace. (4) Direct attacks by the government and opposition on each other, intended to discourage popular support for the other.

and minds" of the populace. These include the kinds of activities conducted by Hamas and discussed above. A discussion of "development" should not be limited to economic or even to economic and social development but must include political development as well. As Kalman Silvert pointed out over forty years ago, development is a total phenomenon.[10] Although sectors can lead and lag, the process will fail if major elements of a sector are left out or an entire sector is not developed. Thus, both the armed opposition and the government have a stake in the outcome of the development process. The government has an overwhelming advantage in development activities, but if it fails to deliver, then that very advantage can become its Achilles heel.

The arrows marked by the number 3 in figure 1 indicate the indirect activities of both sides of a conflict designed specifically to isolate the government and its opposition from the populace. These activities support the shifting of popular support toward the side conducting them. The kinds of activities contemplated here include propaganda designed to show one's own side positively while portraying the opponent as somewhere between simply incompetent and evil. Some of these activities will blend with the development programs at 2, as when a road construction project is undertaken in such a way as to connect a village with its market while at the same time providing jobs for the local people.

The number 4 in the figure indicates direct attacks by the government and the opposition on each other with the specific objective of shifting popular support in their respective favor. These include armed attacks on military and security forces as well as psychological operations directed at the enemy, including both his fighters and his immediate supporters. Examples from the war in El Salvador include government attacks on guerrilla forces base camps or the Farabundo Martí National Liberation Front (FMLN) "spectaculars" such as the March 31, 1987, assault on the Fourth Brigade headquarters at El Paraiso. Military operations of this nature, however, have their downside as well. In another example from the Salvadoran civil war, the army's massacre of residents of the village of El Mozote in 1981 turned countless peasants against the government and thrust them into the arms of the FMLN, as well as turning significant members of the international community, including key members of the U.S. Congress, against the Salvadoran government. By the same token, FMLN murders of off-duty U.S. Marine embassy guards in 1985 and the killing of U.S. military personnel on a downed helicopter in 1989 had the effect of neutralizing much of the international support that the FMLN had been receiving. Similar lessons come from the current intifada between the Palestinians and Israelis, in which excessive use of force by the Israelis is largely offset by the Palestinian suicide bombers' attacks on purely civilian targets.

Unifying and Legitimizing Dimensions
That Lead to Sustainable Peace

The SWORD Model also takes into account the major unifying and legitimizing dimensions of the development of stability, a just civil society, and a sustainable peace. Additional steps toward those ends must be built on a foundation of carefully thought-out, long-term, phased planning and implementation processes that focus on the "offensive" extension of the seven dimensions of the SWORD Model.[11] Three broadly inclusive elements contribute most directly to the allegiance of the populace and the achievement of that end: establishing security, regenerating and bolstering economic prosperity, and nurturing legitimate governance.

Security, which begins with the provision of personal security to individual members of the society (see chapter 2), is probably the most critical societal requirement, as it is the primary basis upon which popular allegiance to the state is built. Providing security to every member of a society includes establishing order and the rule of law in addition to ensuring freedom from intimidation and violence; isolating warring political and criminal factions from all sources of internal and external support; and sustaining life, relieving suffering, and beginning to regenerate the economy.

Regenerating the economy and providing meaningful work—and pay—to individuals is also fundamental. This need not and cannot normally lead to immediate prosperity but only a reasonable hope for things to steadily improve, especially for one's children. Providing meaningful work provides another sense of security and gives people a stake in their society and governing institutions. It also gives people hope for a meaningful future. The evidence strongly demonstrates that if people have no stake in society and no hope for the future, their usual option is to resort to violence to force some kind of change.

The need to provide for the socioeconomic development of a people is generally well understood. But socioeconomic development without political development is clearly not sufficient to generate long-term stability, which requires political competence. To generate a viable political competence that can and will manage, coordinate, and sustain security and economic and political development, two additional goals must be accomplished: first foster political consent, and then establish and maintain peaceful societal conflict-resolution processes. With these additional building blocks in place, a legitimate civil society becomes a real possibility.

Finally, to nurture a sustainable civil society and a durable internal peace, an aggressive *unified* political-diplomatic, social-economic, psychological-moral, and military-police engagement in society must deal effectively with the root causes of the internal conflict. The intent and requirement is to generate the societal acceptance and support that governing institutions need to adequately manage internal change and violence—and to guarantee individual and collective well-being.

Implications

The primary implications of this analysis are clear. The ability of failed, fragile, and menaced governments to control, protect, and enhance their sovereignty, stability, and well-being is severely threatened in the contemporary global security environment. International organizations—such as the United Nations (UN), the North Atlantic Treaty Organization (NATO), the Organization of American States (OAS), and so forth—and individual national powers are increasingly called on to respond to real and perceived injustices and instabilities generated by unreformed political and economic institutions, as well as irresponsible or incompetent political leadership. Furthermore, the international community is increasingly expected to provide the leverage to ensure that legitimate governance—once regained—is given to responsible, uncorrupted, and competent leadership that can and will address the political, economic, and social root causes that created the crisis and forced the intervention.[12]

THE CHALLENGE

The ultimate challenge, then, is to come to terms with the fact that ensuring contemporary security, stability, and peace—at whatever level—

is essentially a political-psychological-moral issue. This issue is too broad for a singular military-police solution. The logical conclusion is to change perspectives.

We must remember, however, that no regime, group, or force can legislate or decree moral legitimacy or political competence for themselves or anyone else. Legitimation, stability, and well-being derive from popular and institutional perceptions that authority is genuine and effective and that it uses morally correct means for reasonable and fair purposes. These qualities are developed, sustained, and enhanced by appropriate behavior over time—and by the achievement of a general sense that life is or can get better.

Nevertheless, in the short term, a failed or fragile regime will likely require outside help in developing these qualities. Probably the best that an outside power or coalition of powers can do is to help establish a temporary level of security that might allow the carefully guided, unified, and monitored development of ethical and professional political competence underpinnings necessary for long-term success in achieving a sustainable peace. This will likely entail finding and selecting legitimate and compatible internal allies and partners.

Critical points about legitimacy must be understood at four different levels. First, regime legitimacy is the primary target of the "bad guys." Second, the "good guys" must protect and enhance their own legitimacy, which is the primary means by which governments might survive being targeted. Third, parties to conflict looking abroad for support—or to deny support—must understand that legitimacy is a double-edged moral issue that will either assist or constrain potential supporters' willingness and ability to become effectively involved. Fourth, the highest priority for a targeted government must be to strengthen and legitimize the state. Without this understanding and the concomitant behavioral changes, governments find themselves in a "crisis of governance." They face growing social violence, criminal anarchy, and overthrow.

To deal with potential destabilizers requires the coordination and implementation of an effective and timely unity of political-diplomatic, social-economic, psychological-moral, and security-stability effort. Unity of effort involves overcoming parochial bureaucratic interests, fighting "turf battles," and ensuring that all efforts are focused on the ultimate common goal: survival. In addition, all the steps undertaken to achieve that goal must be accomplished in a manner acceptable to the peoples of the targeted state (which equates back to legitimacy). Without an organization at the highest level to establish, enforce, and continually refine a national plan, authority is fragmented and will be ineffective in resolving the myriad problems endemic to a violent illegal assault on the state—with failure as a result.

Although national unity of effort is necessary, it is not sufficient. Creating a more complete unity of effort requires contributions at the international level as well (see chapters 2 and 3). To be effective, this international unity of effort requires that the targeted government and its internal and external allies agree on what constitutes legitimate governance and also agree on national goals and associated programs. These requirements reflect a need for an organizational structure to improve coordination and cooperation between and among the targeted entity and its internal and external allies. Finally, all of this requires mutual cultural awareness and sensitivity.

Once guidelines for a mutually agreeable vision of legitimacy and unifying organizational mechanisms are in place, subordinate organizations and programs must be developed to promote and consolidate legitimate governance. The root causes that created the instability and violence must be addressed by these organizations and programs, along with a cooperative and coordinated political stability strategy for sustainable development, the creation of a just civil society, and the establishment of a durable peace. This will probably involve the changing of a failed or failing state's predatory political culture to, in fact, provide physical and structural security; serious political, economic, social, and judicial reforms; and rational ways and means of sustaining these elusive ends.

The special status of the United States and the West allows the opportunity to facilitate positive change. By accepting this corollary to the basic challenge of changing perspectives, the United States and its Western allies can help replace conflict with cooperation and can harvest the hope and fulfill the promise that a strategic populace-oriented paradigm for stability and well-being offers.

CHAPTER 6

The "Almost Obvious" Lessons of Peace Operations

In pursuit of multilateral collective security interests or overriding unilateral national security or humanitarian interests, the United Nations (UN), other regional international organizations, the United States, and other interested parties have become increasingly involved in forms of direct and indirect intervention to achieve a desired level of stability and peace in the current global security environment. Thus, the concept of "peacekeeping" has gone from monitoring agreements between a relatively few sovereign, consenting, and responsible parties to more difficult and ambiguous peace-making, peace-enforcement, and peace-building tasks among a considerably larger number of less-than-sovereign (and sometimes nonconsenting and irresponsible) parties.

The implacable challenge in pursuing nation-state stability and legitimate governance means accepting the responsibilities of political leadership that the international security environment imposes. The task is to mount a coordinated political-economic-psychological-humanitarian-military effort. The purpose of such an effort is to create internal conditions within failed or failing states that can lead to peace and stability with justice (see chapter 5). Even after this has been accomplished, however, "only sustained, cooperative work to deal with underlying economic, social, cultural, and humanitarian problems can place an achieved peace on a durable foundation"—and avoid an eventual relapse into conflict.[1]

Thus, political solutions circling back to "preventive diplomacy" must be a part of the endgame, and all other peace operations in a given context must directly support that agenda. Otherwise, peace operations risk becoming little more than static and limited military occupations.

Adapting the SWORD Model to peace operations required that the names of the seven dimensions of the model be modified to better fit the peace operations environment (see chapter 12). Thus, the factors become the following: military actions of the peace forces; support actions of the peace forces; legitimacy; military actions of belligerents and peace forces; actions targeted on ending the conflict; unity of effort; and support to belligerents.[2]

RELATED LESSONS THAT SHOULD
HAVE BEEN LEARNED

The problems and questions related to the violence of the new world "disorder" imply five highly interrelated and reinforcing lessons that should have been learned from past experience: internal political requirements for successful involvement in complex humanitarian emergencies; the relationship of legitimate governance to stability; the relationship of development to security and stability; the relationship between legitimacy and political competence; and the external political requirements necessary to generate the capability to sustain a durable foundation for peace. The consistency of these lessons in the more than sixty cases that the UN Security Council has declared to be formal threats to international peace and security is impressive. That consistency warrants confidence that these strategic-level lessons take into account the major unifying dimensions of effective peace efforts and should begin the process of rethinking both problem and response in a world of dangerous uncertainty and ambiguity.

Internal Political Requirements for Successful Involvement

The days of delineating a successful international political end-state as simple short-term self-protection, limited adherence to human rights and the election of civilian political leaders, or material compassion for a humanitarian problem should be over. Thus, the main element of U.S. foreign policy, military management, and public diplomacy in the current international security environment must go beyond the notion of democratic enlargement to that of a selective, long-term, patient but firm and vigilant pursuit of responsible and competent (i.e., legitimate) governance that provides a pragmatic foundation for national and international stability and well-being.[3]

The Relationship of Legitimate Governance to Stability

Political legitimacy is based on the moral right of a government to govern—and the ability of the government to govern morally. Popular perceptions of corruption, disenfranchisement, poverty, lack of upward social mobility, and lack of personal security tend to limit the right, and the ability, of a regime to conduct the business of state. Until and unless a population feels that its government deals with these and other issues of political, economic, and social injustice and security fairly and effectively, the potential for internal or external factors to destabilize and subvert a government is considerable.

The Relationship of Development to Security and Stability

The international security dialogue is focusing on national development. That requirement equates to a holistic national capability-building effort. The generally uncoordinated, piecemeal, and ad hoc approach to socioeconomic development must be brought to an end. Unless solutions to development problems are addressed on a coherent and long-term basis, no self-sustaining national development will occur. National development provides the capability for the nation-state to develop the political and economic strength to provide internal order and progress. National development also provides the capability for the state to protect and enhance its interests in the international security arena. Thus, self-sustaining national development provides both security and stability.

The Relationship between Legitimacy and Political Competence

Another lesson that should have been learned, one which helps define an appropriate response to the problem of legitimate governance and contributes to stability, is that of the relationship between legitimacy and political competence. Legitimacy is needed to generate the capability to effectively manage, coordinate, and sustain political, economic, and social development. This capability implies the political competence to develop responsible governance and a resultant national and international purpose and will to which a people can relate and support. This capability thus implies the competence to legitimize and strengthen national political institutions. The degree to which this political objective is achieved at home will determine the level of influence that can be exerted abroad. It will also define, more than anything else, progress toward viable national security and well-being.

The External Political Requirements for Success in
Generating a Durable Foundation for Peace and Stability

The principal circumstance that has plagued efforts by the United States and United Nations to assist Bosnia-Herzegovina, Cambodia, the Congo, Haiti, Panama, Rwanda, Somalia, and any number of additional examples to establish credible and legitimate public security and stability is a lack of commitment to take responsibility for the consequences of intervention. This is part of the battle in both the U.S. Congress and the UN Security Council over support for postwar Iraq and, to a lesser extent, Afghanistan.

Commitment presupposes a great deal more than taking control of a contended area, stopping any escalation of violence, enforcing law and order, and imposing an acceptable level of security. It presupposes knowing where you are going, understanding and implementing the ways and means of getting there, and taking responsibility for action.

An international organization acting multilaterally or a government acting unilaterally that defers to arbitrary "end dates" and fails to make a commitment to a clearly defined vision of ultimate political success enables loss of control of both the process and the end-state. As a consequence, a peace operation or complex humanitarian emergency frequently cycles back to the beginning of the process, and the seeds of the next problem are sown in the present one.

TWO KEYS TO PUTTING IT ALL TOGETHER

The fulfillment of an imperative for holistic responsible governance and just stability consists of two principal elements. They are both conceptual and operational. The first requires a rethinking and restructuring of the notion of stability. The second is end-state planning. Together, they constitute the prime lesson for failed or failing regimes and their international supporters in the coming decades.

Stability

Stability encompasses several ideas discussed in previous chapters. Three components of stability that must be developed are the military-police capability to provide an acceptable level of internal and external security; the economic capacity to generate real security and socioeconomic development; and the political competence to develop a type of governance to which a people can relate and support.

The security and socioeconomic components of stability are generally well understood. Clearly, however, the key concept of political competence is not as well understood, developed, and operationalized as the other two. Classical development theory generally emphasized economic development, assuming that social and political development would automatically follow.[4] However, as early as 1960, Gabriel Almond and James Coleman noted, "The processes of commercialization and industrialization of the economies of these societies have not contributed everywhere to social or political integration, or to the emergence of a politically relevant entrepreneurial or middle class."[5] Nevertheless, both economists and political scientists have persisted in arguing in favor of economic development driving social and political development.[6] For example, Nancy Birdsall and Richard Sabot state, "The conventional wisdom has been that there is a tradeoff between augmenting economic growth and reducing inequality, so that an unequal distribution of income is necessary for, or the likely consequence of, rapid economic growth."[7] According to Robert Bates, "Governments intervene in ways that promote economic inefficiency: they alter market prices, reduce market competition, and invest in poorly conceived agricultural projects."[8] The result has been a significant distortion of the real relationship among the components of stability.

The reality is that stability results from the complex interplay of the three components identified above. Each is essential to the achievement of long-term stability, and although the military/security and economic components can be developed independently of each other, the political competence component is the one that holds them all together. Indeed, the ultimate value of the economic and security elements can be reduced to nothing or nearly nothing if the political/leadership competence component is absent or weak.

Governments that are not responsive to the importance of political competence can find themselves in a "crisis of governance" in which they face growing social violence, criminal anarchy, terrorism, insurgency, and overthrow. Thus, the development of competent political leadership upon a foundation of moral legitimacy is a challenge that governments must meet to survive the growing international instability. Specifically, the challenge is to change perspectives and ensure that every policy, program, and political action contributes directly to the maintenance and enhancement of legitimate governance.

End-State Planning

The key to the implementation of a viable political stability strategy—and strategic clarity—is planning. This depends on a clear strategic vision, based on the above perspective on stability, from which to start (see chapter 4). A viable strategy also depends on a management structure and resources to apply the vision on the basis of a realistic calculation of ends, ways, means, and timing (see chapters 2 and 3). This takes us to end-state planning.

End-state planning starts from Clausewitz' truism that conflict is a continuation of politics by other means,[9] but that concept needs to be accompanied by two qualifying arguments. First, military violence is required only when the conditions or changes sought cannot be achieved through political/diplomatic, social/economic, or informational/psychological means. Second, end-state planning advocates synchronization of all national or international civilian and military instruments of power to gain the most synergism from the interaction of the variables selected for action.

The end-state planning argument concludes that if the United Nations or the United States or any other international player is going to succeed in the future conflicts in which they are most likely to become involved, civil and military forces must be structured and employed in ways that respond to the dynamic political, economic, and social as well as military centers of gravity of the various parties to the conflict. Additionally, there must be a clear definition of what ultimate success looks like.

End-state planning allows decision makers and policy makers to think logically, in synchronized phases, about the conditions they seek to create. It also allows leaders and their staffs to consider the opportunities that may arise and obstacles that must be overcome. The critical requirement is that these high-level participants realize which is which and what the implications for ultimate success might be. The key is to understand precisely what must be achieved, to understand exactly what is required, and to make the decision whether or not to engage in a conflict or complex humanitarian emergency and start down a "slippery slope" that may lead to some form of disaster.

Those efforts cannot be concerned only with the synergized use or movement of national and international instruments of power. They must also be concerned with the long-term effects. It is not a matter of putting the proverbial cart before the horse. It is a matter of knowing where the horse is going and how it is going to get there. Decision makers, policy makers, and planners should never lose sight of that bigger picture.

CONCLUSIONS

Analysis of the problems of legitimate governance and stability with justice takes us beyond providing some form of humanitarian assistance or refugee assistance in cases of human misery and need. It takes us beyond the traditional monitoring of bilateral agreements or protecting one group of people from another or from a government. It takes us beyond compelling one or more parties to a conflict to cease human rights violations and other morally repugnant activities, and beyond repelling simple aggression. Analysis of the problems of governance and stability takes us back to where we began. The core strategic problem is responsible political leadership in the post–cold war world. Foreign policy and military asset management must address this central issue.

The enormity and logic of the establishment of a durable and just peace demand a carefully thought-out, phased, long-term planning and implementation process for sustainable political, economic, and social development. Implementing this extraordinary set of challenges will not be easy. It will, however, be far less demanding and costly in political, social, military, and monetary terms than allowing the problems of irresponsible governance and political instability to continue to fester and generate crises that work to the detriment of all concerned.

The general rule would be that policy makers and decision makers must carefully calculate gains and losses, and when the case warrants, they should intervene earlier rather than later. If done earlier, the initial and intense use of low-cost diplomatic and civilian resources and military support units can be utilized to ensure legitimacy and stability. If done later, the initial and intense use of high-cost military combat units will generally be applied to a losing situation. Ultimately, however, the only test for involvement—whatever its form and level—is national self-interest. That is the only morality within the anarchy of world disorder.[10]

CHAPTER 7

Strategic Vision and Insurgency in El Salvador and Peru

Once again, as they were in the 1980s, political and military leaders are in the process of rethinking the global role and strategies of the United States in terms of military reform and the structuring or restructuring (transformation) of forces to better deal with the security problems that are likely to arise over the next several years. Strategic theory has so far played little part in the debate, which has focused on the ambiguities of modern conflict. Nevertheless, it must be remembered that implementing budgets, force structure, procurement, and planning must be preceded by strategic vision.

Before asking the usual questions—"What are we going to do?" "Who is going to command and control the effort?" "How is it to be done?"—the statesman and commander (as Clausewitz termed them) must first "establish . . . the kind of war on which they are embarking."[1] Determining the nature of the conflict is not only the first but also the most comprehensive of all strategic questions.[2] As a consequence, it is incumbent on senior decision makers and their staffs to correctly identify the primary center of gravity, prioritize the others, and link policy, strategy, force structure and equipment, and campaign plans to solving the central strategic problem. This encompasses what B. H. Liddell Hart, drawing from Sun Tzu, calls the indirect approach to war. "The perfection of strategy would be, therefore, to produce a decision without any serious fighting."[3]

In an attempt to help provide a better understanding of the type of conflict that is most likely to challenge U.S. leadership over the near to long term, we will examine two supposedly dissimilar recent conflicts—those of El Salvador and Peru.[4] The case of El Salvador represents a situation in which the United States was involved for over twelve years in terms of providing money, training, equipment, advice, and much dedication and goodwill. In the end, after a negotiated settlement, the government achieved its goals, which had first been put forth in concrete terms relatively early in the fighting. The former insurgents were reincorporated into the political process, largely on the terms of the government. In contrast, the Peruvian case denotes a circumstance in which neither the United States nor any other outside power played a major role on either side of that internal conflict, although the United States did provide some critical assistance from 1986 on.[5] Nevertheless, the Peruvian government and its armed forces prevailed over the insurgent threat.

An examination of the "strategic problem" in both these cases will provide an understanding of some of the analytical commonalities within the context of insurgency and will serve as a beginning point from which to achieve the vision necessary for success in this kind of "uncomfortable war."

THE INSURGENCY IN EL SALVADOR

The Threat

The primary objective of the Farabundo Martí National Liberation Front (FMLN) was to bring down the incumbent government and replace it with one that would "see [the insurgents] take power" to "make the profound changes needed in [their] society."[6] This was stated repeatedly over the course of the war. The insurgents' strategy altered from time to time in recognition of changing political-military conditions, but the fundamental assumption remained.

The first insurgent strategy was implemented well before the Salvadoran government or the United States determined that a problem existed. This organizational effort was an attempt to develop cadres of future leaders, to politicize and organize the "masses," and to begin the unification of the various "democratic" elements in the country—with the purpose of creating a single revolutionary organization for the prosecution of the struggle.[7] The goal was finally achieved in 1980, when Fidel Castro made it a condition for his support.[8]

The second strategy was oriented toward the government. In late 1979, indirect and direct attacks were initiated, first against the regime of General Carlos Humberto Romero and then against the civil-military junta that replaced him. The indirect part of the strategy was a psychological campaign to discredit the regime in power and to claim the "right" to govern in the name of political, social, and economic justice.[9] The direct attack came in the form of a limited but "final" offensive that began in January 1981. Buoyed by the guerrilla successes in Nicaragua and armed with more than six hundred tons of weapons and ammunition from Cuba, the FMLN leadership attempted to override the preparatory tenets of Marxist-Leninist strategy and take immediate control of the government through the simple force of arms.[10] At the same time, the insurgent leadership overestimated the degree of popular support and underestimated the ability of the Salvadoran armed forces.[11] The result, of course, was initial failure and a rationalization of the effort as the beginning of the "general" offensive that would achieve the final objective.

The failure of the "final" offensive also forced a reassessment of the political-military situation. But instead of returning to the teachings of Lenin, the FMLN leadership adopted a more military orientation. The decision was made that "there was only one road to victory, that of armed struggle and the use of the people's methods of combat."[12] This strategy remained in effect until mid 1984. During this time, the FMLN retired to the countryside and began to mount major conventional-type attacks on the Salvadoran military; it gained control of large portions of the national territory, and France and Mexico granted recognition to the insurgents.[13] However, in this more or less conventional-type war of attrition, the forces of the incumbent government had more manpower, more success in recruiting manpower, and—with the help of the United States—more resources than the insurgents. With those advantages and economic and political reforms perceived as significant at the time—such as agrarian, banking, and electoral reforms—the regular Salvadoran military establishment began to reverse the tide of the conflict.[14]

By the end of 1984, the insurgent leadership apparently agreed that another shift of the center of gravity had occurred. The shift was from the enemy military force to the source of the force's power and to the external support for the government's reform efforts—that being the political, economic, and military aid provided by the United States. The strategy thus became one of taking a relatively low profile militarily, negotiating and waiting for the time when the United States would lose interest in the conflict.[15]

The Salvadoran insurgents were expected to continue to focus on two primary centers of gravity—the legitimacy of the regime in power, and U.S. political, economic, and military support. They were also expected to attempt to achieve their ends through political, psychological, and military actions at the strategic, operational, and tactical levels.[16] Indeed, this is exactly what happened throughout the remaining years of the war.

To discredit the regime in power and to disrupt the community of interest between the Salvadoran and U.S. governments, efforts centered first on the inability to provide real reform. As examples, the FMLN "war of information" continually asserted that agrarian reform was not implemented and was a failure in any case; banking reform was a joke benefiting only the government; export reforms were irrelevant; elections were fraudulent; corruption of civil and military functionaries was widespread; and human rights were a sham.[17]

Second, on the diplomatic front, the FMLN continued the war of information at the international level and worked hard to be perceived as the only entity that really wanted peace and reform. Yet given their "armed revolution" strategy, the Salvadoran insurgents could only be expected to continue to use the Central American peace process and any negotiations for the purposes of appearing legitimate and to gain time.[18]

Third, psychological and organizational efforts with the "masses" were resumed, not only in the countryside, but also in San Salvador.

Emphasis was placed on traditional allies such as student organizations and labor unions. Moreover, the FMLN continued to develop its cadre, train units, refine logistical routes and procedures, and consolidate control over border sanctuaries and areas lacking any government presence.[19]

Fourth, the FMLN broke down into small units to continue assassinations, kidnappings, and general terrorism on a carefully measured scale designed to constantly harass and intimidate the population and the government. These tactics were aimed at lessening regime legitimacy in terms of ability to govern and protect the citizenry. In this connection, the insurgents continued to attack transportation and communications networks and the general economic infrastructure to sabotage government attempts to do anything that might improve the internal economy and the economic component of legitimacy and also to further impress on the United States the futility of its economic and military aid to El Salvador.[20]

Finally, the FMLN mounted occasional spectacular attacks designed to give the impression that it still had good and relatively strong formations capable of a military victory. Again, this type of effort had its effects in the United States as well as El Salvador.[21] Simply put, FMLN efforts were not primarily military. Any military operation had political and psychological objectives as first priorities. Military objectives were—at least at this time—tertiary.

Thus, the threat in El Salvador—as in any insurgency—was multifaceted. In addition to the "guerrilla war," as many as four other wars may be waged simultaneously: a war for legitimacy, a general war of information, a war to reduce outside support to the government, and a war of subversion. This reaffirms the concept of a multifront or multidimensional conflict and provides warning to decision makers that "the first task . . . in planning for a war is to identify the enemy's centers of gravity, and if possible trace them back to a single one."[22] In El Salvador, the primary center of gravity remained related to the moral right to govern, or legitimacy.

The endgame of the Salvadoran insurgency began in 1989 with the fall of the Berlin Wall, the beginning of serious negotiations between the government and the FMLN, and the latter's truly "final" offensive. Following a classic Marxist-Leninist strategy of talk-talk-fight-fight, the

FMLN launched a major offensive in the midst of ongoing negotiations with the government. The offensive, although it never really threatened to gain control of San Salvador, did take place in many of the neighborhoods of the capital, including some that were the residential areas of the elite. The most effective moment for the insurgents was when the acting commander of the city, Colonel Benavides, ordered some of his former junior officers, who were at that time in the Atlacatl Immediate Reaction Battalion, to (in a paraphrase of the words of King Henry with respect to St. Thomas à Becket) "rid him of these troublesome priests." This resulted in the murder of the Jesuit leaders of the Central American University, along with their housekeeper and her daughter.

This atrocity had major repercussions for U.S. support, especially in Congress. The administration of George H. W. Bush, however, applied significant pressure to both the government of El Salvador and the military high command, and the armed forces chose the national solution rather than the parochial military solution and turned an academy classmate (Benavides) over for prosecution. This decision cemented the American-Salvadoran alliance and convinced a large number of Salvadorans as well as much of the international community that reform had really taken effect in El Salvador. When this newfound legitimacy was combined with the withdrawal of Soviet support for Cuba, Nicaragua, and the FMLN revolutionaries, the handwriting was on the wall. The negotiated peace either met the terms the government had offered in 1984 or confirmed actions begun by the government in the intervening years.[23]

The Strategy of Counterinsurgency

If, as we argue here, the government and armed forces of El Salvador won their war against the FMLN, then it behooves us to consider the factors that led to that victory. Among those factors was a credible and effective strategy that evolved over time and was implemented by the government and the armed forces with a supporting strategy by the United States that also was evolutionary. Central to that strategy were the seven dimensions of the SWORD Model.

The strategy began to evolve even before armed conflict had begun, with the attempt by the first and second junta governments to achieve legitimacy through the institution of land, banking, and electoral reform. By the time these reforms were implemented, however, Sir Robert Thompson's observation that "if the [revolutionary] organization is already established, and well-trained and disciplined, it will not be defeated by reforms designed to eliminate the cause. 'It will only be defeated by establishing a superior organization and applying mea-sures designed to break the revolutionary organization.'"[24] This is not to say that reforms designed to achieve legitimacy are unnecessary to successful counterinsurgency but only that they are at this stage insuffi-cient to achieve it.

Fortunately, the Salvadorans and their American supporters did not abandon a strategy of legitimacy. Rather, they began with an approach advocated by the U.S. Military Group (USMILGP) to produce a national campaign plan. The first iteration in 1983 concentrated effort on two departments (similar to U.S. states), with the idea of expanding it to the rest of the country. John Waghelstein, the commander of the USMILGP from 1982 to 1984 and a true scholar of insurgency in general and El Salvador in particular, has summed up the evolution of the national plan extraordinarily well:

> The National Campaign Plan placed emphasis on civic action and developmental projects behind a security screen. This was a radical departure from the purely military, multi-battalion operations extant prior to the plan's inception. Additionally, increased . . . [staff] emphasis on psychological operations indicated a growing awareness of the importance of this dimension of the war. Unfor-tunately, the financial and military support critical to the plan was not forthcoming over the long term. By 1984 the plan was in serious trouble and it would have to wait for the Duarte regime (1984–1989) to resuscitate it at the national level. The Duarte solution to . . . [administrative] inefficiency, graft and corruption problems was to transfer the responsibilities to the ESAF [armed forces]. Duarte's attempt to expand the plan to all fourteen departments, which

further diluted scarce resources, was only partially successful. Even so, the idea of focusing on *all* aspects of the struggle, political, social, economic, as well as military, had taken root and continued to the end of the war. Eventually, it was the simplest solution that had the most success. The plan's third and final form was to give the responsibility and the assets directly to the mayors, thereby cutting out all the sticky-fingered middlemen. This solution also put the OPATTs [U.S. trainers] and the USAID [U.S. Agency for International Development] people in direct contact with the projects, thereby increasing US oversight and plan efficiency.[25]

Unlike the strategy for legitimacy, the American strategy for military support of El Salvador was clearly drawn early on. This was the famous Woerner Report, drafted by a team led by Brigadier General Fred F. Woerner, who would be successively commander of the 193rd Infantry Brigade (the army component of the U.S. Southern Command [SOUTHCOM]) and (simultaneously) deputy commander in chief for Central America, and then, after a brief stint as commander of the Sixth U.S. Army, commander in chief of SOUTHCOM. Thus Woerner was in a position to draft and implement the U.S. military strategy in support of El Salvador from 1981 through 1989. The essential elements of that strategy were to train, advise, and see that the El Salvadoran armed forces (ESAF) were adequately equipped. Critical to its success were the small number (the famous fifty-five-man limit) of highly trained and well-qualified U.S. trainers, who took a role that was primarily one of training the trainers. What they trained their ESAF counterparts in was as important as the fact that they were providing training. The approach was always one of training for technical and tactical proficiency along with the practical values of a strong position in favor of human rights. This resulted in major changes in ESAF behavior over the course of the war in directions that furthered both military capability and the ability to gain legitimacy for the government.

U.S. support actions, while not as consistent as desired, were nevertheless perceived as being strong and for the long haul. As Waghelstein says, "As our Salvadoran allies became convinced we would not let them lose the war, they became more confident regarding other alternatives to ending the war, even through negotiations. . . . We were never committed to the point where the ESAF could go out and kill every guerrilla but neither would we abandon them."[26]

The Salvadoran government and its ally, the United States, sought to mobilize support throughout the war to counter the degree of external support the FMLN was receiving. This major focus of strategy met with mixed success at various stages of the war. Foremost among the objectives was the neutralization of the disputed bits of territory located on the El Salvador–Honduras border, known as the *bolsones*. These were occupied by Salvadorans who were refugees from both the current insurgency and the conventional war between the two countries in 1969. More important, they served as rest and relaxation camps for the FMLN fighters. Neither the United Nations (UN) refugee administrators nor the Honduran government showed much sympathy for the Salvadoran allegations and complaints. Moreover, the political cost of cleaning out the bolsones was far more than the Salvadoran government could afford.

Somewhat more ambiguous was the effort to interdict FMLN supplies smuggled in by land from Nicaragua through Honduras and by sea directly from Nicaragua through the Gulf of Fonseca. U.S. air surveillance using a variety of sensors had some success, as did intelligence monitoring by the United States of traffic in the gulf from the observation post established on Tiger Island. Nevertheless, interdiction proved to be a difficult and thankless task with limited results.

More successful was the diplomatic effort to isolate the insurgents from the support they had received in the early 1980s from France and Mexico. Both countries had recognized the FMLN as a "representative political force" in August 1981. By 1984 Mexico had upgraded its diplomatic mission to El Salvador, "and aid from West Germany was restored."[27] In addition, the public diplomacy effort on the part of the United States had generally neutralized effective opposition to aid for El Salvador at home—especially in the U.S. Congress, where it really counted.

The ESAF, with significant U.S. support, expanded its efforts in operations directly focused on targeting the insurgency, especially intelligence activities, psychological operations, civic action, and civil defense. Over

time, the most successful ESAF operations were those offensive operations based on specifically developed intelligence and conducted by
special operations elements at the national and brigade levels. The
national special operations group (GOE) had the highest degree of
success of any ESAF actions at destroying FMLN guerrilla concentrations.
At the brigade level, GOE successes were mimicked by units known as
long-range recon patrols (PRALs). Supporting them was an intelligence
collection and analysis structure that included a national intelligence
directorate, regional intelligence centers staffed by both U.S. and Salvadoran personnel, and intelligence support and professionalization at
the level of the El Salvadoran brigades and ESAF joint staff.

Psychological operations (PSYOP) were conducted under the auspices
of the joint staff (C5). There were three PSYOP targets: friendly forces,
enemy forces, and neutrals (the civilian population). Propaganda was
developed that focused on each target and, following U.S. doctrine,
was invariably truthful. All forms of media were used, including a government radio station that competed successfully for listeners with the
FMLN's vaunted *Radio Venceremos.*

Military civic action was somewhat less successful in building real
support for the ESAF and the government than were the development
efforts of the various iterations of the national campaign plan. Still, as
adjuncts to psychological operations they made the point of a military
and government presence in the conflictive areas in a manner that
showed the ESAF in a positive light.[28] Perhaps the most successful use of
civic action was in the long-running Operation PHOENIX, designed to
deny the Guazapa Volcano to the FMLN, in which combat operations
were fully integrated with psychological operations and civic action.

The final element targeted specifically on either denying the FMLN
the opportunity to gain popular support or to wean people away from
the rebels was the civil defense program, which created ESAF-supported
and -trained militias. Success varied a great deal in this program—from
very strong and effective civil defense units, through ones that were
barely organized, to a complete absence of civil defense units in some
areas. Nevertheless, the program as a whole was far more successful
than the sum of its parts. The FMLN put enormous effort into attempting

to discredit it and insisted on the disbanding of the civil defense units as part of a negotiated settlement.[29]

Closely tied to the actions specifically targeted on taking the war to the insurgents were a combination of training, doctrine, leadership, operational style, and combat operations required to conduct the war effectively. To begin, the ESAF faced the problem of an enemy that was capable of conducting regular operations against the economy and the armed forces from external and internal sanctuaries. While most of these operations were small scale, the FMLN retained the capability of mounting occasional large "spectaculars" until the end of the war— assuming the insurgents were willing to pay the price in lives, these operations could be maintained for a number of days.

The military strategic problem that the ESAF faced was simultaneously protecting high-value targets (static defense), keeping the FMLN off balance (aggressive small-unit offensive operations—patrolling), and carrying the fight directly to the enemy—all without falling victim to the temptation to treat any civilian found in a conflictive zone as an enemy combatant. This meant that the ESAF had to structure forces for each of these different missions. And so it did. As discussed above, the GOE and the PRALs were organized and employed to carry the fight to the FMLN based on specific intelligence. Regular infantry brigades and "military detachments" (brigade-sized units with areas of responsibility for a part of a department) along with combat units from the three public security forces (national police, national guard, and treasury police) were charged with static defense of high-value targets such as dams. Finally, the ESAF's five immediate reaction battalions (BIRIs) conducted continuous patrolling operations in the various conflictive zones to keep the FMLN fighters off balance.[30]

The capabilities required to carry out these operations were effective training, especially of the special operations units (GOE and PRALs), the BIRIs, and the leaders of the brigades and military detachments. Officer assignments reflected these requirements, as did the distribution of volunteer soldiers versus conscripts, with volunteers making up the GOE, PRALs, BIRIs, and public security force units.[31] Training was clearly improved with the establishment and effective employment of the

National Training Center, while improved discipline was reflected in the drastic reduction of extrajudicial killings attributed to the armed forces.

The last element of the strategy was the unity of effort achieved over time both within the Salvadoran government (including its armed forces) and between El Salvador and its American ally. Both aspects of this unity are well illustrated by events that took place during the final briefing to President José Napoleón Duarte of an assessment of the ESAF, conducted by both the ESAF Joint Staff and the U.S. Southern Command.[32] Before President Duarte arrived, U.S. ambassador Edwin Corr took the opportunity to remind the ESAF Joint Staff that even though the midterm elections had been won by the right-wing party (ARENA), it was not appropriate for the joint staff to be perceived as granting the elected individuals access that they were not due before they took office. The ESAF officers present took the admonition as the friendly advice it was, while recognizing the mailed fist within the velvet glove.

At that same session, after the briefing was completed, President Duarte posed a question that left the teams from both countries somewhat at a loss for words. He asked whether the ESAF was winning the war. After a poignant, if brief, pause, the defense minister, General Eugenio Vides Casanova, said, "Yes, Mr. President, we are winning the war." He was both correct and kind; in a little over a year Duarte was out of office and would die from the cancer that already was wracking his body. Nevertheless, Duarte, Vides, Corr, and General Fred Woerner were all playing from the same sheet of music, which was absolutely essential to achieving the victory that was solidified in the 1992 peace accords.

THE INSURGENCY IN PERU

The Strategic Problem

Peru, in contrast to El Salvador, was faced with two ongoing insurgencies: one rural based, the other urban. The former, that of the Sendero Luminoso (Shining Path), stirred the imagination of most observers of guerrilla wars, as well as long-term observers of Peru. The latter, the Tupac Amaro Revolutionary Movement (MRTA), with a relatively conventional urban focus, generated much less concern. Sendero was by far the largest, the most successful, and the most violent, and it came to be considered the most serious security problem facing the Peruvian government.[33] Thus, we will focus primarily on that organization.

The principal objectives of Sendero were to gain power and to create a "nationalistic," "Indian," and "popular" democracy.[34] Sendero's view of the new state derived from José Carlos Mariátegui, who was the founder of the Peruvian Communist Party in the 1920s. According to Mariátegui, the original basis for Peruvian socialism is in the pre-Columbian Indian (Quechua) community. That communal system was destroyed in the Spanish conquest and kept down by the subsequent colonial and neocolonial elites operating out of the capital city of Lima.[35] As a result, Sendero's founder, Abimael Guzmán, was initiating a third epoch that would reestablish a truly Peruvian democracy.[36]

According to Guzmán (also known as President or Comrade Gonzalo) and in Sendero writings, the organization planned for a protracted struggle focused on a rigid five-stage program for gaining power.[37] The first concerns, beginning in 1962, were to establish a dedicated cadre and rudiments of a revolutionary party, a guerrilla army, and a support mechanism for the entire organization. This would lay the foundations for the subsequent "armed struggle."[38] During the 1960s and through the 1970s, Guzmán concentrated on theory and leadership development from within his academic sanctuary at the University of Huamanga in the highland city of Ayacucho, and on expanding his new revolutionary organization's relationships with relatively isolated peasant communities in the outlying districts around the university. This was largely accomplished by Guzmán's placing graduates of his teacher training program at the University of Huamanga in the rural schools of the region as teachers. As a result of the movement's provision of such needs as paramedical service, farm techniques, and literacy—and its members marrying into peasant families—the revolutionaries gained both the confidence and the support of rural residents in the Andean highlands around Ayacucho with relative ease.[39] Then, in 1978, Sendero disappeared from public view.

In 1980—as Peru was returning to civilian rule after twelve years of military government—the movement reappeared. Sendero leadership moved from what they called the "strategic equilibrium" to the "offensive" (their second stage) and began the attack on the symbols of the bourgeois state. Ballot boxes were burned; the larger cities, including Lima, were blacked-out periodically; public buildings and private companies were bombed; dogs were symbolically hung from lampposts; and a series of attacks on and assassinations of local public figures were initiated.[40]

The third, more violent, stage of the insurgency (the generalization of violence) was initiated in March 1982 with a major attack on the Ayacucho Department prison and the Robin Hood–like release of its prisoners. This operation was followed by a series of relatively small attacks against civil guard (police) posts and various public works, as well as a dynamite attack on the presidential palace in Lima. In December of that year, Sendero Luminoso staged a spectacular event. In an attack on Lima's electrical grid, four high-tension towers were destroyed, causing a complete blackout in the capital and six other cities. Minutes after all the lights went out and everyone was in the streets wondering what had happened, Sendero lit an image of a huge hammer and sickle that glowed from a hill overlooking Lima in celebration of Abimael Guzmán's forty-eighth birthday![41]

At that point, the insurgency had progressed to a stage where it could no longer be ignored. In January 1983, a state of emergency was declared in five provinces of the Ayacucho Department, and the civilian government turned administrative control of the "Emergency Zone" over to the Peruvian armed forces.[42]

Sendero's move to implement the second and third stages of its strategy for taking power took the movement beyond its own core area of Ayacucho. Guerrilla war and counterviolence steadily escalated and spread to other parts of the country. For example, by mid 1984, the state of emergency had been extended from Ayacucho to include thirteen provinces in three different southern highland departments. And Sendero was extending its influence into other key regions. This is the fourth stage of the revolution—conquer and expand bases of support. Logically, the first region into which Sendero moved included the Andean highland departments that extend from Ayacucho (Junín, Pasco, Huancavelica, Apurímac, Cuzco, and Puno). The second geographical region into which

Sendero expanded was that vast area east of the Andes through which the rivers flow into the Amazon system, such as the rich Huallaga Valley. Sendero also began expanding into the northern sierra departments, beginning with Ancash and its large indigenous population. This essentially left the coastal and most of the northern sierra departments and the large cities under relatively firm central government control.[43] However, Sendero also had some significant successes in the economically less well off districts of Lima that were largely populated by migrants from the sierra.[44]

This programmatic isolation of the "center" was exactly that. Sendero won neither the minds nor the hearts of the urban proletariat, simply because it was only beginning to initiate that part of the general strategy. The five-point program for taking control of the entire country was not complete. The last stage of the revolution—besieging the cities and bringing about the total collapse of the state—was not scheduled to take place until the interior support bases were consolidated and the major population centers were either strangled economically or weakened to the point where a relatively small, but direct, military assault would bring about the desired result.[45]

At the strategic level, then, Sendero was moving toward the fifth and final stage of its program to take power. Thus, the strategy became one of increasing sabotage and terrorism, taking a relatively low military profile in the sierra departments where it had grown, consolidating new areas of operation in the northern sierra, and waiting for the time when the interior bases of support were well enough consolidated to make the final attack on the "center" a feasible operation.[46]

At the operational level, by 1987 Sendero Luminoso was on the offensive. Doctrinally and in dialectical terms, other antithetical activities generally considered "defensive" in nature were also pursued in the "offensive" at all levels. For example, Sendero continued to develop its cadre to man the expanding political, military, and support components of the movement; to maintain psychological and organizational efforts with the "masses"; and to consolidate its position in Peru's interior.[47] The thesis in Sendero's offensive strategy at the operational level included—first and foremost—"armed propaganda." Relying on actions rather than words, the leadership chose to attack the economic infrastructure, local symbols of central government authority, and symbols of foreign imperialism and to enforce its own revolutionary order.[48] The primary purpose of this part of the "armed struggle" was, of course, to convince the Peruvian people that Sendero Luminoso was the real power in the country and the only "rightful" heir to government.

Tactically, Sendero operated in small, relatively autonomous units with political, psychological, and military objectives—in that order. Examples of these objectives include assassinations, kidnappings, terrorism, destruction of transportation and communications nets, and the establishment of control over specific areas. All these actions were aimed at lessening regime credibility in terms of ability and willingness to govern and protect the citizenry, and at providing for its own freedom of movement and the security necessary to further the cause.[49]

The Sendero organization of tactically autonomous regional commands (along with the equally tactically autonomous Lima Metropolitan Committee) optimized its operational rule of centralized direction/decentralized execution. The Lima Metropolitan Committee was the only element of Sendero that was authorized by the central committee to conduct operations anywhere in Peru. Guzmán exercised central control over the commands and the Lima Metropolitan Committee by means of a strict interpretation of the party line. Tactical freedom of action extended only as far as the party line permitted and if crossed resulted in effective "excommunication" from the party and movement. This is exactly what happened to the entire leadership of the Lima Metropolitan Committee after it began some very exploratory discussions with the MRTA.[50]

Additionally, spectacular events such as the prison riots in June 1986 were conducted to give the world the impression that Sendero Luminoso really was more powerful and less bloodthirsty than the government and the armed forces and that even in jail, Sendero was organized to "win" the struggle.[51] Aside from such shows of force, direct confrontations with the armed forces did not occur on any large scale. Sendero jabbed and probed and enforced its will against carefully selected targets, but its primary efforts focused on the bases of power, that is, the moral right of an elitist, foreign-dominated and non-Indian minority regime to govern.

In sum, the primary center of gravity in Peru—as in El Salvador—was legitimacy.

The Counterinsurgency Strategy

Like the El Salvadoran armed forces, the Peruvian police and armed forces initially sought to address the challenge of Sendero Luminoso by repression. The Peruvians, however, had less of an excuse for doing so than the Salvadorans since they had already dealt with an insurgency during the 1960s and developed doctrine to address it. That doctrine was remarkably like the dimensions presented in the SWORD Model. Nevertheless, the Peruvian armed forces initially ignored their own doctrine and adopted a strategy based on the Argentine "Dirty War" approach—with the same consequences that the El Salvadoran armed forces suffered.[52]

In relatively short order, the Peruvian armed forces came to see that their strategy was having little success. Still, they were not certain of where to go. Two factors hampered their ability or willingness to modify their approach. First, among the principal advocates of a political-military strategy were some of the former leaders of the military government that had run Peru from 1968 until 1980. In many ways, this group was seen as lacking credibility. Second, the Peruvian military and intelligence services had since 1972 become very dependent on the Soviet Union for military equipment and doctrine. Not only did the Soviets have little to say about counterinsurgency at this time, but they were relatively unwilling to support the suppression of the leftist insurgencies that were plaguing Peru. This was compounded by the desire of President Fernando Belaunde's administration to downplay the threat as much as possible, leave it in the hands of the police, and generally tie the military's hands so that the armed forces would not be so strengthened that they would again resort to a coup to oust President Belaunde a second time. The result was a vacuum for several years that allowed the wound being inflicted by Sendero to fester.[53]

Unlike El Salvador, Peru did not face a generalized problem of legitimacy. Rather, beginning in the transition period of 1979, Peruvians had

enjoyed the benefits of a formal democracy, which polling data indicated they supported broadly. Moreover, the democratic governments
that had succeeded the military regime did not try to turn back the
clock on the social reforms that had addressed many of the problems
related to land tenure and the survival of serfdom. What problems
remained in the 1980s and 1990s, and there were many, were not the
same ones that had brought down President Belaunde in 1968.[54]

The issue of legitimacy in relation to the democratic state and its
extant regimes was largely in the marginalized areas of the southern
sierra—especially Ayacucho and surrounding departments. These were
the areas that had been left behind during the reforms of the late 1960s
and 1970s and, in addition, had not benefited from the return to democracy in 1979–1980. As result, they were relatively ripe for the message
that Sendero had been sending since the early 1960s. Other areas of
the country, however, were not nearly as susceptible. One significant
problem was that the new democratic governments were failing to
deliver effective policy, especially economic policy, and Peru remained
in the economic doldrums. Hence, neither the Belaunde administration
nor that of Alan Garcia, which followed, attained a significant degree of
regime legitimacy—unlike the democratic system as a whole. Nevertheless, although democracy had broad legitimacy in Peru during this
period, there was little depth to that legitimacy, thereby making the
national government vulnerable to appeals from authoritarians of both
the left and the right.[55]

The role played by intervening powers also affected the ability of the
elected government of Peru to deal with the insurgencies. First, as indicated above, the Soviets abdicated their role in advising both the armed
forces and the National Intelligence Service. Second, because of Peru's
stand on the Falklands War and its continuing relationship with the
Soviet Union with respect to military support, relations between the
U.S. government during the Reagan administration and Belaunde were
cool. Military-to-military relations were very limited.[56]

With the election and inauguration of Alan Garcia in 1985, relations
worsened significantly. Garcia's public statement that he would limit debt
repayment to 10 percent of export earnings was taken by U.S. Treasury
Secretary James Baker as insulting, with the result that not only was

American aid to Peru for just about anything frozen, but the United States appeared to look for excuses to apply legislatively mandated sanctions.[57] Nevertheless, the U.S. Southern Command perceived the threat of Sendero as being significant and within the limits of its authority attempted to assist the Peruvians as best it could. This involved low-key subject matter expert exchanges, staff visits, and lectures at the various senior officer education institutions. Moreover, it involved monitoring Peruvian payments for brief periods when Peru was out of the sanctions window and Peruvian military personnel could be sent to the United States for training under the International Military Education and Training program.[58]

Another area of U.S. support was in the intelligence field. Here, a strong relationship was developing as the U.S. Central Intelligence Agency (CIA) moved to fill the void left by the lack of KGB support to the Peruvian National Intelligence Service (SIN). The CIA provided training and assistance to both military and civilian analysts at the National Intelligence Service, as well as support for the nascent psychological operations program of the Peruvian army. Later, the CIA support also extended to the police in the form of both the National Counterterrorism Directorate and its subordinate element, the Intelligence Special Group (GEIN).[59] The latter two organizations were, in fact, responsible for the capture of Guzmán in September 1992.

The key to strategic success in the war against Sendero was a combination of the evolution of effectively employing the army and marines against armed Senderista columns and those forces' ability to relatively rapidly come to the aid of villages that were under attack, along with a developing intelligence capability, a civil defense capability (Rondas Campesinas, or "peasant [civil defense] bands"), and the mistakes of Sendero. Among the latter was Sendero's harsh treatment of villagers in its area of operations—so harsh, in fact, that local people began arming themselves. The army soon took advantage of this development and began to sponsor the *rondas*. A second error was Sendero's overly rapid expansion into areas in which it had not previously operated. Instead of the militants who had been indoctrinated since they were seven or eight years old, the new Senderistas were in their twenties. This opened the organization to infiltration as it had never been before.[60]

The final strategic factor was unity of effort. Here, Peru was fortunate that President Alberto Fujimori's (1990–2001) *autogolpe* (self-coup) of April 1992 and the subsequent rise of Vladimiro Montesinos to be the de facto head of the National Intelligence Service did not have time to destroy the working relationships among the armed forces, the National Intelligence Service, the National Counterterrorism Directorate, and the Intelligence Special Group. Instead, the capture of Guzmán effectively decapitated Sendero, and with the exception of the Huallaga Regional Command and a few holdouts in Ayacucho, the organization largely disappeared. Unfortunately, in 2003 there were signs that it was reconstituting itself as a result of both the incomplete victory of the early 1990s and the failure of the Fujimori government and its successors to do anything to relieve the root causes of rebellion in the largely forgotten southern sierra.

THE CENTRAL STRATEGIC PROBLEM

Analysis of a large number of cases since the end of World War II shows that insurgencies and "revolutionary wars" such as those in El Salvador and Peru are wars for moral legitimacy. Nations whose governments have achieved moral legitimacy are relatively invulnerable to insurgent movements. By contrast, a nation whose government is or has been perceived as lacking in moral correctness is a prime target for Marxist-Leninist "revolution" and its moralistic egalitarian doctrine or other moralistic ideologies.[61]

Thus, the thrust of any given revolutionary program relies heavily on grievances such as political, economic, and social discrimination as the means through which the government is attacked. This was the essential nature of the threat from Peru's Sendero Luminoso, as it is with any other insurgency, and any response must begin there. A campaign that fails to understand this and responds only to "enemy" military forces is likely to fail. As an example, General Edgardo Mercado Jarrin recognized as early as 1967 (in relation to the just-concluded insurgency in the southern sierra and the threat of future similar revolts) that this aspect of the conflict in Peru would be key to the ultimate success or failure for the insurgents or for the government.[62]

Speaking for the Sendero Luminoso organization, Guzmán identified the lack of legitimacy of all Peruvian governments since the Spanish conquest as the primary center of gravity in the "People's War" in that country.[63] Mercado Jarrin understood the strategic problem and long (but until the early 1990s, unsuccessfully) advocated a program to pre-empt the efforts of Sendero Luminoso. His straightforward argument was that "political considerations prevail over military considerations."[64]

It was also recognized early in the El Salvadoran conflict that the political-moral dimension would be key to success or failure in that situation. Speaking for the insurgents, Guillermo M. Ungo identified the legitimacy of the regime as the "primary strategic problem in El Salvador."[65] President José Napoleón Duarte understood the problem and countered with a program designed to nullify the efforts of the FMLN. His argument was simple: "If the Christian Democrats demonstrate in El Salvador that a democratic system can bring about structured changes peacefully, then the polarized choice between domination by the rightist oligarchy and violent revolution by the Left will no longer be valid."[66]

By transforming the emphasis of war from the level of military violence to the level of a struggle for the moral right to govern, an actor can strive for total objectives, such as the overthrow of a government, instead of simply attempting to obtain leverage and influence for "limited" territorial, economic, or political objectives in the classical sense. As a consequence, the concept of indirect force permits political actors to engage in secret and prolonged wars—striking at an adversary's legitimacy and appearing to pursue honorable objectives. This can be the case either before a conflict is recognized to have begun or after it has been considered terminated. Thus, contemporary war is not an extension of politics. The tendency is for it to be at the lower end of the conflict spectrum, multidimensional, and total.

In these terms, a government (including its military establishment) must meet its contemporary security obligations in three basic respects. First, it must understand the strategic problem and be able to deal with more than the strictly military aspects of "small wars," such as legitimacy. This is a conceptual requirement.

Second, the long-term requirement comprises the principles of unity of command and the objective. Adherence to these fundamentals ensures that all efforts are focused on the ultimate common goal. That is, the political, economic, diplomatic, sociological, psychological, and military effort against those who would subvert a given regime must be coordinated and implemented in an effective, organized, and unified way. The ability to accomplish these things and to govern in a manner acceptable to those governed equates to legitimacy.

Third, the short-term requirement for rendering an internal aggressor ineffective comprises the rest of the principles of war—the offensive, economy of force, mass, maneuver, surprise, simplicity, and security. Adherence to these fundamentals ensures that all efforts center on the appropriate means by which a subversive element might be neutralized. This more immediate requirement subsumes three equally essential elements.

Within the context of the short term, the first element is a proactive campaign strategy. The idea is to establish the ability to fight for something rather than react against something else. It must be designed to achieve decisive results; allocate available resources to ensure adequate and sufficient political, economic, psychological, and military power at appropriate points of decision; exploit successes; maintain freedom of action; and maintain security.

The second element in the short term is to ensure adaptability of forces and flexibility of actions. The purpose of this subtenet is to enable forces to maneuver successfully against an adversary; implement strategic planning; integrate the elements that constitute power in a specific situation; and articulate clear and concise objectives to minimize misunderstanding and confusion in a given situation. This, in turn, subsumes direct and indirect action forces that are well trained and mobile.

The final requirement for the short term is to provide an adequate intelligence orientation and organization designed to establish the capability to strike at a time, at a place, and in a manner for which the enemy is unprepared; neutralize an opposing organization; and decisively shift a balance of power. Precise knowledge of who the enemy is and where he is located is a necessary precursor for any effective countering action. If a country such as the United States can understand and implement these aspects of "uncomfortable wars," it will have a better-than-average chance for success in helping its allies such as El Salvador and Peru in their counterinsurgency efforts. Otherwise, these prolonged wars will grind on and the United States will have a better-than-average chance of suffering a series of Vietnam-like defeats, perhaps smaller in scale and less direct but more debilitating in cumulative effect. Not only do these lessons apply to the support of allies with effective governments, but they also apply to the contemporary situations we find in the wars at the opening of the twenty-first century such as Afghanistan and Iraq.

CHAPTER 8

Applying the "Pillars of Success" to the Problem of Homeland Defense

The end of the cold war did not bring an end to threats facing the United States and the global community. Rather, the "unstable peace" and chaos caused by myriad political instabilities and destabilizing forces have become increasingly insidious and more difficult to combat using cold war concepts of security and deterrence. Destabilizers such as rogue states, insurgents, militant fundamentalists, ethnic cleansers, and innumerable other "snakes with a cause" have time and time again proved willing to resort to terrorist tactics and asymmetric warfare to achieve their aims.

Counterterrorism and homeland defense programs hoping to deal with such destabilizers have tended to hide behind a façade of unilateral microlevel criminal sanctions designed to tighten airport and border security, to encourage pharmaceutical companies to step up production and distribution of arbitrary guesswork lists of antitoxins, to impose trade sanctions against foreign companies that do business with nations that support terrorism, and to deny visas to known terrorists. Yet a significant body of evidence worldwide shows that additional and strategic measures are necessary: simply destroying terrorist cells and the governments or other political actors supporting them is not sufficient.[1]

AN OVERVIEW OF THE
HOMELAND DEFENSE PROBLEM

To protect the territory and interests of the United States and its citizens from "all enemies both foreign and domestic" and "to insure domestic Tranquility" are the principal tasks of the U.S. government.[2] The primary reason to emphasize homeland defense is the change in the type, degree, and number of threats to the United States. Now, in addition to traditional regional security issues, an array of "nontraditional" threats—including a hundred different varieties of terrorism, organized crime, drug trafficking, criminal anarchy, ethnic and religious conflict, and the proliferation of weapons of mass destruction—challenges American well-being. These threats to U.S. national security are exacerbated by nonmilitary threats and menaces that have heretofore been ignored or wished away, such as trade war, financial war, and cyber war. All these threats challenge the United States at home and abroad and blur the conventional dividing lines between military, political, economic, and informational security concerns.[3]

The combined effect of these new, evolving, and increasing threats to U.S. national security is profound, limited only by the human imagination. It demands a new approach to both threat and response in terms of homeland defense. Without significant changes in national security thinking, structures, and processes, the United States faces the grave risk of being unprepared to deter and defend against traditional, nontraditional, and nonmilitary threats—and to minimize and contain the harm they will likely cause. In this connection, the homeland defense issue will undoubtedly emerge over and over in the national political arena. Policy makers, decision makers, opinion makers, other civilian and military leaders, and ordinary citizens therefore must be prepared to deal effectively with this vital issue.

As noted in previous chapters in reference to other aspects of response to the current threats in the global security environment, homeland defense should not be treated on a situation-by-situation "crisis control" approach. Instead, serious efforts should be made to develop what former deputy secretary of defense John J. Hamre calls a unified field theory for homeland defense.[4] That type of conceptual framework, although difficult to frame, could provide essential policy and strategy guidance to assist in clarifying objectives (i.e., ends), courses of action (i.e., ways), and the primary human and other resources (i.e., means) required for accomplishing that guidance. Additionally, a unified field theory would empower a new paradigm of federal, state, and local coordination and cooperation. That, in turn, could generate a historically viable and constitutionally supported unity of national effort.[5]

No quick and easy solution to the complex federal, state, local, and civil liberties issues surrounding homeland defense exists as an alternative to the development of a unified field theory. The temptation to give the armed forces a mandate to "lead in support" should be resisted, in favor of wielding all the possible instruments of power in the context of homeland defense—a strategy dictated by good management practice as well as logic. Homeland defense is too big a problem—both in its prevention of catastrophe and in its cleaning up the aftermath of catastrophe—for only one set of societal institutions to deal with.[6] In addition, any given catastrophe is likely to be too big a problem for duplication and triplication of time, money, and effort to be acceptable. A broader deterrence concept with an integrated organizational architecture and a focus on prevention is thus required. The intent would be to supplement or replace the older and narrower nuclear/military deterrence paradigm with one that addresses the traditional, nontraditional, and nonmilitary threats imposed by the diverse state, nonstate, and transnational actors playing in the contemporary global and domestic security arenas. Such a deterrence concept would be more culturally than militarily oriented and would also be more incentive-based than punitive.[7]

TOWARD A UNIFIED FIELD THEORY
FOR HOMELAND DEFENSE

What is to be done beyond doffing shoes at airports and waiting to react to the next crisis? We must go back to the fundamentals.

This is not a premise derived solely from the study of war, although such notables as Sun Tzu and Clausewitz have advocated it.[8] Consider, for example, the National Football League (NFL) and the National Basketball Association (NBA). No coach in the NFL or NBA would go into a season without a "philosophy" for his team. Neither would any coach go into any given game—particularly such critical contests as the Super Bowl and the tournament final—without a carefully thought-out and thoroughly practiced "game plan." These dicta imply a series of highly interrelated and reinforcing strategic-level actions that constitute the basis for a "unified field theory" (i.e., a "strategic concept," a "guiding architecture," a "blueprint for action," or a "theory of engagement"). These actions involve the need to fully understand the strategic environment within which the conflict is taking place; carefully examine and define the nature of a given conflict and its related problems, including the contemporary problem of governance, the complex and multidimensional threat situation, and the "new" centers of gravity; and carefully examine these assessments and put them into a strategic whole from which to understand and conduct the war—that is, develop a theory of engagement.

The central unifying theme of these actions is decisive. If a country such as the United States wants to ensure efficiency and effectiveness in a matter as crucial as war, the civil-military leadership must concern itself with two things. Clearly, the instruments of national power must be organized, trained, and equipped within prescribed budgetary considerations. But those actions must be preceded by clear, holistic, and logical policy direction—and the ends, ways, and means strategy to ensure the achievement of the political ends established in that policy. This fundamental rule is as valid for current and future conflict as it has been in the past. Incredibly, however, the last time this was done in the United States was in 1947, when George F. Kennan initiated the "theory of containment" process that governed the cold war effort to deal with the hegemony of an expansionist Soviet Union.[9] The current global security environment can no longer be framed in terms of one relatively monolithic superpower pitting its will and strength against another. At any one time in this complex new security environment, numerous high-intensity wars, low-intensity conflicts, and small-scale internal wars are being conducted, sometimes overlapping with others. Governments that have not adapted to the new global situation—particularly ones that have left themselves open to accusations of being weak, incompetent, or corrupt—face a particularly potent challenge from nonstate actors that have proved willing to kill and be killed in pursuit of their objectives, which may include basic human rights reform, political autonomy, or overthrow of the existing government.

For many of these actors, terrorism is a very practical form of warfare for the weak to wield against the strong. Such asymmetrical forms of violence are popular in part because of their effectiveness but also because the means of causing mass destruction (as through terror tactics) have become less expensive and more available to those who wish to impose their agendas or desires on others through direct attack. Complicating the nature of this threat is the fact that the root causes of conflict—such as widespread human suffering, a lack of justice, the absence of basic human rights—are often fostered by weak governments, which then become indirect targets of propaganda designed to sway the populace toward supporting the terrorists rather than the government. This, then, is the nature of contemporary conflict.

Governments, international organizations, transnational entities, and other symbols of global power that have not been responsive to the importance of the legitimate governance reality thus find themselves in a "crisis of governance." They face growing social violence, criminal anarchy, and the potential for eventual destruction.[10] The United States and the West confront many such instances of failing and failed states, destabilized by internecine war.[11]

The novelist John LeCarre vividly captures the political implications of the governance problem that must be confronted today. He outlines the answer to the question of "When is a state not a state?" from the point of view of a commonsense practitioner:

> I would suggest to you that, these days, very roughly, the qualifications for being a civilized state amount to—electoral suffrage, ah—protection of life and property—um, justice, health and education for all, at least to a certain level—then the maintenance of a sound administrative infrastructure—and roads, transport, drains, et cetera—and—what else is there?—ah yes, the equitable collection of taxes. If a state fails to deliver on at least a quorum

of the above—then one *has* to say the contract between the state and citizen begins to look pretty *shaky*—and if it fails on *all* of the above, then it's a *failed* state, as we say these days.[12]

The "failed state" phenomenon directly and indirectly threatens the stability of the entire world order. By transforming the emphasis of war from the level of conventional military violence to the level of a multidimensional political-economic-social-moral-psychological struggle centering on the problem of governance, terrorists can strive for the destruction of any symbol of power defined as "bad," instead of simply attempting to obtain leverage and influence for limited political or economic concessions or even the overthrow of a government. By extension, terrorist strategies and tactics may be aimed at the complete overturning of the system of international order.[13]

Attacking the foreign internal development or reconstruction causes and consequences of instability and violence therefore is no longer a matter of grace, of charity, or of patronizing kindness. Because of the very real threat to peace and prosperity, it has become a matter of intense national and global self-interest. The conscious choices that the international community and individual nations make about how to conduct national stability and reconstruction efforts now and in the future will define the processes of national reform, regeneration, and well-being—and thus relative internal and global security, stability, peace, and prosperity. The case of Iraq is instructive in this regard, in that the ultimate resolution of the conflict there weighs heavily on the security and defense of the American homeland because of both Iraq's potential to harbor terrorists and its ability to shift attention and resources from the global terrorist threat toward the deaths of American and allied service members "in a far away land [among] people we know nothing about."[14]

TOWARD A NEW PARADIGM OF COOPERATION

The lack of an evident strategic paradigm and structure for homeland defense has been exacerbated by visions of confused, piecemeal, and ad hoc federal, state, and local responses to relatively recent man-made and natural disasters that have taken place in the United States. The first step in an effective attempt to manage the consequences of any possible attack on the homeland is the development of a new paradigm of cooperation—which, in turn, requires a historically viable and constitutionally supported unity of effort. Preliminary steps taken in this regard are the establishment of the Office of Homeland Security in 2001, the development of *The National Strategy for Homeland Security* in 2002, and the enactment of the major governmental reorganization that resulted in the Department of Homeland Security (DHS), which was fully constituted by March 2003. In addition, the White House published its *National Strategy for Combating Terrorism* in February 2003 along with several more related strategies.[15]

Unity of effort involves overcoming parochial bureaucratic interests; fighting jurisdictional conflicts relating to federal, state, and local jurisdictions; and ensuring that all governmental and private efforts at all levels are focused on the ultimate common goal as defined by these documents and the actions taken by the several agencies and levels of government. For any degree of success, homeland defense must be understood as a holistic process that relies on various U.S. federal, state, and local, as well as other national civilian and military agencies and contingents, working together in an integrated fashion. Otherwise, a response to aggression or catastrophe cannot be made either credible or effective.

For creation of such a unity of effort, the primary federal, state, local, and private (i.e., nongovernmental organizations) parties to the homeland defense issue must first be in general agreement with regard to the objectives of a strategic paradigm, a political vision, and an associated set of implementing operations. Appropriate policy implementation and military management structure—and mind-set adjustments—must also be evident in the several strategies and the new Homeland Security Department. Once those elements are in place, an executive-level management structure will be essential, to ensure continuous cooperative planning and execution of policy among and between the relevant U.S. federal, state, local, and private civilian and military/police agencies (i.e., vertical coordination). That structure must be constitutionally and politically acceptable to the American people and must ensure that all civil-military/police actions at the operational and tactical levels directly contribute to the achievement of the strategic end-state. Although the new Department of Homeland Security is a good organizational start and the strategies provide common statements of ends, ways, and means, multiple problems of interagency and intergovernmental (federal/state/local) coordination remain. Assuredly, these problems will be difficult to overcome, but doing so is not an impossible task.

At another level, steps must be taken to ensure clarity, unity, and effectiveness by integrating allied/friendly/coalition military and civilian, nongovernmental organization, and international organization processes with U.S. civil-military planning and implementing processes (i.e., horizontal coordination). These issues are, in fact, addressed in the *National Strategy for Combating Terrorism.* Nevertheless (as discussed in previous chapters), the political end-state is elusive and operations suffer—and costly duplication of effort occurs—when no strategic planning structure is empowered to integrate key multinational and multiorganizational civil-military elements in a given situation.

Fundamentally, however, unity of effort requires more than reorganizational solutions to minimize the ambiguity, confusion, and tensions that are likely to emerge between and among individuals. Only when and if the various civilian and military/police leaders involved in a homeland defense effort can develop the judgment and empathy necessary to work cooperatively and collegially will they be able to plan and conduct actions that meet the needs of such a complex security situation. At the same time, cultural—both national and bureaucratic—empathy is required to meet the needs and use the appropriate capabilities of the bewildering number and type of organizations that may be involved. Horizontal and vertical unity of effort ultimately entails the type of civilian and military education and leader development that leads to effective diplomacy (both foreign and domestic), as well as to professional competence.

In sum, if the United States is to be successful in meeting the challenges and threats of now and the future, all the agencies in the U.S.

governmental structure must adapt and become integrated, coherent, and proactive in dealing with homeland defense. That must also include state and local governments and even nongovernmental organizations. In addition, the spirit and intent of coordination and cooperation must also extend horizontally to interalliance venues.

Other Western nations have managed at least temporary unity of effort to combat intrastate conflict or terrorism. The two brief examples provided here to demonstrate the principle are not completely analogous to the American homeland defense problem, but they are instructive. The first example indicates how the British have achieved both vertical and horizontal coordination in conflict situations. The second (more fully developed in chapter 9) shows how the Italians overcame a lack of unity in government during the crisis of 1978–1980.

In the British experience, an overall coordinator of all military and civil activities has usually been appointed by the prime minister. A committee of the cabinet provides periodic general direction and support of this individual. The coordinator has the authority to deal with people in his or her own government (i.e., vertical coordination) and with officials in other relevant countries and international organizations (i.e., horizontal coordination). Together, these individuals determine and pursue long-term and short-term mutually supportive objectives.[16]

In 1978–1979, the Italian government understood that unity of effort was a major deficiency in their war against terrorism. The government agreed that the paramilitary Carabinieri understood how to plan and coordinate delicate police operations and could exercise full police power throughout the Italian national territory. The government also agreed that the regular armed forces should be kept in the background, to provide only unobtrusive back-up functions for the heavily committed Carabinieri. Thus, as an emergency national security measure, the government created a temporary counterterrorism task force composed of state police, Finance Guard, and Carabinieri personnel. This organization was headed by Carabinieri general Carlo Alberto Dalla Chiesa, and it took the responsibility for unifying all intelligence collection and police actions. Under Dalla Chiesa's leadership, long-term and short-term mutually supportive objectives were determined and pursued. As a result, terrorism in Italy was brought under control as early as 1980–1981.[17]

TOWARD A BROADER DETERRENCE CONCEPT

In the chaos of the post–cold war era, the threat of devastating attacks on the United States, its interests, and its friends by the former Soviet Union, China, and other actual and potential nuclear powers retains a certain credibility. At the same time, the challenges for contemporary security and deterrence policy intensify with the growing sophistication of biological and chemical war and cyber war. These challenges to deterrence policy are seriously complicated, on one hand, by other nontraditional threats and menaces emanating from adversarial state, nonstate, and transnational political actors. On the other hand, these problems are gravely complicated by the reluctance and the lack of will on the part of some pundits, politicians of both parties, and even some senior military officers in the United States to come to grips with the conduct of asymmetric warfare.

In the anarchic environment of global politics, regardless of perceived intent, what one state or political actor does will inevitably impinge on another. That action will affect some constructively, others adversely. Mutual dependence means that each political actor must take others into account. Interdependence affects nothing more powerfully than it does security. The result can be a vicious downward action-reaction spiral that takes the global community into instability, violence, chaos, and the inevitable destruction of stability, prosperity, and peace. As a consequence, state and nonstate political actors have always tried to deter others from engaging in activities considered to be harmful and to encourage actions thought to be beneficial. A major problem in all of this is that the anarchic environment of global politics allows each political actor to be the only and the final judge of its own interests and actions. Thus, deterrence must be considered the "art of the possible."[18] We address the framing of a successful deterrence policy in terms of a series of rules—primary, intermediate, and advanced—and a focus on realities and conclusions.

Primary Rules

Preventive diplomacy comes into play here. The general rule is that decision makers and policy makers must carefully calculate possible gains and losses and, when the case warrants, apply preplanned indirect and direct deterrent measures earlier rather than later. Earlier application of deterrence measures implies the initial and intense use of low-cost diplomatic and civilian resources and military support units to ensure that the deterrence message has adequate back-up. If applied earlier, preventive measures may reduce tensions that if left to fester could lead to deadly results. In contrast, the later application of deterrence measures implies the initial and intense use of high-cost military combat units to respond to a worsening situation. If applied later, preventive measures may turn out to be either irrelevant or counterproductive. Ultimately, the only viable test for indirect or direct preventive action sooner or later is national self-interest; but in any case, the basic logic of the application of preventive diplomacy is unassailable—the sooner the better.

It becomes apparent, then, that deterrence is not necessarily military—although having a military capability is important. Nor are deterrence measures necessarily negative or directly coercive—although having the availability of those options is likewise important. Deterrence is much broader than that. Deterrence can be direct or indirect, constituting some combination of political-diplomatic, social-economic, psychological-moral, or military-coercive measures. In its various forms and combinations of forms, it is an attempt to influence how and what an illegal internal or a foreign enemy or potential adversary thinks and does. That is, deterrence is the creation of a state of mind that either discourages one behavior or encourages another. Motives and culture thus become crucial. Within this context, political-military communication and preventive diplomacy become vital parts of the deterrence equation.

Intermediate Rules

Once the primary rules have been taken into account, intermediate rules, which may be considered "rules of thumb," are applied. Here decision and policy makers must move from traditional U.S.-centric values and determine precisely what a hostile foreign or militant domestic leadership values most. The "deterrer" must then identify exactly how that cultural "thing," whatever it is, can realistically be held at risk and conversely—as opposed to the proverbial "stick"— identify precisely what "carrots" might also be offered to discourage adverse actions but encourage beneficial behaviors or activities on the part of the "deterree." The task of both deterrence and preventive diplomacy is, as a result, to get into the minds of the diverse political actors and to find viable ways and means of convincing them *not* to use nuclear weapons (or any other kind of weapons) against the United States or others in the global community.

The threats associated with the growing sophistication of biological and chemical war and cyber war are intensifying.[19] At the same time, nontraditional threats and menaces are spreading throughout the entire global community, wreaking havoc wherever they appear. Here again, the deterrence task is straightforward. Culturally effective ways and means must be found to convince these players that it is not in their interest to continue their deleterious behavior.

Advanced Rules

The formula for success in deterrence cannot be reduced to buying more or better military forces, weaponry, and equipment, to superior intelligence, to genius in command, or to relative morality. Deterrence can work only if the intended deterree chooses to be deterred. There is no way that any kind of deterrence can be guaranteed. The problem is that deterrence is a dialectic between two independent wills. As a consequence, the single most important dimension of deterrence is clarity of communication between deterrer and deterree.[20]

In this connection, a successful deterrence policy and strategy must recognize that one deterrent or another may fail. The possibility of failure leads to other requirements. As examples, beyond planning for unilateral conventional and nuclear military reaction, decision makers and policy makers could consider other ideas: enhancing multilateral security measures, going to other proven and ageless unconventional security measures, and developing "new" means of deterrence. Thus, deterrence must also address the relationship with other concepts such as traditional and nontraditional compellence, dissuasion, defense, and denial. Deterrence policy must also address the need to integrate those ideas into policy, strategy, doctrine, training, force structure, and operations with respect to old, new, and emerging adversaries.[21]

Again, deterrence cannot be reduced to a single dominant aspect. Success will be the result of a unified, coherent, long-term, discrete, and culturally oriented policy and strategy that integrates all the civil and military elements of U.S. national power to synergistically influence the behavior of diverse adversaries.

Deterrence Realities for Now and into the Next Century

As long as opposition exists that is willing to risk everything to violently take down a government, destroy a society, or cause great harm to a society, there is war. Guns, bombs, and nuclear, chemical, and biological implements of destruction may be the weapons of choice, as is the case with other governments, rogue states, Maoist insurgents, the Japanese Aum Shinrikyo cult, Mafia families, warlords, or Osama Bin Ladin's terrorists—among others. However, nonmilitary actions such as the deliberate "financial war" attack planned and implemented by owners of international mobile capital—which generated the Southeast Asia financial crisis and inflicted devastating injury on Asia's "little tiger" countries not too many years ago—also can cause socioeconomic and political devastation. This is also the case with the systems analyst, software engineer, scholar, or sixteen-year-old "hacker" who can impair the security of an army or a nation electronically. As one final example, it must be remembered that Germany's former chancellor, Helmut Kohl, breached the Berlin Wall with the powerful Deutschmark—not aircraft, artillery, armor, or infantry. These are the deterrence realities for the twenty-first century. The old strictly "military" model of deterrence is illusion.

This current multipolar world, in which one or a hundred actors are exerting differing types and levels of power within a set of cross-cutting alliances, is clearly more volatile and dangerous than the previous bipolar superpower situation. As they rethink contemporary deterrence, U.S. leaders should think of the country as a "war preventer" more than a "war fighter." Thus, it is incumbent on the United States and the rest of the international community to develop institutional ways and means of understanding and coping with the threats imposed by contemporary nontraditional actors. At the same time, it is important to learn to think "outside the box" and to replace the old "nuclear theology" with a broad and flexible deterrence strategy as it applies to the chaos provoked by the diverse state, nonstate, and transnational nuclear and non-nuclear threats and menaces that heretofore have been ignored or wished away.

IMPLICATIONS

In the confusion of effort that has resulted from trying to deal with homeland defense in the complex contemporary global security environment, strategic considerations have played little part in the debate and actions pertaining to national and global security. The general result in the United States has been the ad hoc and piecemeal crisis management of security affairs. That approach, in turn, has led to ad hoc, piecemeal, and less-than-desirable results—and high personnel, monetary, and political costs.

The United States and the rest of the international community will inevitably face horrible new dilemmas at home and abroad that arise from the instability engendered by the contemporary global security environment. The traditional threat that stems from current and potential nuclear powers is complicated by the many smaller—but equally deadly—nontraditional threats that are generated out of the unevenness of global integration. Clearly the "business as usual" crisis management approach to homeland defense leaves much to be desired in the context of a multipolar world in which innumerable "irrational" political players are exerting differing types and levels of lethal power. Thus, the steps taken since the attacks of September 11, 2001, have started policy makers and decision makers in the right direction. However, it must be remembered that they are, at best, first steps. The government reorganization that produced the Department of Homeland Security will take many years to consolidate—hopefully not the half-century that the Department of Defense required, but many years nonetheless.

THE CHALLENGE, THE THREAT, AND THE MAIN TASK

Over the past few years, decision makers and policy makers have seemed to be consistently surprised at the chaos and violence emerging out of Middle Eastern, Southeast and Southwest Asian, and other societies. They have also appeared to be confused and unable to decide what to do or how to do it, beyond the usual crisis management and spin control. This kind of crisis management approach to global and national security issues reminds one of Alice's conversation with the Cheshire Cat:

> "Would you tell me, please, which way I ought to walk from here?"
>
> "That depends a good deal on where you want to get to," said the Cat.
>
> "I don't much care where," said Alice.
>
> "Then it doesn't matter which way you walk," said the Cat.
>
> "—so long as I get *somewhere*," Alice added as an explanation.
>
> "Oh, you're sure to do that," said the Cat, "if you only walk long enough!"[22]

The Main Challenge

The United States faces a challenge to change perspectives. As has been suggested above, this country needs a central unifying homeland defense concept to replace the cold war concept of "containment"; a thoughtful reorganization of the national security management, coordination, and implementation structures to better deal with the complex new world; and farsighted research and planning mechanisms to give decision makers and policy makers viable options for deterring and reducing the scope, intensity, and duration of contemporary violence. The intent is to learn to culturally understand adversaries and potential adversaries, to influence their thought and behavior for the advantage of the United States and American interests.

Steps to meet the first two parts of the challenge have already been taken. Now those steps must be carried through, modified, and expanded as necessary.

The Main Threat

The ultimate threat is that unless and until American leaders at the highest levels recognize what is happening strategically, reorient their thinking and actions appropriately, and are able to educate and lead their domestic publics into the realities of the post–cold war world, it is only a matter of time before the destabilizing problems associated with global and national security will consume the nation. Additionally, in the current highly integrated global system, we must remember that global defense *is* homeland defense. And "the enemy may be us."

The Main Task

The lessons from over a half-century of bitter experience suffered by governments involved in one form or another of homeland defense show that a given conflict situation (and its catastrophic consequences) often ends short of a desired end-state. Too often this unsatisfactory state of affairs comes about because the endgame is undefined, national and international civil-military unity of purpose remains unachieved, and civil and military/police support is ad hoc. Thus, the admittedly difficult task of developing leaders who can put together a twenty-first-century "game plan" and make it work remains imperative.

PART III

The Application of Grand Strategy at Home and Abroad

CHAPTER 9

STRATEGIC LESSONS OF
ITALIAN TERRORISM

During the height of the terrorist assault on the Italian state, the United States and much of the rest of the Western world was deeply immersed in their own domestic problems as well as the debilitating conflicts in Southeast Asia and Central America. As a result, the most important political phenomenon of the 1970s and 1980s in Italy—and perhaps the West—was generally overlooked or ignored in the United States and elsewhere. The aftermath of the 1978 kidnapping, "people's trial," and "execution" of five-time prime minister Aldo Moro marked the first time in which the Italian state directly addressed the terrorist threat. What made Aldo Moro's assassination significant beyond domestic Italian politics was that it was the harbinger of much of the "new world disorder" that emerged out of the ending of the cold war, as well as the explicit terrorist threat. As a result, this case is particularly useful in terms of its strategic lessons, as they impact on the issues of homeland defense discussed in chapter 8.

The high level of terrorism experienced in Italy from the end of the 1960s through the early 1980s demonstrates a general pattern of the ways and means through which militant intrastate actors can bring their causes into the world spotlight. At the same time, it provides an example of a generalized methodology through which these individuals and groups can illegally challenge governments and force profound political change so that the end-state conforms to their own ideas of how things ought to be.

The Italian case, then, is a logical point of departure from which to examine terrorism as an effective form of warfare for relatively power-less agents to employ against those who are nominally in power. It is also a logical point from which to begin to outline the architecture by which governments can ultimately control or neutralize the strategic challenge of terrorism—and to dispute the notion of some invisible hand creating general international political chaos.

Even though every conflict is situation specific, it should not be considered unique. Analytical commonalities can be identified in each of the "terrorism as war" cases. Thus, we can say that no successful counter-terrorist strategy has been formulated over the past fifty years that has not incorporated the decisive factors also found in the Italian case.[1] Within this context, the primary questions to be dealt with are twofold. First, what were the central problem, the perceived threats or threats, and other concepts that precipitated and guided the response of the Italian state against terrorism? And second, how was the problem dealt with at the strategic level?

THE PROBLEM, THREATS, AND OTHER ELEMENTS THAT DICTATE RESPONSE

The basic problem in the Italian case is that over the ten-year period from 1968 to 1978, violence perpetrated by militant left-wing, right-wing, separatist, pacifist, and other organizations supported by outside forces reached a level and scope too serious to continue to ignore. The assassi-nation of former prime minister Aldo Moro in 1978 at the hands of the Red Brigades was the catalyst that finally brought the state into direct confrontation with terrorism.[2]

The indirect and direct terrorist challenges to the Italian state demanded a rethinking of the problem. Terrorism was undermining the people's faith in the political system, the state's ability to sustain a healthy economy, and the state's capability to provide a lawful environment for basic personal security. In that context, the Red Brigades considered the large-scale killing and maiming of ordinary citizens as well as notable officials "a social duty imposed by the laws of class warfare."[3] Terrorism was also challenging the integrity of the country's political institutions and creating an unacceptable level of instability. The objective was to "destroy the political equilibrium of Italy and give impetus to the conquest of political power and the installation of the dictatorship of the proletariat."[4]

Analysis of the central strategic problem in Italy resulted in the identification of three levels of threat—cause, effect, and response. By 1978 and beyond, however, the Italian government recognized that the greatest single threat to Italian security and stability came from the highest echelons of government failing to recognize and respond to the cause and effect of the dangers posed by intrastate terrorists and their international supporters.[5] Regardless of the level of the threat, however, the capability of the state to cope with the problems imposed by terrorism obviously had to be improved.

Rethinking the Problem: Terrorism and National Well-Being

In 1968, terrorist groups claimed responsibility for 147 incidents, including deaths, woundings, and kidnappings. In 1978, the various Italian terrorist organizations claimed responsibility for 2,498 incidents.[6] This type of effort was considered by the terrorists as a war against the state because "the State, its juristic ideology, and its law are nothing other than instruments through which the bourgeoisie exercises its dictatorship over the proletariat."[7] Yet until 1978 the state had considered terrorism to be only a bit more serious than normal violent criminal behavior.

The aftermath and the investigation of the execution of Aldo Moro indicated that the situation in Italy was more than a complex law enforcement problem: it was a national security problem.[8] In the past, the concept of national security had been primarily associated with the protection of the nation's territory and vital interests against conventional external military aggression. After the Moro incident, however, national security took on a broader meaning. Terrorism, regardless of different internal ideological orientations—exacerbated by outside support—was generally agreed to be dividing, corrupting, destabilizing, and destroying the Italian society as well as the government. As a consequence, the concept of national security expanded to include the protection of the nation's well-being against unconventional internal terrorist assault.[9]

The Complex Threat Situation

The threat of intrastate or terrorist conflict, then, can come in many forms, both direct and indirect. The most visible form of the direct challenge to the state in Italy came in the form of public violence against leading officials who symbolized something that could undercut the terrorist leadership. For example, according to one Red Brigadist, Aldo Moro had to be eliminated because he embodied "all that was the most intelligent and the most dangerous in the (governing) regime."[10]

The indirect threat in Italy came in the form of the progressive discrediting of public institutions to erode the basic public trust that must underlie the legitimate functioning of the state. In any case, Italian terrorists—regardless of political orientation—exploited perceived popular notions of socioeconomic dysfunction as the primary means of attacking the state.[11] Thus, terrorism was both the consequence (i.e., effect) and the cause of instability.

In this context, it may help the analyst to think of a consequence of instability, such as terrorism, as a third-level threat to national security. Root causes—such as a certain level of societal injustice—are second-level threats to national security and stability. The unwillingness or inability of government to develop long-term, multidimensional, and morally acceptable means to maintain and enhance national well-being is the most fundamental first-level threat. The dialogue in the Italian government focused on the fact that since 1968, decision makers, policy makers, and opinion leaders had done little more than watch, pontificate, and improve their personal fortunes while democracy and stability were slowly being destroyed and thousands of innocents were killed, maimed, or kidnapped.[12]

Logically, however, decision makers and policy makers must contemplate all three levels of threat to effectively deal with terrorism. To the extent that unified efforts at all three levels are strongly present in any given counterterrorism strategy, they favor success. To the extent that they are absent or generally weak in a strategy implementation process, they do not favor success.[13]

Nevertheless, once an illegal internal enemy—such as the Red Brigades—becomes firmly established, first-level reform and development efforts aimed at second-level root causes are insufficient to control or neutralize that third-level terrorist threat. The terrorist organization finally can be defeated only by a superior organization and a holistic and unified political, economic, moral, and paramilitary strategy designed to deal with it. The sum of the parts of the desired countereffort to deal with the terrorist threat have to equal a certain capability not only to exert effective deadly military or paramilitary force at the third level, but also to coordinate political, economic, social, psychological, and moral objectives at the first and second levels.[14]

To combat the terrorist threat, the Italian state reluctantly became involved in an unconventional war for survival. This conflict was not simply the result of irrational fanaticism, long-standing socioeconomic injustice, or the inequities inherent in capitalism. Rather, the terrorist groups proclaimed that "revolutionary violence is the highest possible good in overthrowing a moribund capitalist order," and it served as an ideological substitute for conventional war.[15]

Because of the asymmetry of power, the terrorists in Italy and their transnational supporters could not overtly challenge the superior force of the government. By transforming the emphasis of war from the level of military violence to the level of a multidimensional struggle for legitimacy, however, the terrorists could strive for the complete overthrow of the Italian government, instead of simply attempting to obtain leverage and influence for limited economic or political concessions in the more conventional sense. Thus, this war came about as the result of careful political calculation—in conjunction with ideological motivation.[16]

Additional Elements of the Problem That Helped Dictate Response

In a sense, the Italian experience with terrorism was the point of transition into a new age of unconventional conflict in which the use of military power against an elusive foe in an intrastate affair—Italians versus Italians—added ambiguity to the traditional Italian and world vision of war. The "enemy" would have to be very carefully discerned and politically isolated from the rest of the Italian population. This would require the prudent use of power, particularly the more subtle applications of nonmilitary instruments of power, including information warfare, intelligence work, and surgical precision in removing specific individual terrorists from the general populace. Moreover, it would require an almost unheard-of governmental unity of effort to coordinate the multidimensional paradigm necessary for success in an antiterrorist war.[17]

DEALING WITH THE PROBLEM AT THE STRATEGIC LEVEL

To most Americans, involvement in any war—including a war against terrorism—would seem to call for a complex national mobilization process and the allocation of billions of dollars for the effort. In contrast, the realities of many contemporary conflicts appear to require a different approach.

The Italians argued that the moral legitimacy of the republic that emerged out of World War II was sufficiently strong to allow the planning, public dissemination, and implementation of a coordinated and legitimized antiterrorism policy and related "hard law" legislation directed specifically against terrorists. These foundational measures were expected to facilitate an adequate response to the terrorist threat at the judicial, police, and intelligence levels.[18]

In addition, Italian planners understood that an antiterrorist war was in fact a series of "wars" within the war (see chapter 1): (1) the more traditional police-military war against the various terrorist groups; (2) a "war" to maintain the moral right of the incumbent Italian regime to exist; (3) a "war" to unify a multidimensional political-social-psychological-police effort within the fragmented Italian bureaucracy; (4) an informational "war" to convince the Italian people of the moral rectitude of the antiterrorist campaign; (5) a "war" to isolate the terrorists from their internal support; (6) a "war" to isolate the terrorists from their external support; and finally, (7) an intelligence "war" to locate and neutralize the men and women who led, planned, and executed the terrorist violence.[19]

Foundational Legislative Measures Directed against the Terrorists

The first legislation that would allow the prosecution of terrorists for terrorist crimes was enacted as an immediate response to the abduction of Aldo Moro. This legislation amended the Criminal Code of 1930 by increasing penalties for kidnapping motivated specifically by terrorism and subversion of the democratic order. That legislation also empowered the Italian law enforcement agencies to detain anyone who refused to identify himself. Finally, it relaxed restrictions on judicial control of police wiretapping in emergency—i.e., national security—situations.[20]

Additional legislation promulgated in 1979–1980 further amended the criminal code. It specifically addressed conspiracy and actions taken for the purposes of terrorism or subversion. At the same time, pretrial confinement limitations were relaxed for terrorist-related crimes, the penalties for such crimes were substantially increased, arrest warrants became mandatory for terrorist-related crimes, immediate search was authorized for property or entire blocks where terrorists were suspected to be hiding, identification of banking transactions in excess of 20 million lire was made mandatory, and judicial sentences were reduced for terrorists willing to cooperate with the judiciary and the police.[21]

This foundational legislation was adopted inordinately late—ten years after the Italian internal security services recognized that the terrorist threat had begun. Moreover, the measures adopted were ad hoc and piecemeal. As a result, the state belatedly provided the legal means that would allow the security organizations to function relatively effectively but did not reorganize them to function more efficiently.

Adaptation of Lessons Learned to the "Wars"
within the General Antiterrorist War

Because of the continuing absence of a homogeneous and solid parliamentary majority, accompanied by endemic Italian governmental
instability, the diverse "wars" within the antiterrorist war were left to
the discordant elements of the state bureaucracy. Thus, the planning
and implementation of the response to terrorism was not a completely
coordinated and unified effort. The paramilitary Carabinieri understood how to plan and coordinate actions and had full police power
throughout the Italian national territory. As a consequence, planning
and coordination (to the extent that it was achieved) essentially fell to
that organization.[22]

The challenge for those who were to conduct these wars within a
war was to come to a mutual agreement regarding the definition of
success against terrorism and then to plan and implement an integrated effort to achieve that end. The intent was twofold. First, there
would be no strategic ambiguity. Second, there would be no "dirty
war." Together, these unifying and legitimizing efforts would reestablish the kind of stability that was derived from popular perceptions
that the authority of the state was genuine and effective and that it
used morally correct means for reasonable and fair purposes.[23]

THE PARAMILITARY WAR

Successful wars against terrorism demonstrate that they must be conducted by a highly professional, well-disciplined, motivated security
force that is capable of discrete, rapid, and decisive surgical action
anywhere in the country. Moreover, that action must be designed to
achieve political and psychological as well as police-military objectives.
Such a security organization must have the mentality to engage terrorists without alienating the citizenry, because the strength of a terrorist
program is nourished by the alienation of the governed from the
government. Great care must be taken to be sensitive and accommodating
to the general population throughout the process of finding and dealing
with terrorists.[24]

In Italy, the government was reluctant to take the broadened definition of national security to its logical conclusion and correspondingly
broaden the role of the military to a controversial internal protection
mission. Italian planners understood that legitimacy considerations
required that the role of the regular armed forces should be limited to
supporting the major police organizations. They also understood that
the ever-present but relatively unobtrusive paramilitary Carabinieri
would make an appropriate counterterrorism force. As a result, the
regular military took over generally routine, inconspicuous, and unobtrusive police functions to allow the state police and the Carabinieri
freedom to concentrate on the antiterrorism mission.[25]

The Legitimacy "War"

The moral right of a regime to govern is critical in a war against terrorism. The thrust of a terrorist program relies on grievances such as
political, economic, and social injustices as the means through which
government is attacked.[26]

Once the Italian parliament had provided the legislation that would
allow the prosecution of a serious antiterrorist war, legitimacy was
recognized as key to success or failure either for the terrorists or for the
government. The Red Brigades, for example, identified legitimacy as
the primary center of gravity in their strategy to destroy the incumbent
regime. The Italian bureaucracy understood that popular perceptions
of various injustices tend to limit the right—and the ability—of the
government to conduct the business of state. In response, the Italian
government countered with programs designed to preempt the terrorist effort. The coordination task was to ensure that every policy,
program, and action—political, economic, social, opinion making, and
security—would contribute directly to enhancing the popular perception that governmental authority was genuine and effective and was
used in a morally correct manner for reasonable and fair purposes.[27]

The "War" for Unity of Effort

This dimension of an antiterrorist conflict ensures that all governmental efforts are focused on the common goal—maintaining the legitimate

state. The necessary organization to coordinate and implement an effective unity of effort against those who would destroy the government must be established and efforts undertaken in a manner acceptable to the governed people.[28]

In 1978–1979, the Italian government understood that the lack of unity of effort was a major deficiency in the antiterrorist war. The government created a temporary counterterrorism task force including personnel from the state police, Finance Guard, and Carabinieri; this organization was made responsible for unifying all intelligence collection and police operations. Under the leadership of General Carlo Alberto Dalla Chiesa, the organization soon brought terrorism under control.[29]

THE INFORMATION "WAR"

Support of the state on the part of the majority of the populace and well-motivated counterterrorist actions on the part of government forces are directly related to the synergism and effectiveness of informational and public diplomacy efforts. People are the primary source of physical, psychological, and moral strength, becoming the center of gravity in terrorist conflict. Thus, the climate of opinion that might ultimately lead to support for rather than hostility toward the political institutions of the state must be carefully channeled by a legal, democratic, and honest orientation.[30]

In the Italian case, the state and the media embarked on a strong counterterrorist public diplomacy campaign. The objective was to expose and exploit the fact that the various terrorist groups operating in Italy were self-appointed elites with agendas that were their own rather than those of the masses. In the final analysis, the government's antiterrorist information war demonstrated that to the terrorists, Italians who did not prove themselves "true believers" of a given ideology—including, presumably, the 2,384 victims killed, maimed, or abducted by terrorists in 1979—were only "tools of the system," "pigs," and "watch dogs" rather than human beings.[31] The Red Brigadists in particular labeled everyone else—even other leftist ideologues—as "shit."[32]

The "Wars" to Isolate Terrorists from Internal and External Sources of Support

The problem here is to isolate terrorists politically, psychologically, and militarily from the primary sources of aid—whoever and wherever they may be.[33] Internally, the Italian terrorists were isolated from the rest of the community as a result of the effects of the legitimacy war, the information war, and the physical paramilitary war. As the terrorists withdrew more and more into their own compartmentalized organizational structure, their isolation from the rest of the world became nearly complete. That separation from the outside world further restricted access to external reality, the capability to recruit new members, and the ability to organize significant actions.[34] Support to Italian terrorists, however, was not necessarily localized within the borders of the country. Italian terrorist groups were known to be receiving political-diplomatic, logistical-financial, and other support from the Soviet Union, Soviet surrogates such as Bulgaria and Czechoslovakia, and Middle Eastern and North African states including Iraq, Iran, and Libya.[35] More specifically, this aid included "Energia bombs as part of the material provided by Palestinians," "weapons and money as part of the support provided by the Bulgarian secret service," and "revolutionary training as part of the aid provided by Cuba, Libya, and the Soviet Union."[36]

Externally oriented efforts directed against outside aid and support to the Italian terrorists proved to be relatively ineffective, however. By 1978–1979, national security measures intended to isolate terrorists from external sources of support had come to be centered on very porous formal and informal bilateral agreements with all the western European countries, the United States, and other countries interested in facilitating multilateral antiterrorist cooperation. Weak measures intended to deport illegal aliens were also taken. Thus, the stronger and more coherent internal measures taken to isolate the terrorists from the rest of Italian society were those that also isolated them from their outside supporters.[37]

The Intelligence "War"

A major concern in antiterrorist warfare must be removal of the individuals who plan, conduct, and support terrorist activities. This can be accomplished only with the aid of an intelligence apparatus capable of locating and isolating the terrorists so that they can be neutralized.[38]

Italian government efforts to find, discredit, and neutralize terrorists and terrorist leadership focused on the activities of General Dalla Chiesa's counterterrorism task force and the Ministry of the Interior's Central Directorate for Crime Prevention.[39] The Central Directorate for Crime Prevention coordinated the operations of the counterterrorism branch offices organic to the state police in every province of Italy. Dalla Chiesa's task force coordinated the entire intelligence collection effort as well as police operations. An intelligence orientation and organization was thus established that had the capability to strike at a time, at a place, and in a manner for which the terrorists were generally unprepared. The short-term effect was to neutralize a given terrorist group. The long-term effect was to decidedly shift the balance of power toward the legitimate organs of Italian government.[40]

The Other Side of the Equation

The Italian state does not deserve all the credit for bringing terrorism under control. The success of the various "wars" within the antiterrorist war in Italy can also be attributed to a certain level of failure on the part of the terrorists.

In the paramilitary war, the terrorists misjudged the level of the Italian people's commitment to revolution. As an example, Alberto Franceschini—an important Red Brigades (BR) leader—admitted that the Red Brigades had been completely wrong in their analysis of Italian reality: "All of us in the BR were drug addicts of a particular type—of ideology. A murderous drug, worse than heroin."[41] Additionally, terrorist violence was perceived by the populace as wanton and completely beyond that which might be necessary to make a political statement. As a result, the terrorists managed to alienate the citizenry in their attempt to attack the state. That popular alienation cost the terrorists dearly. With the erosion of the terrorists' legitimacy and alienation of their supporters, people began to willingly provide counterterrorist intelligence.[42]

Terrorist legitimacy was called into question from the outset. Even though 259 of the 297 leftist groups claiming responsibility for various terrorist acts were classified as communist, the legal parliamentary Communist Party of Italy denied responsibility for taking a violent approach to achieving control of the state. Throughout the period from 1968 to 1982, indeed, the party "wrapped itself in the flag of the Italian republic," insisted on its commitment to a pluralist society, and withheld its legitimacy from the combatant communists.[43]

The nearly three hundred Marxist-Leninist-oriented terrorist groups likewise did not unify their antigovernment effort. The various Italian terrorist groups maintained their own agendas and their own appreciation of what was to be done and how it was to be done. As a consequence, no single high-level management structure focused on the ultimate common goal, and the goal was not achieved.[44]

An information war is supposed to generate at least tacit support for a cause. Italian terrorist propaganda, information, and public diplomacy were communicated to target audiences in a virtually unintelligible jargon without any serious attempt to educate the public regarding terminology or dogma. Everyone in Italy was evidently assumed to think and talk in a given terrorist group's own terms. The assumption, of course, was erroneous and indicates the level of isolation of the terrorists from the rest of the population. The resultant effect of terrorist information warfare was at best irrelevant and at worst counterproductive.[45]

The physical as well as political isolation of the terrorists was more of their own doing than the result of the Italian state counterterrorism effort. Terrorists tended to remain within their own organizations and in their own friendship groups—venturing out into the community only seldom. As the antiterrorist effort was accelerated, the terrorists withdrew further and further into the protection of their own small, collegial cells. Consequently, they became more and more irrelevant.[46]

Intelligence is key to conflict in general, and terrorist war in particular. Because of the basic isolation of the Italian terrorists, they had little intelligence with which to work; the state, by contrast, had a large and increasingly effective intelligence net at its disposal. Nevertheless, the Italian Communist Party was probably decisive in this matter. The capillary structure of the Communist Party—strengthened by a large number of efficient ancillary organizations—was able to identify and locate specific terrorist organizations, leaders, and members. The party furnished a great deal of this kind of intelligence to the state security organizations (and made them appear to be much more efficient and effective than they really were). In any case, timely and accurate human intelligence provided by the party considerably enhanced the Italian government's efforts to find, discredit, and neutralize terrorist organizations and leadership.[47]

CONCLUSIONS

This discussion of Italian terrorism and its lessons provides a beginning point from which to achieve the strategic vision necessary for success against a variety of terrorist threats. However, one cautionary note must be observed. Even though the terrorist attack on the Italian state is considered to have been a failure, that does not mean that terrorism should be of little or no concern. The destabilizing threats of contemporary terrorism must be taken seriously.

The fact is, Italian terrorism demonstrated to the world a method by which the weak can attack the strong. Red Brigades, Mafia families, archaeo-Trotskyite groupescules, Sendero Luminoso Maoists, Somalian or Southeast Asian warlords, Serbian "ethnic cleansers," militant Muslim fundamentalists, and even perhaps individual loonies have learned that they can hold whole nations at ransom. The specific motivation on the part of a given terrorist or group of terrorists is irrelevant.

The thrust of any given terrorist program relies heavily on grievances such as political, economic, and social injustice as a means through which a government is attacked. A terrorist program also relies heavily on adapting elements of the international system to its transnational advantage. A counterterrorism campaign that fails to understand this and only hides behind a façade of microlevel actions such as those that place criminal sanctions on terrorist-related activities or impose trade sanctions against nations that support terrorism is likely to fail.

For Italians, terrorism was the most important political phenomenon of the 1970s and 1980s.[48] For the rest of the world, terrorism is now the most important current political threat. Precisely how terrorist threats might be accomplished in the future is limited only by the imagination: chemical and biological weapons and the use of cyberspace as a battlefield in a terrorist war are almost certain possibilities. Given the asymmetry between challengers and the challenged, only the foolish will fight conventionally. These are the realities of power and politics in the contemporary "clash of civilizations."

CHAPTER 10

THE PRINCIPLE OF UNITY OF EFFORT

Joint Operations in Panama and the Gulf War

In the original research for the SWORD Model, the quantitative measures of individual dimensions failed to show a significant relationship between unity of effort alone and the outcome of an insurgency.[1] By contrast, the later qualitative analysis of nine peace operations found that along with legitimacy, unity of effort was a powerful individual explanatory factor of success or failure of the operation (see chapter 5).[2] As a result, this dimension as a principle of modern war warrants being addressed in some detail.

Among the Anglo-American principles of war, unity of command is nearly paramount. Yet in interagency operations and coalition warfare, unity of command often is impossible to achieve. As a result, unity of effort may well be the only realistic goal. The challenge of achieving unity of effort requires attention at several different levels: multiservice or joint operations issues, cooperation in the civil-military arena, and multinational alliances and coalitions, or any combination of the above.

UNDERLYING POLITICAL-MILITARY PRINCIPLES

The Classical Theorists

More than two thousand years ago in China, the warrior sage Sun Tzu wrote of the importance of unity, the price of its lack, and the ways to achieve it. Similarly, to achieve victory, he argued the need to attack the enemy's unity. "When he is united, divide him."[3] Sun Tzu presented this argument in multiple dialogues.

- *Chang Yu*: Sometimes drive a wedge between a sovereign and his ministers; on other occasions separate his allies from him. Make them mutually suspicious so that they drift apart. Then you can plot against them.[4]

Sun Tzu, however, was not finished. He addressed various aspects of unity, the first being the enemy's strategy. "Thus, what is of supreme importance in war is to attack the enemy's strategy":[5]

- *Mu*: . . . The Grand Duke said: "He who excels at resolving difficulties does so before they arise. He who excels in conquering his enemies triumphs before threats materialize."
- *Li Ch'uan*: Attack plans at their inception. In the later Han, K'ou Hsun surrounded Kao Chun. Chun sent his planning officer, Huang-fu Wen, to parley. Huang-fu Wen was stubborn and rude, and K'ou Hsun beheaded him and informed Kao Chun: "Your staff officer was without propriety. I have beheaded him. If you wish to submit, do so immediately. Otherwise, defend yourself." On the same day Chun threw open his fortifications and surrendered.

    All K'ou Hsun's generals said: 'May we ask, you killed his envoy, but yet forced him to surrender his city. How is this?'

    K'ou Hsun said, "Huang-fu Wen was Kao Chun's heart and guts, his intimate counsellor. If I had spared Huang-fu Wen's life, he would have accomplished his schemes, but when I killed him, Kao Chun lost his guts. It is said, 'The supreme excellence in war is to attack the enemy's plans'."[6] Next best is to disrupt his alliances.
- *Yu*: Do not allow your enemies to get together.
- *Wang Hsi*: . . . Look into the matter of his alliances and cause them to be severed and dissolved. If an enemy has alliances, the problem is grave and the enemy's position is strong; if he has no alliances the problem is minor and the enemy's position is weak.[7]

Finally, Sun Tzu asserted the almost obvious positive argument, "He whose ranks are united in purpose will be victorious."

- *Yu*: Therefore Mencius said: "The appropriate season is not as important as the advantages of the ground; these are not as important as harmonious human relations."[8]

Thus, Sun Tzu staked out the position that in war, unity of effort is what Carl von Clausewitz would call "a center of gravity."

Count Carl von Clausewitz, in his treatise *On War*, also articulated the principle of unity of command for the modern student. Nevertheless, he states, "Friction is the only concept that more or less corresponds to the factors that distinguish real war from war on paper."[9] In that friction lies the challenge not only to unity of command, but also to the broader notion of unity of effort. Clausewitz observes, "The military machine . . . is basically very simple and therefore seems easy to manage. But we should bear in mind that none of its components is of one piece: each part is composed of individuals, every one of whom retains his potential for friction. In theory it sounds reasonable enough: a battalion commander's duty is to carry out his orders; discipline welds the battalion together. . . . A battalion is made up of individuals, the least important of whom may chance to delay things or somehow make them go wrong."[10]

In essence, Clausewitz is saying that in the friction of war, unity of command is not enough to guarantee unity of effort. Rather, the military leader must—through the training of his men—make certain that unity is achieved in the effort that is the engagement or campaign. Consider, then, how much more difficult it is likely to be to attain effective unity in a campaign conducted by multinational forces in coalition. Clausewitz comments on this point when he says, "If two or more states combine against another, the result is still politically speaking a single war. But this political unity is a matter of degree."[11]

As a matter of degree, it will vary with the circumstances. When, as in World War II, the very survival of all of the allies was at stake, the supreme allied commander could enforce both unity of command and unity of effort. When, however, the survival of no member of the coalition is at stake, as is perceived to be the case in the "drug war" in South America today, unity around the strategic and operational goals will be loose, at best.

Here Clausewitz gives us a major assist in understanding the nature of unity of effort when he posits, "This unity lies *in the concept that war is only a branch of political activity; that it is no sense autonomous."*[2] In other words, for Clausewitz, unity of effort rests on the proposition that the coalition partners agree on the nature of the political objective. Thus, another principle—the objective or end-state—comes into play.

The End-State

The concept of the end-state is fairly simple: it is what we wish the battlefield to look like after the fighting is done. If, however, there is no battle, then "battlefield" becomes a figurative term but one that in no way vitiates the concept of end-state. In other words, the end-state refers to the descriptive outcome of the operation—but it may also be prescriptive in the sense that it is what our plans call for. The end-state is also more than the objective. Rather, it is a painting of the landscape on which the objective is located.

In a commonplace combat example, the objective may well be a particular hill on which is located an enemy observation post in a farmhouse. The objective will be given as the hill. The end-state might be described as the occupation of the hill and the farmhouse with our troops—and the removal of the enemy troops. It might be further described as the farmhouse intact, the enemy troops captured or dead but, at a minimum, unable to constitute a counterattack.

This brings us to one other aspect of the end-state; it is not simply a single outcome but rather a range of acceptable outcomes. In our simplistic example, the outcome described is near the maximum end of the acceptable. Toward the minimum end would be the following: the hill occupied, the farmhouse destroyed, the enemy forces driven off with sufficient losses that they are unable to regain the hill with a determined counterattack. Clearly, this end-state is not as desirable as the first, but it does fall within the acceptable range.

Another important aspect of the end-state is that it needs to be the subject of agreement among the decision makers engaged in the operation. Having a commander envision one end-state while his subordinate air and naval commanders envision different end-states, for example, does little good. If the political leaders have still another vision, then the force commander may well find himself in some other job much sooner than he expected. Furthermore, if other, nonmilitary government agencies are involved and their view of the end-state is different, then a successful outcome is problematic, at best. Finally, if other nations, intergovernmental organizations, or nongovernmental organizations are involved, then their desired end-states must be accounted for as well.

As John Fishel has noted elsewhere, "achieving unity of effort is often elusive and . . . the premier pitfall is in the failure to reach agreement on the desired end state or strategic objective. If there is no agreement on the range of outcomes that can be defined as acceptable end states, then there will be no effective unity of effort. Lack of an agreed upon end state clearly dooms any effort to failure."[13]

This principle has been operative in conflicts throughout the cold war and the post–cold war period to varying degrees. Even cases of apparent success have been marred by the lack of a coherent political-military end-state. At best, those cases leave the United States with an interminable military commitment, as in Korea or northern Iraq; at worst, the United States is forced to withdraw its forces ignominiously, as in Lebanon (1983) or Somalia (1993–1994). In between are ambiguous cases like Operation DESERT STORM, in which the immediate military objective was achieved but the strategic political end-state of regional stability remained beyond our collective reach. This ambiguity leaves the nagging question of whether the entire effort will have to be undertaken again at some future date to finally resolve the unresolved issues—as, indeed, has been the case of the Iraq war that began in 2003.

While the end-state is critical to strategic success, that is not to say that it is unessential at the operational level. Rather, operational as well as strategic success depends on the existence of an agreed-upon end-state. At the operational level, the end-state is more military than political, but it is not exclusively military. An example of an appropriate operational end-state from Operation DESERT STORM is the occupation of Kuwait

City by Arab coalition forces—including the Kuwaitis—aided by U.S. forces (especially special operations forces and including civil affairs) in a way that ousted the Iraqis, restored the Kuwaiti ruling family, and precluded extrajudicial reprisals.[14]

Despite the demonstrated criticality of the end-state, it is an insufficient condition for unity of effort. Without an agreed-upon objective defined as an end-state, there will be no unity. Nevertheless, the mere existence of such an end-state in no way guarantees unity of effort. Rather, there are many shoals on which a ship may founder on its way to unity of effort.

TOWARD FULLY INTEGRATED OPERATIONS

The Shoals of Jointness

The new "American way of war" is joint warfare—that is, it encompasses the forces of several services. Although Americans have fought jointly since the Revolutionary War, "jointness" in the modern sense dates only from the 1986 Department of Defense Reorganization Act, known (after its sponsors) as the Goldwater-Nichols Act. Prior to 1986, all "joint" U.S. military operations were conducted with the individual services pulled kicking and screaming into harness. The Goldwater-Nichols Act shifted the focus of operations away from the services to the unified combatant commander and gave him the authority required to effectively practice genuine joint operations.[15]

That authority is summarized by the command relationship called combatant command. Under this authority, the commander of a unified command has combatant command of any assigned or attached forces in his operational area. Combatant command essentially consists of operational control and directive authority for logistics. Operational control gives the commander the authority to direct his forces, organize them, and reorganize them by task, while directive authority for logistics allows him to assign one service component to provide logistical support for another. Combatant command thus gives the commander the authority to mold the joint team in ways that were impossible prior to 1986.

One example of this new approach to joint warfare is drawn from the planning for what became Operation JUST CAUSE in Panama in 1989. In that case, the commander in chief, General Fred F. Woerner, determined that he needed operational control of naval forces supporting his operation. The navy argued that its normal procedure was to operate "in support of" a commander in chief, not under his operational control. What General Woerner objected to in such an arrangement was the idea that the naval commander while "in support" could undertake some other mission, thus depriving the commander in chief of forces he was counting on. With the battle lines thus drawn on the bureaucratic map, the issue was referred to the chairman of the Joint Chiefs of Staff, Admiral William Crowe, for resolution. Admiral Crowe surprised his fellow admirals when he ruled in favor of General Woerner.

Nevertheless, the issue was not completely dead. It raised its head again during Operation DESERT SHIELD in the Persian Gulf; this time the commander in chief for the Pacific, Admiral Arthur Larson, sided with fellow commander in chief General H. Norman Schwarzkopf and assigned the naval component to U.S. Central Command in operational control status, relieving the commanding admiral of his duties for his continued objections in the process.

Jointness does not mean that forces are wholly interchangeable or that the United States is engaged in an experiment, like Canada's, of merging all services into one. Rather, jointness means that each service brings its unique capabilities to the operation to be used in the most effective way possible with the capabilities of the other services. The U.S. military is getting pretty good at this most of the time, as we have seen in the many operations undertaken between 1989 and 2003. In spite of our general success in attaining effective unity of effort in joint operations since 1986, however, we still face significant challenges.

The principal vehicle for conducting a joint operation is known as a joint task force. By doctrine, the joint task force is an organization made up of two or more services for an operation of limited duration.[16] In spite of this definition, at least one joint task force has achieved an endurance record of twenty years with no indication of an end date.[17] When creating a joint task force, a combat commander is faced with two basic choices: he can create it from the base of an existing organization or build it from scratch. In the first case, the joint task force will have the advantage of a staff that has worked together, but it will also have the flavor of its parent service (with all the associated parochialism). In the second case, the joint task force will likely be specifically tailored to the mission with (one hopes) the appropriate mix of forces, but its staff will almost certainly be a bunch of strangers who will have to learn to work together, while at the same time learning each other's service language, as well as the joint language.[18]

Examples of both types of joint operation are Joint Task Force South, which carried out Operation JUST CAUSE in Panama; Joint Task Force Restore Hope (also known as UNITAF) in Somalia; and Joint Task Force Provide Comfort in Turkey and northern Iraq. Joint Task Force South was composed of the Eighteenth Airborne Corps plus augmentation from the air force, marines, navy, and army forces assigned to Panama. In essence it was an army organization and did business the army way. Even though its staff had to be significantly augmented, that did not change the army orientation very much because most of the augmentation came from the staff of the army component permanently assigned to Panama. Joint Task Force South clearly demonstrates both the advantages and the disadvantages of achieving unity of effort in this way. The Airborne Corps staff had worked together and had also worked with the army component staff in Panama; they knew each other and shared a common worldview. Nevertheless, Joint Task Force South was a parochial organization that clearly did not understand the nature of the threat posed by the Panama Defense Forces, its enemy.[19]

Similarly, Joint Task Force Restore Hope, built around the First Marine Expeditionary Force, was an augmented Marine Corps staff. Essentially, it did business in the Marine Corps way and, although successful in accomplishing its stated mission, was subject to criticism for its methodical approach.[20]

By contrast, Joint Task Force Provide Comfort was an ad hoc organization built around the doctrinal concept of a foreign internal defense augmentation force.[21] As such, its organization was specifically tailored to the mission. Its staff was more clearly joint, but it had the definite disadvantage of staff members having to learn to work together from scratch. This problem was mitigated by the use of a number of staff elements that had worked together in both the two subordinate task forces and the joint task force itself.[22]

The U.S. armed forces are becoming more and more used to playing the joint game. Moreover, it is being taught to field-grade officers (majors and lieutenant commanders) at the several staff colleges, with a selected group intended to be joint staff officers attending a twelve-week second phase at the Joint Forces Staff College. Thus, the future combatant commanders with their staffs and the service chiefs with their staffs are being nurtured in soil well fertilized with "jointness." This is not to say that parochialism has gone away. It continues to appear in battles over budget and doctrine, as well as in conflict over roles and functions. "However, because the joint game is far more institutionalized than any of the other games," as Fishel has noted, "it is far more subtle. The joint game has been played in the U.S. military for years and even such major rule changes as the Goldwater-Nichols legislation have only changed the game at the margin, although in some very profound ways."[23]

The Interagency Problem

In modern conflict, the joint game will hardly be the only one in town. Rather, for U.S. forces involved in the conflicts of the post–cold war age, there has been and will continue to be a bewildering array of governmental and nongovernmental players. The principal question to be considered in this environment is "Who is in charge?"

The environment of modern conflict tends to put U.S. military forces into situations in which the U.S. command structure is less than totally clear. In most instances, U.S. civilian governmental agencies and structures were in place where the operations were taking place. The single exception was Operation PROVIDE COMFORT in northern Iraq (which proved an important difference in the conduct of this operation). In all the others, an American ambassador was on the ground, which sets some particular ground rules for how business is done. The only problem with the rules is that their interpretation can sometimes lead to conflict.

Every U.S. ambassador appointed to a post since the presidency of John F. Kennedy has received the same letter of instruction. In essence, this letter states that the ambassador is the personal representative of the president and is responsible for every action undertaken by the U.S. government or its representatives in that country.[24] The exceptions to this oversight responsibility are personnel assigned to international agencies and "major military commands."[25]

What constitutes a major military command to create the exception is somewhat undefined. For example, clearly the U.S. ambassador to Panama did not have jurisdiction over Headquarters of U.S. Southern Command when it was located in that country, or over the service components of the command that were also based there. By contrast, Joint Task Force Panama (consisting of the army component and much of the air force, navy, and marine components) was clearly present there in support of the U.S. ambassador and needed to respond to his guidance. In the more normal environment, in which the military is represented by a defense attaché office and a security assistance office, officials from both are members of the ambassador's country team. Both are subject to the ambassador's policy guidance and can be ordered out of country by him, and their senior members receive "letter input" to their formal ratings from him.

What this means during a significant military operation where war has not been declared and the president has not specifically stated that the ambassador is to support the military forces is that the letter of instruction still sets the ground rules. In other words, the ambassador is formally "in charge." The real relationship, however, is one of negotiating with the ambassador and the other agencies on the country team (or represented in-country) to try to achieve common objectives and mutually supporting actions. Interagency coordination can founder on the shoals of turf battles, personality conflicts, and petty disputes, as well as on real policy disagreements.

These disputations tend to be aggravated by the porous boundary between the strategic and the operational levels of any war or operation. As suggested above, the strategic end-state tends to be more political than military, while the operational end-state tends toward the reverse.

If the boundary between the two is unclear, then the probability of conflict between the wielders of the military and political instruments of power increases with the increasing lack of boundary definition. A good example of sharp boundary definition is that of the Gulf War, in which the political leadership of the coalition determined that the only way to achieve the desired political end-state was through the exercise of the military instrument. The plan of the campaign was then worked out by General Schwarzkopf and agreed to by the commander of the Saudi joint forces, General Khalid bin Sultan, and supported by the diplomatic representatives of the coalition and their civilian governments. By contrast, the decision to use the military instrument of U.S. power to defend Saudi Arabia was led by the political instrument in diplomatic guise and supported with military assets—most notably, Schwarzkopf himself.

The second part of the interagency problem has to do with American nongovernmental organizations. As the term suggests, these are private agencies not under the control of the U.S. government. They are usually in-country by agreement with the host government (or with an international agency), but they still expect to be supported by the U.S. government organizations that are in place there, much as any citizen would expect. Moreover, the U.S. government often finds nongovernmental organizations to be of use in carrying out its policy, which it may do by funneling resources through them. This funneling is commonly done by the U.S. Agency for International Development's Office of Foreign Disaster Assistance, thus creating a symbiotic relationship with the nongovernmental organizations. All of this is supposed to be coordinated by the senior U.S. governmental officer present, typically the ambassador, but this situation, too, is complicated by personality and organizational culture.

What happens when the "take charge" organizational culture of the military meets the "studied ambiguity" of the State Department, the "street cop" smarts of the Drug Enforcement Administration, the "developmentalism" of the U.S. Agency for International Development, and the "single-minded goal orientation" of a nongovernmental organization? Confusion is likely to reign unless the several organizational leaders can develop the empathy necessary to achieve unity of effort.

Multinational and Intergovernmental Organization Games

Both Sun Tzu and Clausewitz remarked on the problems of alliances. Some new angles to the classical problem were added in the last two decades of the twentieth century even as we rediscovered the difficulties of multinational operations. In the process, some old issues were apparently resolved, only to have new ones rise.

In the classical multinational game, two basic kinds of relationships exist: alliances and coalitions. Although alliances are usually thought of as being longer term, more institutionalized, and more stable while coalitions are perceived as more ad hoc, such is not always the case. At the beginning of the World War I, for example, Europe was divided by a system of alliances and coalitions. On one side was the Triple Alliance of Germany, Austria-Hungary, and Italy; on the other was the entente built around a formal alliance between Russia and France and informal understandings and combined military maneuvers between France and England. In that event the coalition arrangement proved stronger than the formal alliance.[26]

Despite such cautionary facts, formal alliances may well be the key to achieving unity of effort among both military forces and their governments. The American experience in Operation PROVIDE COMFORT is a case in point. This operation was an intrusive humanitarian assistance mission into northern Iraq to protect the Kurds who had fled their homes in the wake of their failed revolt against Saddam Hussein following the Persian Gulf War in 1991.[27] In this operation, under the command of the American lieutenant general John Shalikashvili, with a mainly U.S. force augmented significantly by a large number of countries, most of the participants were members of the North Atlantic Treaty Organization (NATO). While PROVIDE COMFORT definitely was not a NATO operation, General Shalikashvili conducted it using NATO procedures, which gave all the critical participants a common way of doing business and a common language. In such a case, it is difficult to discount the impact of such a long-term organization, even when it was not acting as such.

The lack of such common ground does not preclude success but does make it more difficult to achieve. During the several operations in

Somalia from 1990 to 1994, some of the difficulties faced by the coalition forces resulted from expecting unity of effort from a number of nations that had rarely worked together. Recent experience indicates that a coalition is more likely to achieve effective unity of effort if its members are familiar with each other's way of doing business by virtue of being members of an alliance of long standing with an integrated command-and-control system. Nevertheless, that familiarity will not overcome the divisiveness of conflicting political objectives and differing end-states, as is evident in the recent difficulties suffered by peacekeeping operations in Rwanda and Bosnia.

The multinational environment (like the single-nation interagency environment) is also complicated by nonmilitary and nongovernmental players. Among the more important nonmilitary players are the intergovernmental organizations, especially the United Nations (UN) family of organizations.

Many erroneous expectations about the UN abound—the central one being that it is a single organization that acts in the same way a government does. The UN is not a single entity; it is instead a family of intergovernmental organizations, each of which can act in its own sphere only to the extent that its members allow it to do so. Thus, a UN Security Council resolution is binding on all members of the United Nations (if the Great Powers that are the five permanent members are willing to enforce it). A resolution of the General Assembly is merely a recommendation. Loan conditions imposed on a member by the International Monetary Fund can be very powerful and compelling while, at the same time, in complete conflict with the policy positions of the secretary general. In short, in a UN-mandated operation, one may find UN intergovernmental organizations working at cross-purposes with each other.

Again, as all this is taking place, the nonmilitary agencies of several national governments (not all of which are members of the coalition) may very well be working in the area of the operation along with a host of international nongovernmental organizations. Although this multiplicity of involved parties does not produce a wholly anarchic international system, it does verge on the chaotic. Achieving unity of effort in this environment requires both diplomatic and political skills on the part of all key players. It also requires a strategy.

ACHIEVING UNITY OF EFFORT

Through the development of a strategy one can perhaps come to closure with the problem of unity of effort. A strategy consists of three parts: ends, ways, and means. The ends can be stated in general terms as goals or aims or in more specific terms as objectives. An effective strategy will do both and carry the process a step further by describing one or more acceptable end-states. Ways answer the question of "how." They are best laid out as courses of action and may be usefully detailed in a campaign plan. Among the key parts of the courses of action should be a description of the nature of the controlling relationships for the operation or activity. Finally, means refer to resources: financial, material, and personnel. This strategy then should be tested against the three critical questions of strategic development. First, will the courses of action proposed accomplish the goal? Second, can they be executed with the resources that are available or can be made available? Third, is the cost—human, social, political, material, and financial—acceptable? If not, then unity of effort is unlikely to be achieved and the strategy is likely to fall short.

A successful strategy to achieve unity of effort requires the knowledge to determine which of the several possible games are being played. In the post–cold war world, all three games—joint, interagency, and multinational—will be taking place simultaneously. This simple fact requires that each key player's real objectives be understood. Merely agreeing to vote for a resolution in the UN Security Council or offering to contribute troops to a peace operation authorized by that resolution does not mean that one government has the same objectives as another that appears to have taken the same stance. Moreover, no government wholly gives up its freedom of action in any kind of operation. The first prerequisite of successful unity of effort is for the leaders to know the goals, objectives, and aims of their partners. This is equally true of the military services, government agencies, intergovernmental organizations, and nongovernmental organizations.

Once the objectives of the relevant players have been identified, the common ground with respect to the objective and its attendant end-state must be determined. That common ground provides the necessary but insufficient condition for unity of effort. Mutually compatible goals and objectives will provide the leaders of the effort a clue as to how best to organize the effort without asking any player to do something that is not in keeping with its objectives.

The next step in the development of a strategy is to determine the ways to achieve the common objectives as well as how to best prevent the attainment of those that are clearly not compatible with one's own. Objectives that are "value neutral" can be left to those who desire them—they need neither to be helped nor to be hindered. In approaching the decision of which ways are to be pursued, one needs to consider the procedures available, because they offer the operational and tactical common ground that makes unity of effort easier to achieve if they exist or more difficult if they do not. It is here that long-standing alliance relationships can come into play.

The final step in developing a strategy is to assign resources against objectives. The general principle to be followed here is that specific organizational assets should be assigned against objectives that a coalition partner or cooperating organization has identified as its own. At the same time, care must be taken to avoid giving a participant the opportunity to undertake an objective that is contrary to the common goals of the mission.

Once the overall strategy is developed, the question of basic command-and-control procedures for any particular mission arises. For the United States, it is especially useful if the president will make a decision as to whether the ambassador or the military commander is in charge of the mission. Experience shows that American political authorities at several levels are reluctant to do this. It is therefore incumbent on the operational planner to make every attempt to gain a decision, which may be best accomplished by stating the force commander's intent to "take charge" in the formal planning process that is referred to the president and secretary of defense for approval. In this way, a decision on civilian or military authority may be forced.

Unfortunately, this approach will not solve the basic problem in the multinational setting. Still, one can reduce the problem to the extent that the participating nations understand and follow common procedures. The evidence strongly suggests that the most effective unity of effort has been achieved when the coalition is dominated by nations who have long worked together in a standing alliance with an integrated military command and well-established political institutions.

Finally, the process of achieving unity of effort with intergovernmental and nongovernmental organizations is mainly accomplished in two ways. First, the operational leader can be of use to the individual organization. By creating some dependency, he can to some extent control their behavior. He should also be aware of the likelihood that a mutual dependency will be created and that—to the extent that it is— he will be influenced by the very organization that he wishes to influence. Second, the operational leader can cut off support for the organization that he wishes to influence. The danger in this approach is the access that the organization has to the operational leader's political authority.

Achieving unity of effort in modern conflict is thus a complex process. At its base it entails effective politics and skillful diplomacy— and neither of these qualities is thought to be the common currency of military leaders. Throughout history, however, the successful military leader has possessed them both in abundance, as demonstrated by the likes of Alexander, Napoleon, Eisenhower, and Schwarzkopf.[28] Less successful military leaders may well have been deficient in these skills.

TWO CASES OF UNITY—MORE OR LESS

The following case studies consider the relationship between civil and military authority and serve as an informal test of the hypotheses implicit within the preceding discussion. Operation JUST CAUSE was essentially a simple situation involving only the U.S. government (and the host country). Operation DESERT STORM was a more complicated picture because of the involvement of other nations within the context of a UN-authorized coalition. Commonalities are suggested in the successes and the failures of both operations. Moreover, a significant amount about unity of effort was learned from Operation JUST CAUSE and was applied to DESERT STORM. Unfortunately, planners either forgot what was learned or misapplied it during the UN mission in Somalia (see chapter 12).

Operation JUST CAUSE, the December 1989 invasion of Panama, and its attendant postconflict operation, PROMOTE LIBERTY, were the result of a command-and-control structure significantly modified by the 1986 Department of Defense Reorganization Act.[29] This act had given the commanders in chief of the unified commands (including U.S. Southern Command) significantly greater authority than they had held in the past. It had also strengthened the role and power of the chairman of the Joint Chiefs of Staff at the expense of the service chiefs. The full impact of the new law, however, had yet to be felt. Rather, it was a process of bureaucratic revolution by evolution taking place in some of the minor skirmishes over command relationships—among other engagements—as discussed previously. Thus, in 1989, while the extent of combatant command still was not exactly clear, it was significantly greater than the command relationship that had existed a mere six years before, during the U.S.-led invasion of Grenada.[30]

From February 1988, when planning for what became Operation JUST CAUSE began, until September 30, 1989, the commander in chief of U.S. Southern Command was General Fred F. Woerner. A scholarly Latin Americanist who was a superior troop leader, General Woerner had attempted to stay ahead of the military implications of the constantly shifting sands of U.S. policy toward Panama since the beginning of the "crisis" the day after he took command in June 1987. Although he disagreed with many aspects of that policy, he loyally implemented it and took the lead in attempting to achieve realistic civil-military positions that stood a chance of success in attaining the objectives of the U.S. policy makers, which included the departure from power (and Panama) of the de facto dictator, General Manuel Antonio Noriega, peacefully and without any obvious U.S. intervention.[31]

Woerner's efforts resulted in a plan that he called Fissures. Fully coordinated with the U.S. State Department, the plan was devised to divide the Panama Defense Forces from the civilian supporters of the regime and drive a wedge between the Panama Defense Forces and Noriega. Woerner sent the plan through his channels to the Joint Chiefs of Staff and, when he heard nothing, developed a revised version called Fissures II. This he sent forth with his recommendation that it be adopted as a complete package. He specifically requested that he not be ordered to execute individual paragraphs of the plan because it had been developed as a unified concept with each part dependent on every other part in concert with the other agencies of the U.S. government. All he ever was directed to execute were individual, unrelated paragraphs.[32]

This abortive effort at interagency planning marked the boundaries of the interagency process through the execution of Operation JUST CAUSE and well into Operation PROMOTE LIBERTY. The perception was that an activity that had been developed in coordination among several agencies clearly belonged to no agency and therefore could hardly be worthy of serious consideration. The joint military planning process that produced Operations Orders Blue Spoon (the combat operation) and Blind Logic (civil-military operations), by contrast, was well established as part of the Joint Operations Planning System's Crisis Action Planning. As such, conflicts—which indeed existed among the several planning commands—were played out according to fairly well established rules.[33]

The most significant military planning conflicts occurred during the period from May 18, 1989, through October 1989. During this period, General Woerner (on the advice of his director of operations, Brigadier General Marc A. Cisneros) had activated the Eighteenth Airborne Corps as Joint Task Force C to take over the execution planning for Blue Spoon, thereby relieving Joint Task Force Panama (which was at that time U.S. Army South plus augmentation) of this planning responsibility. The army component was being stressed so hard that its theater responsibilities were suffering.[34] This activation entailed, in addition, the coordination between the Airborne Corps planners and the Southern Command staff who were responsible for the commander in chief–level orders. Moreover, it required coordination with the civil-military operations planning cell, which was developing the commander in chief's civil-military operations order as well as the operations order for the Civil-Military Operations Task Force. In the event, action officer–level agreements that had been incorporated into the civil-military operations order (Blind Logic) were not included in the corps' plan.[35]

Part of this lack of action had to do with the fact that General Woerner's retirement was announced on July 20 and scheduled for September 30; the identity of his successor, General Max Thurman, was announced at the same time. The corps was not particularly happy with Woerner's Blue Spoon and felt that the Southern Command staff was dictating how the corps should conduct their mission rather than what that mission should be. For its part, Southern Command was concerned that the corps planners showed no understanding of the political-military nuances that characterized the Panama situation.[36]

When General Thurman assumed command on September 30, he formally activated the corps as Joint Task Force South for planning purposes. Between July and September, however, he had been working with the corps to restructure General Woerner's concept of the operation. Interestingly, this restructuring was in the direction of rethinking that the new director of operations at Southern Command, Brigadier General William Hartzog, initiated.[37] Hartzog's predecessor, General Cisneros, had taken command of U.S. Army South in late June and, in an ironic twist, in his new capacity as Joint Task Force Panama commander, had become somewhat resistant to the idea that the corps was needed.

Nevertheless, Thurman was explicit about one thing. He wanted unity of command and designated the corps commander, Lieutenant General Carl Stiner, as his "warfighter" and sole subordinate commander for the operation. As a result, the corps staff took charge of the planning. Some of the friction of this time is reflected in an article by "Tacitus" (a pseudonym for one or more staff officers from the 193rd Brigade or U.S. Army South):

> U.S. Army South (USARSO), in its role as Joint Task Force–Panama (JTF-PM), was thought to lack the organization and experience to execute the original plan, so the XVIII Airborne Corps was designated the war-fighting headquarters. But the Corps wasn't deployed to the theater; instead, XVIII Corps, like JTF-South (JTF-SO), stayed in CONUS until just before the attack. It then tried simultaneously to deploy, absorb the JTF-PM staff, assume command of in-place forces, and control the flow of H-hour and follow-on forces. This was a prescription for failure.[38]

When Operations Orders Blue Spoon and Blind Logic were executed respectively on December 19–20, 1989, as Operations JUST CAUSE and

PROMOTE LIBERTY, there was no question as to who was the commander of all combat operations—Stiner was the "warfighter." When General Thurman activated his director of strategy, plans, and policy, Brigadier General Benard Gann, as the commander of the Civil-Military Operations Task Force, however, there was some question as to whom Gann worked for. Gann was directed to execute a separate commander-in-chief plan in addition to his duties as a director of the Southern Command staff. Moreover, General Stiner later declared that he (Stiner) had no responsibilities for restoration operations. Yet for several days, the position of commander of the Civil-Military Operations Task Force formally was located under Joint Task Force South, after which it was returned to the commander in chief's control. At no time did Stiner take effective control over it.[39]

The issue of command and control of the Civil-Military Operations Task Force vindicated General Woerner's concept that the civil-military operation to restore government services to Panama was the key to political-military success and that it was much too sensitive to leave in the hands of the joint task force commander. Thus, a separate headquarters, reporting to the commander in chief, was appropriate, especially so that the commander in chief would determine the priorities between the requirements of the joint task force and those of the Civil-Military Operations Task Force.

Nevertheless, General Thurman's effort to centralize all of the operations directed by Operations Order Blue Spoon was also appropriate. Where Woerner had three separate headquarters reporting to him and carrying out a combination of combat and civil-military operations, Thurman had only two headquarters: one that dealt with combat operations while the other addressed civil-military issues. The key was that the Joint Special Operations Task Force had been made subordinate to the joint task force. This decision resolved a point of conflict that had been very much in evidence prior to Thurman's assumption of command.[40]

One additional unity of effort issue that needs to be addressed in this case is that of civil-military cooperation and coordination with respect to the operations orders. In the planning phase of the operation, the U.S. embassy was aware only of Operations Order Klondike Key (the noncombatant evacuation) in any detail and only loosely aware of the existence of Blue Spoon.[41] With respect to Blind Logic, the order with the greatest policy implications, the chief planner was refused permission to coordinate with the embassy and was allowed to discuss the U.S. government's goals for a post-Noriega Panama in only the most general way.[42]

Once Operation PROMOTE LIBERTY was being executed, significantly more civil-military coordination took place. When Deane Hinton arrived as U.S. ambassador, he clearly was in charge of all activities by elements of the U.S. government, including the military, but only to the extent that he actively took action. In a number of areas he allowed separate agencies, nominally under his control, to continue bureaucratic infighting long after any such conflict might have been productive. This was particularly true of the relationship between the U.S. Military Support Group–Panama (which succeeded the Civil-Military Operations Task Force) and the International Criminal Investigative Training Assistance Program. Also a player in this conflict was the Administration of Justice Program of the U.S. Agency for International Development.[43] Nevertheless, all three organizations were either officially or de facto members of the ambassador's country team, so a specific forum was available for the resolution of conflict. The existence of such a forum hardly suggests that it will be successful—success is driven by personality, institutional position, and power both in-country and in Washington. Suffice it to say that the civil-military arena was somewhat more chaotic than the joint military one.

However, unity of effort in Operations JUST CAUSE and PROMOTE LIBERTY was a significant improvement over what had gone before in the joint arena. Under both Woerner's and Thurman's concepts, span of control was limited. Where Woerner had perhaps retained too many decisions in his own hands, Thurman possibly had not intended to retain enough. The civil-military environment, by contrast, was hardly unified at all. Initially—that is, in the planning stage—this lack of unity was due to two factors. First, for much of the critical period no ambassador was in-country. Second, when dealing with operations orders under the Joint Operations Planning System, the planners were specifically prohibited from coordinating outside of military channels. After the operations were under way, civil-military coordination was hampered by a laissez faire approach to control on the part of the ambassador and the parochial interests of the several agencies on the ground. The country-team mechanism, although it provided a forum for conflict resolution, was insufficient to achieve genuine unity of effort in the absence of leadership willing to force the contending parties to resolve their differences. A final manifestation of interagency conflict was the perception in the joint staff that the Department of Defense had been left holding the financial bag for other agencies in Panama despite commitments made at the time.[44]

One other conclusion can be drawn from Operations JUST CAUSE and PROMOTE LIBERTY. Where the military objective of destroying the fighting capability of the Panama Defense Forces was clear, there was unity of effort. Similarly, where the political-military objective of restoring government services was clear, there was also unity of effort. Where the political objectives were not clear and different nuances were understood by different players, however, then there was no unity of effort.

Unity of effort in and during the Gulf War had a significant advantage over the situation in Panama in that the principal strategic objectives were relatively clear and the end-state reasonably well defined. This was accomplished through a series of policy pronouncements, UN Security Council Resolutions, and the campaign plan and operations plans of U.S. Central Command and the coalition.[45] The immediate strategic/operational objective was the deterrence of Iraq from any further aggression into Saudi Arabia and its withdrawal from Kuwait. The end-state was defined as the restoration of the legitimate government of Kuwait, the elimination of Iraq's ability to make aggressive war (including the elimination of its weapons of mass destruction), and stability in the region. The latter was further defined as leaving Iraq intact as a state and preventing its dismemberment into its three ethno-religious components—the Shia of the south, the Sunni of the Mesopotamian heartland, and the Kurds of the north.[46] A complicating factor lay in the escalation of President George H. W. Bush's rhetoric, which at times suggested that the United States would not be averse to an Iraq divided, "like all of Gaul," into three parts. This factor, however, would hardly come into play until the end of the campaign.

U.S. command in Operations DESERT SHIELD and DESERT STORM was fairly uncomplicated and informed by the Goldwater-Nichols Act of 1986. Because these were military operations taking place on the sovereign territory of a number of countries in the Middle East, the military commander was clearly the dominant U.S. player. U.S. ambassadors generally were "in support of" the military effort.

Military command was the combatant command of U.S. Central Command and its commander in chief, General H. Norman Schwarzkopf.[47] Thus, all U.S. forces operating in the commander in chief's area of responsibility were under Schwarzkopf's direct control. In practice, this authority meant that Schwarzkopf could—and did—attach U.S. Army forces to U.S. Marines and cross-attach forces between units. It also meant that army lieutenant general Gus Pagonis's Twenty-second Support Command provided logistical support to all U.S. Central Command forces. It further meant that all air assets (at least on Day 1 of the air campaign) were covered by a single air tasking order developed by the staff of the Joint Forces Air Component commander, Lieutenant General Chuck Horner (U.S. Air Force).[48] These air assets included not only U.S. Air Force and Navy planes, but also Marine Corps aircraft and Army helicopters. (Later, army aviation was not included, and marine aviation was granted the authority to give highest priority to sorties to close air support in accordance with Marine Corps doctrine.)

Like the air operations, maritime operations came under the operational control of the commander in chief. This was only the second time that U.S. Navy forces had ever been under operational control to a commander in chief from another service—the first time had been in the Panama planning. The U.S. Navy historically preferred to operate "in support of" a ground-based commander, and operational control was not accomplished without some conflict. When the situation was finally sorted out, the U.S. Central Command naval component, under the commander in chief, had operational control of all U.S. naval forces in the Gulf area.[49]

One additional command relationship—tactical control—complicates the situation of the combatant commander and his subordinates. In this relationship a force may be given a mission by a commander who does not acquire the authority to task-organize that force. Thus, when naval air was given a mission by the Joint Forces Air Component commander under the air tasking order, the Joint Forces Air Component commander was exercising tactical control.

Although these relationships describe the command-and-control situation within U.S. Central Command, they do little justice to the arrangements among the U.S. unified commands or with coalition forces. The U.S. command-and-control system begins with the president of the United States as the constitutional commander in chief of all the armed forces and runs through the secretary of defense to the commanders of the unified commands.[50] Under the law, the chairman of the Joint Chiefs of Staff is not in the chain of command but is in the chain of communication. The chairman is the conduit through which all orders are relayed, in addition to being the principal military advisor to the president and the secretary of defense. Thus, it would be a rather foolhardy combatant commander who would choose to challenge the chairman directly.

When a conflict is taking place within a combatant commander's area of responsibility, all other commanders and service chiefs operate "in support of" the primary combatant commander to the degree directed by the president. In Operations DESERT SHIELD and DESERT STORM, that degree was nearly absolute. The general rule is that the "supported" combatant commander tells the "supporting" commander what he needs, and the supporter provides it. Again, the system worked as the textbook said (with the usual minor glitches, mostly unintentional) during the Gulf War. Thus, the Pacific and Atlantic commanders in chief both provided ships to the naval armada of U.S. Central Command. Meanwhile, the commander in chief of U.S. forces in Europe provided a joint task force (Joint Task Force Proven Force) under tactical control of the commander in chief of Central Command to conduct the second front of the air campaign out of Turkey.[51]

Command and control of coalition forces was quite a bit more complicated. During the Gulf War, there was no formal alliance among the coalition partners. Nevertheless, NATO relationships were important to the overall success of the coalition. Forty years of maneuvers and the development of common procedures and vocabulary stood the members of the coalition who were also NATO members in good stead. This was especially true of the coalition's air and naval forces. For the ground forces, it applied to the United States, French, and British forces. Even in the absence of an alliance relationship, however, procedural unity had developed through many years of security assistance and combined exercises, which served the same end. Egyptians, Saudis, and members of the Gulf Cooperation Council had been recipients of U.S. equipment and training over the years and had conducted a number of combined exercises. Together, these factors went a long way toward putting disparate forces on the same procedural footing.[52]

Formal command and control was parallel, which is to say that the United States and Saudi Arabia were officially equal partners. Saudi joint forces commander Lieutenant General Khalid was General Schwarzkopf's formal equal. It was important that their headquarters were in the same building, making direct coordination between the two commanders physically easy. What in fact made this arrangement workable was the Coalition Coordination, Communication, and Integration Center (C³IC), which was formed under the lead of the U.S. Army component.

The C³IC became a clearinghouse for coordination of training areas, firing ranges, logistics, frequency management, and intelligence sharing. Manned by officers from all coalition forces, the C³IC served as the primary tool for the coordination of the myriad details inherent in combined military operations. It soon expanded and was divided into ground, air, naval, logistics, special operations, and intelligence sections. The C³IC became a vital tool in ensuring unity of effort among coalition forces, remaining in operation throughout Operations DESERT SHIELD and DESERT STORM.[53]

This set of arrangements allowed the forces of the coalition to pursue their common goals effectively. When Operation DESERT STORM began, some coalition forces were rearranged so that British and French forces operated under the tactical control of U.S. forces.[54] Arab coalition forces operated under the control of Khalid's two commands: Joint Forces Command North and Joint Forces Command East. Although not under Schwarzkopf's command, these forces acted in full coordination with the U.S.-developed plans. The preservation of formal independence of operation permitted the practical integration of Khalid's forces with Schwarzkopf's, given that the coalition was fully united on its operational objectives.

One other tool for achieving unity of effort was the use of U.S. Army Special Forces as liaison personnel with the Arab coalition partners. These liaison elements provided an effective communication link among elements whose technical communications were not compatible and who did not fully share doctrine or experience. The special forces liaison teams often were the glue that made the coalition effective at the tactical level.[55]

One final aspect of unity of effort in Operations DESERT SHIELD and DESERT STORM is the management structure for planning post-conflict operations in Kuwait and the command-and-control system for their execution.[56] As had earlier been the case for Generals Thurman and Stiner in Panama, postconflict operations in Kuwait were the least of the worries facing Schwarzkopf and his subordinates when planning for the war. In Washington, however, the assistant secretary of defense for special operations and low intensity conflict (SO/LIC) recognized that this would become a necessary mission. At the same time, the G5 of the 352nd Civil Affairs Command, a U.S. Army Reserve unit, Colonel Randall Elliott (who in civilian life was the Middle East desk officer in the State Department's Bureau of Intelligence and Research and a close friend of the ambassador-designate to Kuwait, Edward "Skip" Gnehm), saw a similar need. Together, Elliott and the SO/LIC staff, with Gnehm's support, energized the bureaucracy to begin postconflict planning. It finally got under way with the activation of the Kuwait Task Force under Elliott's direction with the call-up of a number of Reserve Civil Affairs officers.

The Kuwait Task Force was controlled by an interagency steering committee group from the Departments of Defense and State. Although it was supposed to be in coordination with U.S. Central Command, this never materialized to anyone's satisfaction. Thus, when the Kuwait Task Force arrived in Saudi Arabia in late January, its plans were not synchronized with those of U.S. Central Command or the U.S. Army component. They did, nevertheless, provide a basis for the long-term reconstruction of Kuwait. Moreover, once the Kuwait Task Force arrived, it came under combatant command to the commander in chief, thereby alleviating much of the confusion as to the role of the Kuwait Task Force.

The Kuwait Task Force soon was incorporated into the Combined Civil Affairs Task Force (built around its parent unit, the 352nd Civil Affairs Command). During Operation DESERT SHIELD, U.S. Central Command had given "executive agency" for civil affairs to Army Central Command. Executive agency, an anachronism from pre–Goldwater-Nichols days, was hardly the appropriate vehicle to plan or execute postconflict operations. This was especially true because the commander in chief had retained command of the land component, thus precluding the army central commander from effectively planning and controlling all civil military operations.

When the time finally came to execute plans for the restoration and reconstruction of Kuwait, the army central commander established a combined task force, Task Force Freedom, under his deputy. It included not only the Combined Civil Affairs Task Force but also combat, combat support, and combat service support elements, as well as coalition units from the British, Saudis, and Kuwaitis. Of special import was that Task Force Freedom had inherited, with the Kuwait Task Force and Combined Civil Affairs Task Force, an interagency subordinate element, a Disaster Assistance Response Team from the U.S. Agency for International Development's Office of Foreign Disaster Assistance. The Disaster Assistance Response Team came with its own civilian contractor support. Nothing like this interagency arrangement had been seen since the disappearance of the CORDS (Civil Operations and Revolutionary Development Support) organization of the Vietnam War. Finally, Task Force Freedom greatly resembled the U.S. Military Support Group–Panama, which had been developed from a doctrinal construct now called the Foreign Internal Defense Augmentation Force. In short, whether intentional or not, a large number of command-and-control lessons had been learned as a result of the Panama experience, coupled with trial and error.

CONCLUSIONS

Operations JUST CAUSE and PROMOTE LIBERTY in Panama and DESERT SHIELD/DESERT STORM in the Middle East and Southwest Asia clearly reinforce the theoretical contentions of the first part of this chapter. In both sets of operations, unity of effort was dependent on participants' agreement on common objectives. The delineation of common objectives, however, while necessary for unity of effort, was certainly not sufficient. Achieving unity of effort was made more difficult by differences in organizational cultures and personalities. Unity of effort was, however, enhanced by the commonality of tactics, techniques, and procedures institutionalized by formal alliances, joint and combined exercises over time, and study at the staff colleges of the principal coalition members. Other factors enhancing unity of effort were the various liaison mechanisms developed ad hoc, such as the C³IC and liaison officers.

Finally, the inability to achieve a full measure of unity of effort can be seen in the relationships that existed between the military and civilian government agencies. Interagency operations and activities, however well developed they may be in Washington, leave much to be desired in the field. Unfortunately, this situation has improved little during the years that have elapsed since the end of the first Gulf War.

CHAPTER 11

CONFRONTING THE "WAR ON DRUGS"

Probably the most insidious security problem facing the United States and the rest of the world, now and for the foreseeable future, centers on the threats to a given nation-state's ability and willingness to deal with transnational threats to the control of national territory as well as on the internal organizations seeking violent change within that territory. The major players involved in these threats to the stability of targeted nation-states generally include nonstate actors and nongovernmental groups that may or may not be supported by other nonstate entities or nation-states. This is what some have called the gray area phenomenon[1] and represents what we have chosen to call "uncomfortable wars" throughout this book.

This phenomenon is not new. What is new is that with the ending of the cold war, threats associated with uncomfortable wars are now being recognized as real and have begun to emerge as major problems in their own right. These threats—the consequences of instability—range from terrorism, insurgency, and illegal drug trafficking to warlordism, militant fundamentalism, ethnic cleansing, civil war, and regional wars. Despite the pervasiveness of these problems and despite the fact that they have been a part of the international security environment for a long time, opinion makers and decision makers appear to be doing little more than watching, debating, and wrangling about how to deal with these seemingly unknown phenomena. As a consequence, territory, infrastructure, and stability are being quietly and slowly destroyed, while untold numbers of innocents continue to die.

However, the basic architecture has been developed for a theory of engagement with a better-than-average chance of controlling the conflicts inherent in the gray area phenomenon. The principal components of the resultant paradigm can be applied to the so-called drug war (as an example of the gray area phenomenon), revealing additional implications that pertain to the development of U.S. defense and foreign policy more generally. By coming to grips analytically with the most salient commonalities that dominate modern conflict, political and military leaders should be able to develop the strategic vision necessary to maximize international opportunities and to win a contemporary war—not just the battles but the war itself.

THE BASIC ARCHITECTURE FOR
A THEORY OF ENGAGEMENT

When the major aspects of the transnational threats and violence inherent in the gray area phenomenon are carefully considered, the analytical commonalities in each of the struggles can be delineated (as discussed throughout this book). They provide a conceptual framework (i.e., paradigm) for defining the kinds of conflict in the contemporary world and the basis for a peremptory theory of engagement. Although the emphasis on each component may vary with the context of the specific situation, all successful strategies to win these uncomfortable wars that have been formulated over the past half-century have incorporated these principal analytical commonalities (see chapters 1 and 5). The underlying premise of the resultant paradigm is that the ultimate outcome of any contemporary conflict—including the drug war—is primarily determined not by the manipulation of violence but by factors such as perceived legitimacy, outside support for both an illegal challenger and the targeted government, and internal political-military activities. The latter include the credibility of objectives and degree of organization for unity of effort, the level of discipline and capabilities of security forces, and the effectiveness of the intelligence apparatus and other measures specifically directed at terminating the threat. To the extent that the seven strategic dimensions of the SWORD Model are strongly present in any given conflict situation, they favor the incumbent government's success in controlling it.[2]

PRINCIPAL COMPONENTS OF THE PARADIGM AND LESSONS FROM THE ANDEAN RIDGE

These analytical commonalities transcend different regions and stages of political-economic development and apply to virtually any nation-state facing the transnational threats and internal violence pertaining to the gray area phenomenon. As such, they exert a high degree of influence on the perceived success or failure of antidrug politics and programs in the Andean Ridge countries of Bolivia, Colombia, and Peru in Latin America (known as the White Triangle).[3] The metaphorical relationships of the principal components of the paradigm to the transnational cocaine war in Latin America are not specifically associated with either the supply or the demand side of the illicit drug problem. Rather, they focus on the often-forgotten societal dimension of conflict that constitutes the central strategic program that is the hub of all power and movement and on which everything in the gray area phenomenon equation depends. Moreover, they appear to define "the most likely model for the future."[4]

Degree of Legitimacy

This concept concerns the moral right of a government to govern. Popular perceptions of corruption, disenfranchisement, poverty, lack of upward mobility, and personal security limit both the right and the ability of a given regime to function. Until a given populace generally perceives that its government is dealing with these and other basic issues of political, economic, and social injustice, instability and the threat of subverting or destroying a targeted government are real.

Because of these problems, the governments of cocaine-supplying countries in the Andean Ridge are considered "fragile democracies." In vulnerable nation-states, the efficiency of the state apparatus has consistently been low in all branches of government. These weaknesses are apparent in areas as diverse as provision of basic social services, agrarian reform, tax collection, income distribution, law enforcement, and general security. They stem from long-standing political, economic, and social problems perpetuated by a generally inadequate public administration.[5]

At the same time, these governments are further challenged by the "revolution of rising expectations," sluggish or stagnant economies, growing population densities, and internally and externally organized violence. The nation-state in the White Triangle tends to be weakest in frontier zones and areas outside the major cities. Its failure to extend an effective presence in basic social elements such as the judiciary, police, health, and education leaves a vacuum in which guerrillas and insurgents, the political and narco-Right, and the government all compete for power.[6]

A brief description of the town of Tocache in the Upper Huallaga Valley of Peru during the early 1990s illustrates this kind of situation. Tocache had six banks (for laundering money), six fax machines, several stereo dealerships, a discotheque, and one of the largest Nissan outlets in Peru. Tocache also had no paved streets, no drinking water, and no sewage system. Whatever education that took place in or around the town was controlled by Sendero Luminoso officials; commerce between coca producers and narco-traffickers in the area was controlled by Sendero Luminoso officials; and tax collection and conflict adjudication in and around the town were performed by Sendero Luminoso officials. On various occasions, the Peruvian government sent security forces into Tocache to provide "law and order," but they exerted no permanent involvement, influence, or control of that portion of the national territory.[7]

The problem in the Upper Huallaga Valley of Peru is not unique. The struggle for legitimacy is based on the various contenders' credibility of cause (i.e., objectives) and perceived right or ability to govern. No group or force can legislate or decree these intangibles for themselves, but all parties can develop, sustain, and enhance them through specific actions. These intangibles derive from popular perceptions that authority is genuine and effective and uses morally correct means for reasonable and fair purposes.

If these goals and the goals of winning an uncomfortable war are to be compatible, internal efforts and external support must concentrate on the ways and means of legitimizing and strengthening weak governments (see chapter 3). The elements that define state legitimacy and nation-building include free, fair, and relatively frequent elections; additional and effective political participation in the governmental process by the populace, to include the vibrant interest-group activity that characterizes what is now called "civil society"; a fair and just judicial system that can keep up with its caseload; the incumbent government's ability to extract and distribute resources fairly and to reduce the level of corruption; the regime's ability to enhance the economic and social development of the country; and the active or tacit approval of the major social institutions of the country. All of these indicators are highly interrelated and must be operative and positive for a government to survive and win against a gray area phenomenon such as the narco-trafficking scourge in the White Triangle.[8]

The implications for the paradigm are obvious—every policy, every program, and every action of a targeted government and its external allies must contribute positively and directly to developing, maintaining, and enhancing the ability and willingness of that regime to control its territory and govern its people in a culturally acceptable manner. This is the "umbrella of legitimacy" and will be the prime lesson for vulnerable nation-states in the coming decades.

Cocaine Revenues

Cocaine revenues are the basic source of physical strength and psychological balance of the illegal narcotics industry. This variable illustrates the fundamental need to isolate the "bad guys" in gray area phenomenon–related conflicts from their outside support regardless of the form that support may take. As long as the narco-traffickers—or any other illicit challengers—are not isolated, the credibility of their activities in a targeted country becomes greater and their legitimacy becomes stronger relative to that of the government.

Because of the criminal nature of the illegal narcotics industry, revenue estimates vary from source to source and are often contentious. However, there is no dispute over the enormous amounts of money derived from the production, distribution, and sale of illegal drugs. These vast revenues are spent in seven general areas: (1) to purchase weapons and hire paramilitary forces to protect laboratories, airfields, drug shipments, and key personnel; (2) to neutralize law enforcement institutions by bribing civil servants, police, and military personnel to overlook or support illegal activities; (3) to maintain elaborate intelligence networks to gain advance information on raids and other antidrug measures directed at the industry; (4) to undermine and make irrelevant the judicial systems that might cause problems; (5) to influence public opinion and the political process in a given country; (6) to create power brokers within various important political systems; and (7) to invest in acceptable business enterprises to make more money and gain social legitimacy.[9]

The illegal cocaine industry in the White Triangle is fast becoming a strong transnational political actor in its own right. Because of the amount of revenue and the level and type of expenditures involved, its foreign policy instruments include force, economic leverage, propaganda, and diplomacy. Thus, the multinational narco-trafficking organizations are beginning to exert a dominating political influence throughout Latin America and the Caribbean region.[10] But the traditional nation-states of the area seem not to understand the ways and means of dealing effectively with the threat that particular nonstate actor represents.

The "cocaine revenues" variable indicates that a realistic antidrug strategy should address the demand side as well as the supply side of the illegal narcotics equation. No other approach could provide anything but a partial solution. As a consequence, in any kind of antidrug effort the "outside support to the illegal challenger" variable (i.e., the "cocaine revenues" variable, in the context of the drug war) cannot be ignored or passed off as too hard to deal with at the strategic level. This dimension of the paradigm further demonstrates the need for a besieged government to separate its illegal nonstate challengers from their external material, political, and diplomatic support as well as from their network of sanctuaries.

The war against outside support to the disloyal opposition is critical in its own right. If pursued successfully, it provides a power multiplier in all the other critical areas of a given struggle.

Type and Consistency of External Support for a Targeted Government

Outside aid to a targeted government is as important as outside aid to a challenger. The difference is that nonstate political actors can accept with impunity monetary and other types of support from various non-traditional sources that range from criminal organizations to rogue states to church groups, whereas a targeted government tends to accept relatively conditional economic, political, and military support from other traditional nation-states. Large numbers of outsiders and large amounts of external influence on a government in a nationalistic environment for any length of time have tended to be counterproductive in terms of the sovereignty of the targeted country, implicit acquiescence to what may be called "foreign interests," and the consequent legitimacy of the incumbent regime. Moreover, external support to a targeted government must be cooperative, consistent, and realistic to be effective.[11]

Various agencies of the U.S. government support a number of relatively independent programs meant to reduce the supply of coca and its derivatives. Lessons learned from the North American counternarcotics involvement in the Andean states indicate that these programs are generally perceived to be imposed by the U.S. agencies involved, inconsistent in terms of being carried to their logical conclusions, and therefore unrealistic.[12]

As examples, direct crop substitution and crop eradication programs have offered almost no real incentives and are considered impractical. An examination of the situation indicates that coffee producers and other workers are still moving into new areas to begin coca-leaf production. This continued migration and the switch from a traditional crop or profession indicates that these migrants believe that they can make more money producing coca than coffee. They estimate that if coca-leaf prices are approximately $2.00 per kilogram, the number of hectares required to produce the same income from coffee would be 4.6 hectares per hectare of coca-leaf. Other traditional crops such as cacao (chocolate) and achiote (a dye) would require 13.9 hectares and 11.1 hectares, respectively. Even if the price of coca-leaf dropped to as low as $.33 per kilogram, a little more than 2.3 hectares of cacao and 1.1 hectares of achiote would be needed to equal the income from a hectare of coca.[13]

It is also important to note that prices for all products other than coca-leaf (e.g., corn, rice, sugar) are generally 20 percent of free on board cost at the farm gate in the Upper Huallaga Valley of Peru. This pricing is arbitrary and is enforced in the market centers by government bureaucrats. Additionally, payment to the farmer may take from two to six months. In contrast, coca-leaf is paid for at what is considered the full and fair market price; payment is in cash, on the spot, and with no bureaucratic problems.[14]

As with crop substitution programs, crop eradication programs are likewise considered unrealistic. For example, a coca farmer in the Chapare area of Bolivia expects to receive an income of about $2,600 a year per hectare for his coca-leaf. This is more than four times the price he can get for the next-most-profitable crops: oranges and avocados. The U.S. government has been indirectly providing a one-time $2,000 incentive payment for each hectare of coca eradicated in Bolivia. Given the long-term income that coca farmers can expect to receive, there is no economic reason for them to accept that kind of offer. However, some wily farmers have reportedly taken eradication grants to get rid of old and unfruitful coca farms and underwrite the costs of planting new ones in more remote locations.[15]

In any case, the monetary cost of a more serious crop eradication and substitution program has been estimated at approximately $7,000 per hectare.[16] Even if this seemingly low price were acceptable to the farmers, such a program is not likely to be carried to its logical conclusion. The cost of coca substitution at the $7,000 figure in Bolivia would come to a half-billion U.S. dollars. If that same formula were applied to the more than 250,000 hectares of coca in Peru, the bill would come to $1.75 billion!

Thus, the outside support programs for the eradication and substitution of coca-leaf in the Andean states appear to indicate a lack of seriousness and dedication on the part of the United States, which tends to discourage those host-country officials and citizens who understand the necessity of a holistic approach to the drug phenomenon. The common-sense logic of a Bolivian coca farmer is powerful: "I cannot get my bananas and orange crop out because of the bad roads. But even if I could, I can't make any money. If the government and you Yankees are going to take coca away from me, I need credit, profitable alternative crops, good roads, a market, and security."[17] A winning strategy designed to support a targeted country's counterdrug effort must therefore develop programs that sponsor and support major cooperative political and economic nation-building reforms. Such efforts to attack endemic "root causes" of instability must be coordinated horizontally at the international level and vertically within a given nation-state to provide for a complete unity of effort and ultimate success.

The implications of the external support component of the paradigm are also clear. The "outside support to a targeted government" variable requires macro-level political and economic aid for an embattled government to carry out micro-level measures such as crop substitution and crop eradication programs. Otherwise, long-term political, economic, and social development will not be forthcoming, a regime's ability to govern and control its territory will decline, and the country will continue to suffer.

An additional aspect of external support to the targeted government concerns military and public security forces. The temptation is for the United States to take over the planning and execution of military and police operations. For the same reasons outlined above, this has proved to be a very bad idea. Instead, the best strategy for military and public security force assistance is often the least. That is, a very limited number of Americans should be deployed to the targeted country—and then in a "train the trainer" or technical advisor role. At the operational level, this approach has had some success in both Bolivia and Colombia.[18]

Type and Consistency of Internal Political-Military Activities

This component of the general paradigm addresses the elements that must be established, coordinated, and empowered before a given conflict can be effectively dealt with. This umbrella concept includes at least three powerful dimensions: (1) the credibility of objectives and degree of organization for unity of effort, (2) the discipline and capabilities of security forces, and (3) the effectiveness of intelligence apparatus and other security organizations whose activities focus on terminating the threat. Without unified organization at the highest level able to establish, enforce, and continually refine the purpose and end-state (i.e., the political objective), authority is fragmented, the society is confused and unresponsive to the requirements for a given counterdrug effort, and security forces and intelligence organizations cannot perform appropriately. Thus, only one result is possible—failure.

In this connection, most of the governments in the White Triangle have dismal records in planning and implementing U.S.-supported antidrug programs over the past several years, largely for two reasons. First, the generally weak state apparatus lacks the ability to confront powerful opponents with strong outside support of their own; and second, these governments have what they consider to be reasonable economic, political, and security concerns about the possible impacts of successful drug control programs.[19] In addition, leading government actors—such as Peru's former intelligence chief, Vladimiro Montesinos—have been so deeply involved in drug corruption that they poison the entire government apparatus. Montesinos was hardly the only case; as early as 1980, President Garcia Meza of Bolivia ran the region's first narco-dictatorship, setting the "standard" for Panama's General Manuel Antonio Noriega.

Economically, coca production is thought to be of great benefit to Colombia, Bolivia, and Peru. For example, narco-dollars have been hailed as a major contribution to the economic growth of Colombia and the well-being of a significant number of individual Colombians.[20] Many in the region also fear that if antidrug campaigns were successful, hundreds of thousands of people would be unemployed.[21] It is not hard to imagine the short-term impact on the economic and political system of Bolivia if approximately 200,000 coca-leaf producers lost their livelihoods. Indeed, the mere threat—coupled with a lingering depression and an unpopular plan to sell Bolivian natural gas to the United States and Mexico (through Chile)—resulted in strikes led by politicians such as Evo Morales and his coca-farmer followers that toppled the elected president, Gonzalo Sanchez de Lozada, in the fall of 2003. Colombia and Peru likely would experience similar consequences if the same thing should happen to the thousands of Colombians employed by the coca industry in that country and the 300,000 to 500,000 Peruvians thought to be involved directly or indirectly in coca production there.[22]

Politically, most Latin Americans generally tend to see illicit drugs as a North American problem that the United States would rather deal with outside its own boundaries. Thus, antidrug measures are perceived as externally imposed. In these terms, U.S. and U.S.-supported eradication, extradition, interdiction, military and police operations, and other sanctions are seen as serious affronts to national sovereignty and serious degradations of personal dignity. Thus, courting the support of the United States is politically unacceptable in a strongly nationalistic milieu such as Bolivia today. The 1993 presidential election campaign and the events of the fall of 2003 in that country demonstrated that political actors in all parts and levels of society find these "interventionist" actions to be powerful focus points for developing and mobilizing constituencies for their own personal agendas. As a consequence, Bolivia continues to be "the quintessential coca nation; . . . a veritable cocalandia."[23] Given the mobilization of an important segment of the voting population against U.S. "imperialism," any new government in that country is not likely to be as supportive of U.S. counterdrug efforts as its predecessor. At the least, civilian, police, and military officials thought to be cooperating too closely with the United States in its "neo-colonial efforts" are likely to be politically suspect, and their careers may be in jeopardy.[24]

From a security perspective, insurgency is considered the major internal concern in several of the countries of Latin America. In Colombia and Peru, U.S. counternarcotics requirements were perceived as taking resources away from the counterinsurgency struggle. Also, U.S. training, equipment, and other counterdrug aid is thought to exacerbate the age-old destabilizing rivalry between the police and the armed forces when provided to the police rather than the army, or to the army rather than the police. At the same time, people see the strengthening of security forces and intelligence organizations to be as much a threat to fragile civilian governments and legitimate opponents of those governments as to the illegal narcotics industry. This is the case in virtually every country involved in the war against drugs. Finally, making criminals of minor drug-industry employees and coca farmers in the relatively inaccessible areas of the White Triangle encourages territorial disintegration and provides a ready source of recruits for any organization violently threatening the national territory or the incumbent government.[25]

As a result of these economic, political, and security perceptions, it should be no surprise that the Andean Ridge countries' counternarcotics organizations for unity of effort, intelligence, and military-police operations have left something to be desired. One observer has pointed out that the only thing the counterdrug effort in the White Triangle has accomplished has been to force the narcotraffickers to change their means of transport, their routes, and their residences from time to time.[26]

Nevertheless, the tools of the law and law enforcement, strike operations against drug labs or insurgents (or both), military civic action coupled with civilian government development activity, psychological operations, and population and resource control measures can be used creatively and effectively to defeat the threat. Organization, objectives, and the operational instruments of conflict control are resources that (when developed and integrated into a legitimizing and holistic strategy) could make the difference between winning and losing the illicit transnational challenges inherent in the drug conflict. Nevertheless, the problem of preparing specifically for law enforcement interdiction-type operations, low-intensity insurgency–type operations, or conventional operations against possible and probable challengers is moot. The solution to the problem is to prepare for "warfare as a whole" within the context of popular involvement.[27]

The three internal political-military dimensions postulated here concern the necessary basic objectives and organization that must be established and empowered to pursue a long-term struggle. Each dimension is an imperative that elaborates on the concept of unity of effort through the coordinated action of all elements—political and security—toward a commonly agreed-upon, mutually advantageous strategic political objective. All parties concerned must consider how their actions contribute to the generation of public support and the strengthening of legitimate societal institutions—the ultimate political objective in any uncomfortable war. Every effort in the struggle must be directed at that objective. Otherwise, the effort becomes irrelevant.

CONCLUSIONS

Developing a theory of engagement for the "new" wars represented by the gray area phenomenon requires a focus on solving the central strategic problem. The general task for leaders and their staffs is to incorporate the political, economic, psychological-informational, and moral dimensions of these uncomfortable wars, especially the "war" on drugs, into a strategy for improving the ability and will of governments to deal with the problems and consequences of instability.

In addition, the task and the challenge in the contemporary security environment are to change the perspectives, approaches to problems, corresponding tools, and measures of effectiveness. Leaders and opinion and policy makers must therefore come to terms with the fact that contemporary conflict—whatever type and at whatever level—is not a strictly military-police effort. It is essentially a political-moral effort. The most refined tactical doctrine and operational art carried out by the optimum military or police structure in pursuit of a strategy that ignores the populace in any specific situation will be irrelevant. The realization that success in contemporary conflict depends on strategic societal factors—and that winning battles at the tactical and operational periphery may make little, if any, contribution to winning the overall conflict—is a critical first step toward dealing with the central strategic problem.

It has been argued that the "good guys" are winning most, if not all, of the battles involving transnational threats to a traditional nation-state, but it appears that the "bad guys" are winning the war.[28] This is not taking place by chance. If a country such as the United States can understand and implement the seven aspects of the paradigm—enhance legitimacy, isolate the "bad guys," provide appropriate and consistent external civilian support for a targeted government, provide the right kinds of support to the military and public security forces, establish credible objectives and organize for unity of effort, improve the discipline and capabilities of a government's armed forces, and enhance its intelligence, psychological operations, and civil affairs organization and capabilities—it will have a much better chance of helping its friends and allies in their efforts against these threats. Otherwise, these uncomfortable wars will grind on, and the United States will likely suffer a series of Vietnam-like defeats, perhaps smaller in scale and less direct but more debilitating in cumulative effect. This is the primary operative strategic reality of the gray area phenomenon.

CHAPTER 12

THE CHALLENGE OF
PEACE ENFORCEMENT

Somalia

On December 3, 1992, the United Nations expanded its traditional role of peacekeeping operations to a more ambitious peace-enforcement intervention in an attempt to resolve the root causes and the resultant violence in Somalia. In this first attempt by the international community to deal with the new post–cold war phenomenon referred to as the "failed nation-state," participating states of the coalition were authorized to use "all necessary means" to carry out the United Nations Security Council mandates.[1]

By the spring of 1993, what had begun as a mission to provide security for the delivery of humanitarian assistance was quickly evolving into one of nation-building. However, the operation would undergo a major transformation in its structure and organization prior to taking on these new and substantially greater responsibilities. On May 4, 1993, the U.S.-led Unified Task Force transferred civilian as well as military control of the Somalia operation to the United Nations (UN). This transition was more than a change in leadership, for it marked a planned turning point in the scope of the mission.

At transition the new mandate of UN Security Council Resolution 814 came into effect. The narrowly focused mission of the Unified Task Force, as executed by the administration of President George H. W. Bush and U.S. allies under UN Security Council Resolution 794, had been to provide security for humanitarian relief efforts so that these endeavors could continue without further interruption and rescue a starving population. The stated mission of the UN Operation in Somalia II (UNOSOM II) in Resolution 814, by contrast, was not only to provide a secure environment for the continuation of humanitarian relief operations, but also to provide the secure environment needed to achieve national reconciliation with the establishment of a transitional government, as well as to advance economic rehabilitation. Significant tasks included the disarmament of the armed Somali factions and the return of hundreds of thousands of refugees to their homeland. These objectives implied a distinctly different end-state from that of the Unified Task Force, with very different implications for the military forces committed to Somalia. The short-term mission of the Unified Task Force ended with the successful delivery of humanitarian aid; UNOSOM II would end with the reestablishment of a functioning government.[2]

By its very nature, UNOSOM II was a mission that could place UN forces in direct opposition to one or more of the belligerent clans, which had been at war with each other for nearly two years. In particular, the UN forces would clash with Mohammed Farrah Hassan Aideed, a prominent clan leader who had his own political ambition for the end-state of the nation—one that would establish him as head of the new government. Within a week following the transition of the mission to the United Nations, Aideed's militia skirmished with UN forces near the city of Kismayo. Three weeks later, his militia initiated a deliberate ambush of UN forces in the capital, Mogadishu, resulting in the deaths of over thirty peacekeepers. This attack embroiled the United Nations in a protracted conflict that would ultimately end with the withdrawal of UNOSOM II from Somalia without accomplishing the mission given in its mandate.

The failure of UNOSOM II to achieve its objectives makes it an instructive case study from which to derive lessons for the future. Analyzing that mission in terms of the several dimensions of the SWORD Model helped to both refine the paradigm's utility and cast light on the reasons for the inability of a multinational peace-enforcement operation to end the violence and factionalism in war-torn Somalia.

"COSMETIC" MODIFICATIONS
TO THE SWORD MODEL

The seven dimensions of the SWORD Model are statistical constructs, called factors, that group a number of variables together in a metric scale (see chapter 5).[3] The factors themselves could be called just about anything from numbers to letters to names that attempt to impart connotative meaning. The latter is what we have chosen to do with the naming of the dimensions of the model. Unfortunately, this effort to achieve connotative clarity falls apart when we apply some of the dimension names to peace operations instead of to the insurgencies for which they were developed (see chapter 6). The simple solution to the "problem" created was to rename some of the dimensions—and that is precisely what we have done below, with the original name given to each dimension on the left and its peace operations name on the right.

unity of effort	unity of effort
host government legitimacy	legitimacy
degree of outside support to insurgents	support to belligerents
support actions of the intervening power	support actions of peace forces
military actions of the intervening power	military actions of peace forces
host government military actions	military actions of belligerents and peace forces
actions versus subversion	actions targeted on ending conflict

Unity of Effort

If a necessary but insufficient condition for achieving unity of effort is agreement on the objective of the operation among the parties to it, then UNOSOM II was in trouble from the beginning.[4] Although this operation had a clearer mandate than its predecessor, Operation RESTORE

HOPE, it was plagued by the fact that the administration of President Bill Clinton did not know exactly what it had signed on to, any more than did the other participants. As the implications of the lack of analysis of the meaning of the mandate sank in, other players began to deny that they were indeed party to the agreement. The impact of this issue would only increase as time passed.

Lack of agreement about the meaning of the mandate was compounded by the command relationships that structured UNOSOM II. UN operations usually employ a force under a single force commander appointed by the secretary general with the approval of the Security Council. The force commander reports either to the special representative to the secretary general or directly to the secretary general.[5] While this is the norm, if a special representative is appointed, the force commander typically has a high degree of autonomy.[6]

The first deviation from the norm of UNOSOM II was in the relationship between the special representative to the secretary general and the force commander. At American insistence, the special representative was the former deputy national security advisor to the president of the United States, Admiral Jonathan Howe, while the force commander was Lieutenant General Cevik Bir of Turkey, a member nation of the North Atlantic Treaty Organization. Moreover, the deputy force commander was American Major General Thomas Montgomery, who wore a second hat as commander of U.S. forces in Somalia. This arrangement made for a much closer relationship among the principal leaders of the mission than usually is the case. Moreover, it gave a particularly strong leadership role to the special representative to the secretary general and made the command relationships an American show in everything but name.

Below this level, the UNOSOM II force commander, General Bir, established operational and tactical control as the working command relationships for forces in Somalia. Operational control usually means that the force commander can both assign missions to forces and organize and reorganize the forces as needed by attaching elements of one unit to another. Tactical control usually is short term and means that the force commander can assign a mission to a unit but cannot task-organize the forces. All national contingents were under the operational control of the force commander. General Bir intended to exercise operational control of contingent forces through brigade commanders, each of whom had been assigned an area of responsibility. In practice, these command relationships and the UNOSOM II command-and-control structure proved ineffective. Some national contingents simply would not serve under the operational control of other contingent commanders. Instead, they would prefer to work "in coordination with" or "in cooperation with" other contingent forces.[7]

The multinational character of UN peace operations warrants particular attention. National interests and organizational influence may compete with doctrine and efficiency, as well as with the objective of the mission. Consensus building is difficult (and often contentious) and continuous, while solutions often are national in character. Commanders can expect contributing nations to adhere to national policies and priorities, which at times can complicate—or even derail—the multinational effort.[8]

The command relationship between UNOSOM II and the U.S. Quick Reaction Force (which was prescribed by the commander in chief of U.S. Central Command and outlined in the terms of reference for U.S. forces in Somalia) illustrates the problem. The Quick Reaction Force, located in Somalia, was under the operational control of Central Command. Tactical control of the Quick Reaction Force was delegated to the commander of U.S. forces in Somalia for "normal training exercises within Somalia. . . . [and] in situations within Somalia that exceed the capability of UNOSOM II forces and required the emergency employment of immediate combat power for a limited period or show of force operations."[9] Any tasking for the Quick Reaction Force outside these guidelines required explicit approval by Central Command. The terms of reference provided adequate flexibility for the UNOSOM II deputy force commander to employ the Quick Reaction Force in emergency situations. However, to conduct critical nonemergency combat operations that exceeded the capability of UNOSOM II forces, the terms of reference proved to be quite inflexible.[10]

Thus, the American version of its grant of operational control of U.S. forces to the force commander flew in the face of its own normal definition of operational control, which, in any case, was reserved by the commander of Central Command. Needless to say, the grants of "operational control" by other force providers were similarly restrictive. As a result, when the mandate given by Resolution 814 expanded because of the ambush of Pakistani peacekeepers on June 5, 1993, with the passage of UN Security Council Resolution 837 the next day, several force providers indicated that they had not agreed to use their forces for the capture of a factional leader. This was most true of Italy, which had maintained—and continued to maintain—a unilateral, direct dialogue with the leaders of Aideed's militia.

In short, UNOSOM II failed to achieve unity of effort as a result of two critical factors. First, whatever agreement on the objective that had existed broke down following the passage of Resolution 837, largely owing to the fact that the force providers had not been consulted. Second, the command-and-control arrangements were flawed, especially with respect to U.S. participation, which was circumscribed by the inexplicable American political and military failure to support the very arrangements it had put in place. That is, neither the political leadership of the Clinton administration (including the secretary of defense) nor the military leadership of Central Command was willing to follow U.S. military doctrine with respect to command and control.

Legitimacy

The dimension of legitimacy in the analysis of UNOSOM II is closely related to unity of effort, especially with respect to defining and agreeing on the objective.[11] The fact that the objectives of UNOSOM II were neither entirely clear nor agreed upon by all the force providers had significant impact on the operation's legitimacy.

Legitimacy clearly is a matter of perception. It revolves around the degree of support for both the operation and the peace force from the participating nations and the belligerents alike. The community authorizing the operation needs to see its objectives as both worthwhile and capable of being accomplished, while the belligerents and the people of the area of the operation need to see the peace force as an impartial arbiter of their conflict. Moreover, the legitimacy of the operation depends on the perception among the people of the operational area that the

peace force can provide the security required to begin the establishment (or reestablishment) of appropriate governmental functions.

In the case of Somalia, during Operation RESTORE HOPE, the Unified
Task Force apparently met most, if not all, of these requirements. The
Unified Task Force generally was perceived as an impartial arbiter of the
conflict. The task force demonstrated the capability to provide security
for the delivery of humanitarian assistance and to begin the reestablishment of governmental functions. Yet its very success sowed the seeds
of the potential delegitimization of its successor, UNOSOM II. Aideed
was the one factional leader who was unwilling to accept a restored
Somalia under any terms but his own and was astute enough to see that
he would have an opportunity to create a new reality as the Unified
Task Force transitioned to UNOSOM II.

In February 1993 Aideed had lost the southern city of Kismayo to
the forces of another factional leader, Hersi Morgan (son-in-law of the
deposed dictator, Siad Barre), a loss that became a festering wound
for him and reinforced his already firm belief that foreign intervention in Somalia was not required. Thus, Aideed began to regard the
United States and the United Nations not as neutral humanitarians
but as political adversaries.[12] However, he had not sought a direct
confrontation with the Unified Task Force, which demonstrated an
overwhelming military presence in the form of U.S. and other Western
forces. He knew, though, that he could simply wait out these forces,
all the while preparing military actions to be used against UNOSOM II
should his political position deteriorate further during the continued
UN intervention.[13]

On May 7 Aideed's forces attempted to seize Kismayo, and although
they were defeated by the Belgian peacekeepers, the United Nations
failed to eject them from the area. Two days later the Galcayo peace conference began. Although this was an Aideed initiative, it turned out to
be a major political setback for him. The UNOSOM II political division
successfully opposed Aideed's attempt to manipulate the conference,
thereby leaving him extremely frustrated over his inability to control the
political process in Somalia.[14] With his political stature threatened and
having been defeated by a Western military force in Kismayo, Aideed
lashed out on June 5 against the Pakistani peacekeepers.

These events clearly set the stage for the contest for legitimacy that would take place in Mogadishu, the other cities and towns of Somalia, New York, the capitals of the force providers, and media sources such as CNN. In Somalia, the issue of legitimacy ultimately turned on whether the peace force could provide the required degree of security in the face of Aideed's opposition. A critical part of UNOSOM II's problem was that to be effective the operation needed to be perceived as at least impartial and at best neutral in terms of the factional fighting. Without that perceived impartiality, UNOSOM II lost consent. Aideed's grant of consent had been tenuous and was withdrawn completely following the failure of his political plans at the Galcayo conference. Thus, from June 5 on, Aideed's actions were aimed at undermining the legitimacy of UNOSOM II among the people of Mogadishu and—to the maximum extent to which he was capable—the people of Somalia. He also aimed at exploiting cracks in the coalition of nations and forces that made up UNOSOM II.

The juridical legitimacy of UNOSOM II stemmed from Resolution 814, that is, from the agreement of the members of the UN Security Council in New York. The practical legitimacy that flowed from that resolution was found in the terms of commitment by the force providers. For example, the United States committed to provide significant forces on the condition that the special representative to the secretary general was an American with a military background, the force commander was from NATO, and the deputy force commander was likewise an American. No nation committed its forces under the full operational control that the special representative and force commander envisioned or desired, not even the United States. Nevertheless, the terms of Resolution 814 and the commitment of forces agreements set the practical and juridical limits of legitimacy. The events of June 5 were to change that.

As a result of Aideed's ambush of the Pakistanis, the UN Security Council passed Resolution 837 on June 6. The resolution strongly condemned the unprovoked attack and the use of radio broadcasts to incite such attacks, and reaffirmed "that the Secretary General is authorized under resolution 814 to take all necessary measures against all those responsible for the armed attacks . . . including against those responsible for inciting such attacks, to establish the effective authority of UNOSOM II throughout Somalia, including to secure the investigation of their actions and their arrest and detention for prosecution, trial, and punishment."[15] The resolution was written and passed overnight. While resolutions of the Security Council are supposed to be binding on all UN members, the council depends on enforcement by force providers who may not be Security Council members. Such was especially the case of Resolution 837. At American urging, the council rushed the resolution through to demonstrate, "as one senior administration official put it, that the United Nations, engaged in a major multi-national peacekeeping mission, could not be 'pushed around' by some renegade warlord."[16]

Even before the passage of Resolution 837, the Italian ambassador to Somalia had expressed reservations to the force commander over the perception that UNOSOM II was taking sides against Aideed.[17] As one of the force-providing nations not consulted about Resolution 837, Italy essentially chose not to participate in its enforcement. In a cable to New York the special representative to the secretary general expressed Force Command's concerns regarding the "passive presence" of the Italian forces and the negative impact of a virtual Italian sanctuary for Aideed in Somalia.[18] The Italian case provides strong evidence of the rapid loss of legitimacy within UNOSOM II.

Finally, the events of October 3–4, 1993—when eighteen members of U.S. Task Force Ranger were killed and seventy-five wounded (all shown live and in living color on CNN, including the dragging of the body of a dead American soldier through the streets of Mogadishu as well as pictures of a wounded U.S. helicopter pilot as Aideed's prisoner)—raised serious questions with the American public over whether this peace operation was worth doing. When the Clinton administration made no attempt to counter the impact of the view according to CNN, the American public withdrew its grant of legitimacy to the operation. At that point, the president announced a phased withdrawal of U.S. forces and the end of American participation as of March 31, 1994. Both Resolution 814 and Resolution 837 were dead. The peace operation in Somalia had lost its mandate and its legitimacy.

Support to Belligerents

One of the complicating factors in the case study of UNOSOM II is the initial identification of the belligerents. The problem is analogous to threat analysis in conventional military operations, with the caveat that all belligerents are potential allies of the peace force as well as potential adversaries. To understand the belligerents in this situation requires a brief review of some of the major aspects of Somali society and the nature of the Somali state.

Somalia was made up of the fusion of British Somaliland in the north and Italian Somaliland in the south. Although the two had been separate colonies, they were united by the Somali language and their Islamic religion. The Somalis are, however, a clan culture reckoning descent from six major clan families. While each major clan tends to control discrete territories within (as well as outside) Somalia's borders, significant overlap occurs, more in the south than in the north.[19] Still more important is the fact that the clans further divide into any number of competing subclans. At the same time, political and militia organizations are overlaid on the subclans, resulting in the potential for (and often the reality of) conflict between the traditional and the "political" leadership. Ultimately, an oversimplified picture of the belligerents appeared around rivals from the same clan who held leadership in Mogadishu and loose alliances with other militia leaders: Ali Mahdi and Mohammed Farrah Aideed.

At the several peace conferences held in Addis Ababa and at Galcayo during the Unified Task Force and UNOSOM II interventions, fourteen militia factions were recognized as participants in the peace process.[20] In effect, this recognition gave primacy to the militia factions, their "political" organizations, and the "warlords," over the traditional clan leaders. Moreover, it reinforced the picture of the belligerents as falling into two distinct political-military coalitions. The result of this process was two-edged. As suggested in the previous section, it tended to isolate Aideed from the rest of the players, but it also strengthened his hand by cementing his coalition of subclan leaders and supportive factional forces and militias.

While Ali Mahdi generally had supported the Unified Task Force and later UNOSOM II, this support had not won him sufficient external support for his cause. Rather, the United States and United Nations tended to treat him as simply the other factional leader, like Aideed, but a "good boy." In the end this left Ali Mahdi as isolated in fact as Aideed seemed to be. Yet Aideed was not isolated. Rather, most of his subclan supported him; several other militia leaders did as well; so, too, did key economic leaders such as Osman Atto. As important as these supporters were, Aideed also received indirect external support from the Italians.

Soon after Resolution 837 triggered UNOSOM II military operations aimed at capturing or otherwise neutralizing Aideed, the warlord struck back. On July 2 his militia ambushed Italian forces, inflicting casualties of three killed and thirty wounded, causing the Italian force to abandon several key strong points. Later that month the Italians negotiated with local elders from Aideed's clan to reoccupy those strong points. In effect, UNOSOM II forces were allowed to operate in that portion of North Mogadishu only at the discretion of Aideed's forces.[21]

Following the July 2 attack, the Italian force commander virtually reverted his troops to a consensual peacekeeping status. In so doing, cordon and search operations and aggressive checks at strong points ceased. This was evidenced in Force Command's July 6 cable to the under secretary general for peacekeeping operations: "National authorities and local commanders feel free to ignore direction and urging for aggressive action. . . . [A national contingent] is insistent on further negotiations with faction elders who have no actual influence on the . . . militia."[22] This concern was also highlighted in a July 7 UNOSOM II Force Command situation report, which states that national "military officials have forbidden [their national forces] to conduct indiscriminant violent reprisals against Aideed's forces. This prohibition places [their brigade commander] in a difficult position because he is required to negotiate before engaging in military operations against Aideed."[23]

This inaction on the part of the Italians had deeper effects on coalition operations. Many coalition partners were hesitant to share operational and intelligence data with the Italian forces, fearing that such matters would be compromised. Even within the headquarters, the UNOSOM II chief intelligence officer, an Italian, was excluded from the planning process on numerous UNOSOM II–directed operations.

The situation clearly did not improve for UNOSOM II over time. Rather, the impact of Italian inaction (which amounted to de facto support for Aideed) strengthened Aideed's hand and increased the boldness of his subordinates, as reflected in an encounter with a Mr. Gullit, a clan elder supporting Aideed, near a strong point in North Mogadishu. The operations officer commented that Gullit "was the leader and did most of the talking. . . . He stated that . . . [Aideed's militia] would not accept any other contingent than the one (the Italian Brigade) that currently occupied the area and that they were ready to die before they would cooperate with UNOSOM. . . . We killed seven Nigerians because they violated the occupation agreement established for the strong point by sending the reinforcing platoon of APCs."[24] In short, the effective "defection" of Italy from the coalition and that nation's de facto support for Aideed much increased the capabilities of the latter by creating sanctuaries for him within the confines of Mogadishu. In these areas he could hold meetings in relative safety to plan his next moves. Moreover, his forces could use the safe areas to rest and recuperate as well as rearm.

However, an even greater problem for UNOSOM II with respect to external support to the belligerents existed. As Clausewitz advised, those who would conduct a war must first establish "the kind of war on which they are embarking."[25] Aideed was receiving aid in the form of trainers and fighters from a group of "Afghan Arabs" that would later become known as Al Qaeda—a fact that was discovered in the wake of the terrorist attacks of September 11, 2001. These jihadists brought tactics and techniques that had proved effective in the war against the Soviets in Afghanistan and applied them during the events of October 3–4, 1993, in Mogadishu. They enjoyed initial tactical success, although in the end the tactical defeat of Aideed's forces was overwhelming. Nevertheless, with this support—both internal and external—Aideed became, over the months between June and October 1993, increasingly more formidable. His increasing strength ultimately was manifested in the aftermath of UNOSOM II's pyrrhic victory on October 3–4, when Task Force Ranger took significant casualties in the attempt to arrest Aideed. The result, of course, was the U.S. withdrawal from the mission and the collapse of UNOSOM II a mere six months later.

Support Actions of Peace Forces

The perception of the nature of the commitment controls this dimension; that being the case, the commitment was stated as a mandate in a series of UN Security Council resolutions. Beginning with the passage of the first, Resolution 794, a dispute between the United States and the secretary general arose over the meaning of the key words of the mandate— to "use all necessary means to establish as soon as possible, a secure environment for humanitarian relief operations." At a December 22, 1992, meeting with the secretary general, Secretary of State Lawrence Eagleburger reemphasized the U.S. position of a limited mission in Somalia.

The Clinton administration entered office determined to concentrate on domestic policies and early on echoed President Bush's call for a rapid handover of the U.S.-led Operation RESTORE HOPE to UNOSOM II. With the continued desire of the secretary general to expand the mandate to one of nation-building, there was much disagreement as to the shape of UNOSOM II. The first indication of a major adjustment in the U.S. position came on March 26, 1993, when the Security Council adopted Resolution 814, which outlined in detail the mission and tasks of UNOSOM II—to include disarmament and nation-building. This resulted in relatively early indications that the international community had achieved a consensus to strongly support a complex peace operation. More importantly, these rhetorical indicators were backed up on the ground by the clear strength of the Unified Task Force.

The core of the Unified Task Force was the U.S. Joint Task Force Somalia, organized around the Marine Expeditionary Force (I MEF), under the command of Lieutenant General Robert Johnston of the U.S. Marine Corps. In addition, the joint task force included the U.S. Tenth Mountain Division (light infantry) with substantial support forces and a high degree of mobility owing to significant numbers of helicopters.

Precision firepower was available to the force from AC 130 Spectre gunships. Augmenting the Americans were allies, mostly from NATO nations and some others, including units of the vaunted French Foreign Legion. At its peak, the Unified Task Force numbered some 38,000 troops. Indicative of its effectiveness was that its forces rarely were challenged by the militia of Aideed or any of his lieutenants; when they were, they defeated the challenge with hardly any friendly casualties.

When Operation RESTORE HOPE transitioned to UNOSOM II on May 4, 1993, the UN force was programmed to be nearly as strong as the Unified Task Force (at the end of its tenure), with some 28,000 troops. However, on transition day UNOSOM II numbered a mere 14,000, with few of the combat capabilities that the Unified Task Force had shown. Instead of two U.S. divisions as the core of the fighting force, UNOSOM II had only one infantry brigade of the Tenth Mountain Division available as a Quick Reaction Force for emergencies. The principal combat forces belonging to Force Command were a number of battalions and brigades from Belgium, France, Italy, Malaysia, Nigeria, and Pakistan, all with incompatible equipment, different command-and-control commitments, and different levels of capability. The face the UNOSOM II force showed to Aideed was one of much less support from the world community than UN rhetoric and the Unified Task Force had demonstrated.

The perception of the length of the commitment likewise was as mixed as the signals the international community sent. Whereas the series of Security Council resolutions indicated that the United Nations and its force-supplying members were prepared to stay as long as necessary to restore civil government and civil society to Somalia, the clarity of the message was diminished beginning with the dispute between the United States and the secretary general over the meaning of Resolution 794. The United States made it clear that the Unified Task Force had a mission of limited duration. President Bush even speculated that U.S. forces could hand over the mission to the United Nations by January 20, 1993: inauguration day. That date was obviously unrealistic, but it shows that an early transition to UNOSOM II was desired.

With the inauguration of the Clinton administration, the appointment of General Bir of Turkey as UNOSOM II force commander, and the passage of Resolution 814, the goal of a seamless transition from the Unified Task Force to UNOSOM II forces on a schedule driven by events and not by time seemed feasible. Given the nature of the problem, the date of passage of Resolution 814, and the time required to deploy forces and equipment, May 1993 appeared to be a realistic date for transition. This tentative "planning" date, however, soon became fixed in many minds.

As May approached, some concern was expressed in the United Nations as to when Force Command would assume theater responsibility and whether establishing the command was premature. All parties involved in the transition process had a position on the subject. The Unified Task Force, seeing its mission as completed, wanted the transition to occur as expeditiously as possible;[26] the force commander believed that members of the Unified Task Force were "extremely aggressive in their insistence on a 1 May 1993 deadline for transition."[27] The Unified Task Force staff did not share an understanding of the constraints of the United Nations in terms of resource procurement.[28] The position of planners for UNOSOM II was that transition should occur based on the capabilities of Force Command to assume the mission and effect a seamless transition. The result of these apparently small discords rebounded, perhaps, giving the impression that the contributors to Operation RESTORE HOPE (many of whom were also contributors to UNOSOM II) had lost their will to stay the course.

Later events such as the response of a number of force providers to the June 5 attack on the Pakistanis and the passage of Resolution 837 reinforced the impression that the nations making up UNOSOM II lacked the will to stick out the fight. The events of October 3–4, in which U.S. Task Force Ranger took its large number of casualties, simply confirmed the perception that Aideed had outlasted UNOSOM II.

The final element of this dimension involves the perception that the commitment of military forces will be consistent with the threat posed to the accomplishment of the mission. Rather than look at all the force providers to UNOSOM II, it is instructive to consider the changing commitment of the United States to the mission. In Operation RESTORE HOPE, the United States led the military effort, committing a Marine Expeditionary Force headquarters (the equivalent of an army corps) under the command of a three-star general, a Marine Corps division, an army division, and significant air and naval forces, along with major sustainment elements. That the force commander controlled all the U.S. forces was equally important. By contrast, under UNOSOM II, the United States committed less than a single division and did so with reluctance. When it later increased its forces, it did so unilaterally, without giving any control to UNOSOM II Force Command, thereby raising significant questions as to the depth of the U.S. commitment to the UN mission. Thus, by all three criteria, the support actions of the peace forces were lacking.

Military Actions of Peace Forces

Force size is the first variable of this dimension. In a peace operation, particularly a peace-enforcement operation, the peace forces need to be of sufficient size and strength to deter the use of force against them or their mission. A related factor is that they need to be introduced as a body and not piecemeal, since the latter allows the belligerents to adjust to the new realities as well as giving them time to probe the peace force for weaknesses with relatively low risk to the belligerents. The Unified Task Force and the UNOSOM II forces present a stark contrast with respect to both aspects of this variable.

First, as noted above, the Unified Task Force was a large force, and most of it arrived quickly—literally overnight. The marines undertook a nighttime amphibious landing under combat conditions, after having made a show of force with numerous U.S. Navy and Marine air sorties in the days immediately preceding the landing. They were quickly followed by the U.S. Army's Tenth Mountain Division, French Foreign Legion troops, and the forces of the other contributing countries. Almost before anyone had realized it, the peak of 38,000 had been reached, and forces were being reduced to about 28,000, the level at transition. Even more than the numbers was the combat capability those numbers represented. The Unified Task Force was an integrated combined-arms force with resources including infantry, mechanized, and armor units, attack helicopters, AC 130 gunships, F-14 and F/A 18 jet fighter bombers, and naval gunfire.

The contrast with UNOSOM II is striking. Planned for 28,000, on transition day the force numbered a mere 14,000. Its component combat elements would trickle in from May to September 1993. Beginning in the late summer, as new units from additional force-providing countries arrived, units from countries already there withdrew, leaving the force somewhat below its optimal strength.

The combat capability of the UNOSOM II force also compared unfavorably to that of the Unified Task Force. Most of the UNOSOM II combat elements were in battalion strength, or less, from a variety of contributing nations with widely differing equipment, training, doctrine, and leadership. The U.S. combat forces were reduced from two divisions with all their support to the brigade-sized Quick Reaction Force, which was under the control of Force Command only during bona fide emergencies. Quality of other combat forces varied greatly.

The principal purpose of the UNOSOM II peace force was to contribute by its actions to the de-escalation of the conflict. To that end, the force commander undertook a series of show-of-force operations at transition. The intent of these operations was to show that a seamless transition had occurred between Operation RESTORE HOPE and UNOSOM II and to demonstrate to the Somali people that the security for humanitarian relief and political reconciliation would continue and grow under the United Nations.

The effect of these show-of-force operations on the populace was uncertain, however. Less than seventy-two hours after the assumption of command from the Unified Task Force and in the middle of a show of force, UNOSOM II faced its first major confrontation with militia forces. This showdown occurred not in Mogadishu, where it was most expected, but in the southern port city of Kismayo. During the late evening hours of May 6 and extending into the morning of May 7, 1993, a band of approximately 150 armed men attacked Kismayo, where they engaged elements of the Belgian Parachute Battalion. During the engagement, one Belgian officer was wounded, and an estimated forty Somalis of the attacking force were either killed or wounded.[29]

A Force Command investigation team determined that the attack was conducted by forces allied to Aideed. Despite the fact that Belgian forces had soundly defeated the hostile militia, the Belgian commander's actions suggested to Force Command that he was unwilling to risk further casualties to his force. Indeed, his actions prompted Force Command to remind the Belgian commander that UNOSOM II, while operating under Chapter VII, found itself in the role of peacemaker and that "the intent is to aggressively establish and maintain a secure environment by force of arms, should the situation in your AOR become untenable."[30]

The failure (which began early in the operation) to undertake military and associated diplomatic actions to de-escalate the conflict clearly increased Aideed's confidence that his intransigence and skillfully directed violence against individual national contingents of UNOSOM II would result in his ultimate victory. The UN Security Council and the special representative to the secretary general played directly into his hand when, after the June 5 ambush of the Pakistanis, they pushed through Resolution 837 without building a consensus for it among the force providers. In turn, this pushed the United States into dispatching Task Force Ranger, whose mission to capture Aideed only escalated the level of violence. The results became apparent in the October firefight that left eighteen members of the task force dead, seventy-five wounded, and some three hundred or more Somalis, not all of whom were militia fighters, killed and many more wounded. Since all-out war was not what the Clinton administration had in mind, these events prompted it to set a date for the withdrawal of U.S. forces and the abandonment by the United States of the mission. The U.S. withdrawal, of course, doomed UNOSOM II to failure.

Military Actions of the Belligerents and the Peace Forces

Events developed this dimension of the analytical paradigm in a particularly interesting way. As Operation RESTORE HOPE gave way to UNOSOM II, the military effectiveness of the peace force deteriorated. Meanwhile, the tactical skills of Aideed's militia improved, as did his effective employment of those skills (owing largely to the advice and training provided by the "Afghan Arabs"). As militia professionalism grew, the tactical employment of the peace force became significantly less resolute and more tentative. Thus, the relationship between the peace force and Aideed's militia in terms of their military professionalism was an inverse one. Following the passage of Resolution 837, Force Command initiated offensive actions to restore order and security in Mogadishu. The aim of the operations conducted from June 6 through August 31 was to reestablish a secure environment (including control of key facilities and supply routes) and to neutralize Aideed's militia and his radio station. Regaining control of the city was crucial for the UN forces for two reasons. First, the adverse effects on the morale of the peace forces that the June 5 attack engendered had to be negated. Second, the UN civilian staff as well as personnel of many nongovernmental organizations and UN relief agencies had departed the country after the attack and would not return until a secure environment was restored.

One important operation by the peace forces was conducted on June 17 against what was called the Aideed Enclave. While this operation attained a tactical victory, its positive effects were short lived. The counterattack against Moroccan forces precipitated their withdrawal from the city and denial by their national authorities for future employment in Mogadishu.[31] The failure to secure a strong point in the enclave allowed militia infiltration back into the area. French forces were asked but were reluctant to retake the ground previously fought over, and their government ordered them out of Mogadishu.[32] Italian forces, who had participated reluctantly in the operation, were not prepared to do so again.

Aideed's militia were not idle in these circumstances. On June 22 they began what became nightly harassment of UNOSOM II installations with small-arms and rocket-propelled-grenade fire.[33] Weekly anti–UNOSOM II demonstrations were held at the soccer stadium near the Aideed Enclave, and the militia began erecting roadblocks in areas they controlled on a number of key streets and roads in the city. Although Force Command initially saw the roadblocks as harassment and protest, their tactical significance became apparent when Pakistani forces accompanied by U.S. engineers were ambushed while clearing one.[34] Over the next few months, this escalation of violence by Aideed's

militia became increasingly more frequent. Attacks often were characterized by the use of improvised explosive devices of the type we are
seeing again in Iraq.[35] Moreover, the ambushes fueled the reluctance of
UNOSOM II units within the city to get out on the streets in lightly
armored vehicles or on foot, which would have increased the visibility
and show-of-force effectiveness.

A unilateral operation in July raised the U.S. profile beyond what the
Clinton administration desired. As a result, getting U.S. aviation assets
approved for anything beyond force protection proved vastly more
difficult, and the use of U.S. ground forces in search operations other than
those immediately adjacent to U.S. facilities was significantly limited.
This policy was in keeping with the original command intent to maintain
a low signature so that U.S. combat forces could revert to an "over the
horizon" mission by the end of summer. However, the policy of with-
holding U.S. troops negatively impacted the coalition forces and their
willingness to place soldiers at risk. The Pakistani Foreign Ministry
stated that without U.S. attack helicopter strikes, there would be "chaos
in the country."[36] Attempting to prod coalition forces into action without
continued use of U.S. forces, especially attack helicopter assets, slowed
any UNOSOM II follow-on action and effectively lost any initiative
gained by the operation. This U.S. policy (with the exception of Task
Force Ranger and its unilateral special mission) would not change for
the duration, despite the fact that levels of violence increased and success
for the UN mission was significantly more at risk than it had been in
May, when the policy had first been developed.

In contrast to some of the developments noted above, August brought
an increased dedication of resources to capture Aideed and his senior
advisors, and Task Force Ranger was introduced into the theater to
carry out this mission. Admiral Howe, the special representative to the
secretary general, had requested additional forces from the United
States for this effort. He either saw the lack of initiative by the coalition
or understood that no properly configured force existed in-theater that
could execute the mission to arrest, detain, and bring to trial those
responsible for the armed attacks against UN forces. At this point, one
U.S. official noted, the Pentagon argued that "'if it is us against Aideed,
we might as well try to actually get Aideed.' . . . Howe . . . wanted more

force and said, 'you have approved the U. N. . . . resolution to go after [Aideed] and you have to provide the forces to do it.'"[37]

After a series of unilateral operations in September (during which Aideed and his troops—with important help from the "Afghan Arabs"—learned a great deal about the capabilities and tactics of U.S. forces supporting Task Force Ranger, as well as their vulnerabilities), a major operation that would become the decisive event in the UNOSOM II mission took place. On October 3 the task force received information that a number of Aideed's senior advisors were meeting in a building in downtown Mogadishu. Task Force Ranger assaulted the area and quickly captured twenty-four detainees, including two senior Aideed advisors. Taking advantage of what had been learned in previous operations, Aideed's militia shot down a Task Force Ranger UH-60 helicopter near the raid site. As ranger ground forces moved to the crash site to recover survivors, they came under a barrage of fire from surrounding buildings and streets, taking a number of casualties. This force formed a perimeter around the crash site. Two miles to the south, a second UH-60 (Blackhawk) was shot down. Although the U.S. Quick Reaction Force had a back-up company ready to reinforce Task Force Ranger, it was mounted in soft-skinned vehicles and would be unable to punch through the hostile resistance and link up with the rangers by itself.

As a result, the UNOSOM II reserve of a Pakistani tank platoon and two Malaysian mechanized companies was ordered into action. Although this reserve force was ready to launch in less than an hour, Task Force Ranger notified headquarters that the embattled rangers had fortified several buildings as strong points and were not in danger of being overrun. Force headquarters therefore slowed the rescue operation to implement a fully developed tactical plan that made use of the capabilities of the U.S. Quick Reaction Force and the Pakistani and Malaysian armored vehicles. After encountering heavy resistance, the rescue column reached the two crash sites and evacuated the rangers. In the course of the action eighteen U.S. soldiers were killed and seventy-five wounded; three Malaysian armored personnel carriers were destroyed, one soldier killed, and ten wounded; and two Pakistani soldiers were wounded. Estimates were that between three hundred and five hundred Somali militia were killed and some seven hundred wounded.[38]

Clearly, the events of October 3–4, 1993, amounted to a major armed clash between the U.S. and UNOSOM II forces on one side and Aideed's militia on the other. Although the coalition forces exhibited no lack of professionalism and in fact achieved a significant tactical victory, the events indicated just how far Aideed's forces had come. They had the capability to make any effort to subdue Aideed extremely costly—more costly, as it turned out, than the United States was prepared to pay.

Actions Targeted on Ending Conflict

Of the actions comprising this dimension, one—intelligence—represents classical military thought. As the ancient Chinese sage Sun Tzu put it, "Now if the estimates made in the temple before hostilities indicate victory it is because calculations show one's strength to be superior to that of the enemy; if they indicate defeat, it is because calculations show that one is inferior. With many calculations, one can win; with few one cannot. How much less chance has one who makes none at all!"[39] By contrast, the other actions—population and resources control, psychological operations, and civic action—often get short shrift from the warriors; in Somalia, they received the sobriquet of "mission creep." Yet lack of preparation and attention to the actions of this dimension in Operation RESTORE HOPE and carried on into UNOSOM II contributed in significant ways to the failure of the latter mission.

A lack of what is sometimes called "basic intelligence"—that is, an understanding of the political, cultural, and social nature of the society—created obstacles to success from the beginning of Operation RESTORE HOPE. Where that basic intelligence was strong, as in the U.S. Liaison Office of Ambassador Robert Oakley, it was not responsible to or required by the Unified Task Force commander, General Johnston.[40] Thus, the Unified Task Force largely worked in the dark at the strategic level. Moreover, as the army forces stated in their after-action report, "National and Strategic systems were unable to provide detailed information prior to deployment."[41]

Second, U.S. forces at the tactical level also had serious problems. Although the Marine Corps had a relatively effective tactical intelligence collection system that relied on human sources, the army's intelligence units generally were not organized to operate in a human source environment. For the army, "commanders must task some units, other than intelligence, to perform detailed collection tasks. The units tasked often do not have the background or training . . . [needed]. As a result, reports sometimes lack detail and leave gaps in the collection plan."[42] As a result, army forces relied heavily on the intelligence capabilities of the special operations forces, especially Army Special Forces. Although field commanders certainly would have made use of the intelligence capabilities of civil affairs and psychological operations personnel, these were in short supply, resulting in a lack of basic intelligence useful at the operational and tactical levels.

The transition to UNOSOM II did not improve the picture either. Resistance to the notion of intelligence in a peace operation on the part of the United Nations was compounded by the fact that Force Command's U2 was an Italian who, because of his government's policy, was excluded from staff planning of UN operations. In addition, as Sun Tzu observed, "What is called 'foreknowledge' cannot be elicited from spirits, nor from gods, nor by analogy with past events, nor from calculations. It must be obtained from men who know the enemy situation."[43] Although tactical intelligence support for the hunt for Aideed was relatively effective in that it was able to locate specific high-priority human targets for capture, it never did identify that Aideed's militia had developed effective tactics to make aviation operations increasingly costly. It also failed to identify the degree and kind of support being provided to Aideed by the "Afghan Arabs."[44]

Although the Unified Task Force rejected the larger mission of nation-building, it did undertake a significant number of activities that could fall under such a rubric. Among these were road building and the establishment of local governments and police. U.S. officers tended to speak somewhat disparagingly of these efforts as "mission creep," but they were clearly inherent in the UN secretary general's perception of the mandate. This was, of course, the definition prescribed by Resolution 814 that was to be executed by UNOSOM II.

Early in May, the UNOSOM II political staff forwarded a paper to Force Command that outlined what they perceived to be an opportunity for early commitment of forces to the central region of Somalia, outside Mogadishu. This paper offered an assessment of multiple factions awaiting UNOSOM II deployment, which represented both a challenge and an opportunity to place a permanent force in the town of Galcayo to ensure its demilitarized status.[45] Rather than being seen as simply one logical course of action for a unified effort by all the agencies, the document became an implementation policy for the political staff and the special representative to the secretary general. Plans for a methodical, controlled buildup of forces gave way to guidance to determine how soon a deployment could be made into the central region. Expansion was thus becoming a time-driven process rather than being driven by events or capabilities.

A related shortfall in the establishment of a coordinated strategy to end conflict was the lack of a humanitarian relief policy. Feeding sites were scheduled to be closed at the end of May 1993—a phasing out of the Unified Task Force's humanitarian mission. Yet follow-on funds and a plan for their investment—required to rejuvenate the Somali economy—were lacking. To be successful the United Nations needed a coordinated military, political, and economic strategy. A secure environment needed to be established so that local political structures could be reestablished. These structures (including police, judiciary, schools, and public administration) required initial economic support. Once basic government services were restored, local economies could develop and become self-sustaining, thus ending the need for major continued humanitarian assistance. Such a strategy never developed. Efforts made to correct this situation in the late summer failed. This resulted in the political and economic instruments of power becoming dependent on the military strategy for dealing with hostile militia forces. Complementary strategies never were developed, nor was the appropriate mix of capabilities—including civil affairs and psychological-operations forces—emplaced to address the hostile clans or to capitalize on those areas where peaceful reconciliation was progressing. Thus, the limited success in establishing district and regional political councils did not translate into similar successes in restoring basic government services.

In short, the focus of both the Unified Task Force and the UNOSOM II forces in terms of their actions was much too narrow to end the conflict.

The Unified Task Force discounted the need for basic intelligence on Somalia and saw the necessary nation-building activities as mission creep. While UNOSOM II forces recognized the need for effective intelligence, the effort was so compartmented that it failed to achieve the required degree of synergism. It also fell afoul of the political disagreements among the force-contributing nations. As implemented, UNOSOM II had neither the military organizations—including civil affairs and psychological operations—in sufficient numbers to effect a lasting peace, nor the civil development organizational capabilities to produce or implement a coordinated plan for effective nation-building. As a result, the entire process reverted to guerrilla warfare of Aideed's militia against the UNOSOM II forces.

CONCLUSIONS

Somalia may be considered the first post–cold war peace-enforcement operation. Application of the SWORD Model, dimension by dimension, to the events in Somalia yields an analysis that fairly screams of a doomed operation, which by its failure to appropriately address the several variables making up each dimension, as well as the whole of the paradigm, ultimately had no chance of success.

After a promising start by the Unified Task Force, unity of effort foundered on the shoals of a flawed command-and-control structure, lack of coordination and cooperation among the agencies making up UNOSOM II, and (escalating from a relatively minor problem in Operation RESTORE HOPE) the profound lack of agreement on the objectives of UNOSOM II among the force-providing nations. The lack of unity of effort both influenced and reflected the ebbs and flows of the perceived legitimacy of the operation. Whereas Operation RESTORE HOPE had a high degree of legitimacy—owing in part to the agreement among all parties on the objective of humanitarian relief, which resulted in a degree of consent from the belligerents, however grudging—UNOSOM II rapidly lost its legitimacy as consent was withdrawn by one faction and then agreement among the force contributors on the objectives of the operation slipped away.

The loss of consensus among the members of the coalition was soon reflected in the tacit and overt support given to Aideed by Italy. This, in turn, further weakened the strength of the UNOSOM II coalition, as the various contributors reassessed their support. The changing degree of support for the operation was reflected in the military actions of the peace force as the various national and functional components of UNOSOM II sent mixed signals regarding the strength and focus of the effort. The inverse relationship between the increasing professionalism of Aideed's militia (buttressed by the training and support of the "Afghan Arabs") and the decreasing professionalism of the several UNOSOM force contingents reflected especially the nature of the support Aideed was receiving—both from Somali clans and factions and from the Italians—as well as the weaknesses of the peace force in the other dimensions.

Finally, the inability of the several components of UNOSOM II to identify clearly the actions required to end the conflict greatly contributed to the failure of the operation. When the special representative to the secretary general and Force Command finally did identify the required actions, they could not get the other components to deliver what was needed in a timely fashion. What was accomplished was both too little and too late.

CHAPTER 13

Taking the "Enemy" into Consideration

Colombia's Three Wars, Plus One

Since the terrorist attacks on U.S. soil on September 11, 2001, political and military leaders in the United States have been reconsidering the global role and supporting strategies that the nation should carry into the future. They are now discussing these issues in terms of the political and military transitions required to deal more effectively with the global security problems that were submerged in the morass of the East-West conflict and unleashed by the Eastern European revolutions of 1989. In these terms, Colombia has emerged as the most compelling issue on the hemispheric agenda. That country's deeply rooted and ambiguous warfare has reached crisis proportions in that Colombia's "Hobbesian Trinity" of illegal drug trafficker, insurgent, and paramilitary organizations are creating a situation in which life is indeed "nasty, brutish, and short."[1]

The first step in developing a macro-level vision, policy, and strategy to deal with the Colombian crisis—in a global context—is to be clear on what the Colombian crisis is,[2] and what the fundamental threats implicit (and explicit) in it are. This is the point from which political and military leaders can start thinking about the gravity of the terrorist strategy employed by Colombia's stateless adversaries. It is also the point from which to begin developing responses designed to secure Colombian, hemispheric, and global stability.

THE CONTEXT OF THE COLOMBIAN CRISIS

In the 1930s and 1940s, chronic political, economic, and social problems created by a self-serving civilian oligarchy began to foment yet another crisis in a long list of internal conflicts in Colombian history, the most recent of which—the so-called War of 1000 Days—had ended in 1902 with the utter exhaustion of both the Liberals and Conservatives. In 1930, Liberal reformists came to power and deprived Conservatives of the control of the central government and extensive local patronage. The Liberals also initiated an ambitious social agenda that generated increasing civil violence between Conservative and Liberal partisans.[3]

With the end of the World War II, a new generation of Colombian politicians had come to the fore; they had grown up in the relative peace that had existed since 1902. By 1946, violence between Liberal and Conservative factions had begun to be felt, although its effects were largely confined to the rural parts of the country.

The catalyst that ignited the eighteen-year period called "the violence" (*la violencia*) in April 1948 was the "assassination" of Liberal populist Jorge Eliecer Gaitan. That murder sparked a riot known as the Bogotazo that left much of the capital destroyed and an estimated 2,000 dead. Although the government was able to contain the situation in Bogotá, it could not control the violence that spread through the countryside. Rural violence became the norm as an estimated 20,000 armed Liberal and Conservative combatants settled old political scores. Over the period from 1948 to 1956, *la violencia* claimed the lives of more than 250,000 Colombians.[4]

Within this unstable environment of uncontrolled violence, rural poverty, political disarray, and government weakness, the illegal drug industry began to grow and prosper. That prosperity in turn provided resources that allowed insurgent organizations to grow and expand. And later, as the Colombian government proved less and less effective in controlling the national territory and the people in it, the self-defense paramilitary groups emerged.[5] The common thread that permitted these violent nonstate actors to develop, grow, and succeed was—and is— adequate freedom of movement and action over time. The dynamics of the Hobbesian Trinity, within the context of the almost constant instability and violence that have plagued the country over the past several decades, have substantially expanded the freedom of movement and action of these insurgent and paramilitary groups and correspondingly eroded that of the state.[6] Virtually anyone with any kind of resolve can take advantage of the instability engendered by the ongoing Colombian crisis. The tendency is that the best-motivated and best-armed organization on the scene will eventually control that instability for its own narrow purposes.

COLOMBIA'S THREE WARS

The problem in Colombia is that that country (and its potential) is deteriorating because of three ongoing, simultaneous, and interrelated wars involving the illegal drug industry, various insurgent organizations (primarily the Revolutionary Armed Forces of Colombia [FARC]), and "vigilante" paramilitary groups (the United Self-Defense Groups of Colombia [AUC]). This unholy trinity of nonstate actors is perpetrating a level of corruption, criminality, human rights violations, and internal and external instability that, if left unchecked at the strategic level, can ultimately threaten Colombia's survival as an organized democratic state and undermine the political stability and sovereignty of its neighbors.

The Narcos

The illegal drug industry in Colombia can be described as a consortium that functions in much the same way as a multinational Fortune 500 company. Products are made, sold, and shipped; bankers and financial planners handle the monetary issues, and lawyers deal with the legal problems.[7] The consortium is organized to achieve super efficiency and maximum profit. It has its chief executive officers and boards of directors ("*capos*"); its councils, system of justice, public affairs officers, negotiators, and project managers; and its enforcers. Furthermore, it operates in virtually every country in the Western Hemisphere and Europe.[8]

Additionally, the illegal drug industry has at its disposal a very efficient organizational structure, the latest in high-tech communications equipment and systems, and state-of-the-art weaponry. With these advantages, decisions are made quickly that can ignore or supersede laws, regulations, decisions, and actions of most of the governments of the nation-states in which the organization operates. Narcos have also assassinated, bribed, corrupted, intimidated, and terrorized government leaders, members of the Colombian Congress, judges, law enforcement and military officers, journalists, and even soccer players. As such, the illegal drug industry is a major agent for destabilizing and weakening the state governmental apparatus.

At the same time, narco-cosmetic patronage to the poor, creation of their own electoral machinery, open participation in traditional political parties, and financing of friendly election campaigns has facilitated even greater influence over the executive, legislative, and judicial branches of the Colombian government. That activity exacerbates the necessity of meeting the narcos' needs and demonstrates the necessity of meeting their expectations and demands. Finally, all of these elements mitigate against responsible government—and against any allegiance to the notion of the public good and political equality. In that process, the consortium has achieved a symbiotic relationship with the state and in a sense is becoming a superstate within the state.[9]

The Insurgents

The FARC insurgents are essentially a Marxist-Leninist *foco* (i.e., insurrectionary armed enclave) in search of a mass base.[10] Because of their general lack of appeal to the Colombian population, the insurgents have developed a military organization designed to achieve the "armed colonization" of successive areas within the Colombian national territory.[11] The intent is to liberate and mobilize the "disaffected and the dispossessed" population into an alternative society.[12] That is, FARC responded to the lack of popular support by attempting to dominate the "human terrain," as did the communists in Vietnam. In this effort, FARC has proved every bit as ruthless as the Vietcong. Torture and assassination—to say nothing of kidnapping, extortion, intimidation, and other terrorist tactics—are so common as to go almost without comment except in the most extreme cases.[13] Strategically, operationally, and tactically, the FARC approach is the Vietnamese approach.[14]

All of this probably would have remained more or less out of sight and out of mind of mainstream Colombia in the underpopulated and underconsidered rural areas of the country if not for the financial support provided by the illegal drug phenomenon. In 1982, a decision was taken by the Seventh Conference of the FARC to develop links with the Colombian drug industry that would provide the money—and manpower—necessary for the creation of a "true democracy."[15] As a result, FARC expanded from approximately 2,000 guerrilla fighters in 1982 to more than a hundred "fronts" (company-sized units) with approximately 18,000–20,000 fighters in 2001. This illicit funding has provided the FARC with the capability of confronting regular Colombian military units up to battalion-size and of overrunning police and military installations and smaller units. Moreover, insurgent presence spread from 173 municipalities in 1985 to 622 in 1995, out of a total of approximately 1,050 *municipios*.[16]

Thus, Colombian insurgents have taken control of large portions of the "countryside" and placed themselves in positions from which to move into or dominate the major population centers. The stated intent is to create an army of 30,000 with which to stage a "final offensive" against the regular armed forces and "do away with the state as it now exists in Colombia."[17] Through the control of large parts of the Colombian national territory, the insurgents are thus replacing the state. In that connection, the insurgents are denying the state its traditional "monopoly on violence" and are challenging central government authority over the other parts of the country still under government control.

The Paramilitaries

The AUC self-defense organizations are semiautonomous regional alliances relatively independent of each other. Nevertheless, a central organization exists, primarily to develop a national coordinated strategy against the insurgents. Additionally, the AUC national front organization provides guidance, training, and other help to member organizations as necessary. Strategy and tactics of the AUC, interestingly, mirror those of the insurgents. These organizations seek to expand their control of grassroots levels of government—municipalities or townships (municipios) and rural areas (corregemientos)—and to exercise political influence through the control, intimidation, or replacement of local officials. And like the insurgents, the paramilitaries profit from drug trafficking.[18]

These "vigilante" groups began as self-defense organizations for the protection of family, property, and the law and order of a given geographical area. Because of the AUC's orientation against the insurgents and willingness to provide fundamental justice and personal security to those defined as noncollaborators with the insurgents, the paramilitary groups have consistently improved their standing in Colombian society. As examples, the number of small AUC groups has increased from 273 to more than 400, with an estimated current total of up to 8,000 active combatants. In 2001, AUC groups were estimated to have an armed presence in about 40 percent of the municipalities in the country. Moreover, the paramilitaries have organized, trained, and equipped "shock brigades" that since 1996 have become capable of successfully challenging insurgent military formations.[19]

Since the election of Alvaro Uribe as president in 2002, the situation with the AUC and other paramilitary groups of the Right has become more complicated. Uribe began a negotiation process that resulted in 2003 in a ceasefire and an agreement with the AUC to disband over the course of two years.[20] If this agreement works out, it will both remove a key player from the game and give the government time to replace the illegitimate paramilitary groups with legitimate auxiliary forces.

Despite paramilitary success against insurgents where the state has been absent or ineffective and despite the growing popular support for these purported self-defense groups, the Colombian government disavowed the AUC and other paramilitaries. Also, despite the truce with the AUC, the other groups have failed to go along—as have some disaffected elements of the AUC. As such, the paramilitaries have became a third set of competing nonstate actors—along with the various insurgent organizations and the illegal drug consortium—challenging

the authority of the state and claiming the right to control all or a part
of the national territory.

♦ ♦ ♦

Each of the three armed nonstate players in the Colombian crisis sepa-
rately generates formidable problems, challenges, and threats to the
state and the region in its own right. What, then, might be the effect of an
alliance of the willing against the state—even if that alliance represents a
complicated mosaic of mutual and conflicting interests?

THE NARCO-INSURGENT-PARAMILITARY NEXUS

Within the past three or four decades, the nature of insurgencies has
changed dramatically throughout the world with what Steven Metz
calls "commercial insurgency and the search for wealth."[21] One of the
most far-reaching transformations was first noticed (despite its having
been extant for many years) in the 1970s with the growing involvement
of insurgent forces with narco-traffickers in the Middle East and Asia—
Lebanon and the Golden Triangle come quickly to mind.[22] Thus, the
narco-insurgent connection is not new, and it is not confined to Latin
America. The question is not whether there might be an alliance between
the illegal drug industry, the insurgents, and the paramilitaries in
Colombia, since that reality has been understood and admitted to since
the 1980s.[23] The question is whether the threats associated with that
union warrant real concern and a serious strategic response.

Motives and Linkages

The motives for the narco-insurgent-paramilitary alliance are straightforward: accumulation of wealth, control of territory and people, freedom
of movement and action, and legitimacy. Together, these elements represent usable power—power to allocate values and resources in a society.

The equation that links illegal narcotics trafficking to insurgency and
to the paramilitaries in Colombia—and elsewhere—turns on a combina-

tion of need, organizational infrastructure development, ability, and the availability of sophisticated communications and weaponry.[24] For example, the drug industry possesses cash and lines of transportation and communication. Insurgent and paramilitary organizations have followers, organization, and discipline. While traffickers need these human resources to help protect their assets and project their power within and among nation-states, insurgents and paramilitaries are in constant need of logistical and communications support—and money.[25]

Together, the alliance has the economic and military power equal to or better than that of most nation-states in the world today. This alliance also has another advantage. All three groups possess relatively flat organizational structures and sophisticated communications systems; in combination, these elements create a mechanism that is considerably more effective and efficient than any slow-moving bureaucratic and hierarchical governmental system. That combined organizational advantage is a major source of power in itself.[26]

Internal Objectives

The narco-insurgent-paramilitary alliance is not simply individual or institutional intimidation for financial or criminal gain. Nor is it just the use of insurgents and AUC groups as "hired guns" to protect illegal drug cultivation, production, and trafficking—those are only business transactions. Rather, the long-term objective of the alliance is to control or substantively change the Colombian political system.[27]

Narcos may not seek the overthrow of the government, as long as the government is weak and can be controlled to allow maximum freedom of movement and action.[28] The insurgents, by contrast, seek the eventual destruction of the state as it exists. Whether or not the insurgents are reformers or criminals is irrelevant; their avowed objective is to take direct control of the government and the state.[29] Likewise, the paramilitaries want fundamental change, although they appear to be interested in creating a strong state that is capable of unquestioned enforcement of law and order. Whether or not the vigilante groups are "democratic" or authoritarian is also irrelevant, because for their own self-preservation, they have little choice but to take direct or indirect control of the state,[30] or surrender. The main group, AUC, has taken the second option, while AUC splinters and other paramilitaries have opted for the former. The common effort by the triad of narcos, insurgents, and paramilitaries—governmental change or overthrow—is therefore directed at the political community and its institutions. In this sense, the nexus is not simply criminal in nature. It is a major political-psychological-moral-military entity. At the same time, the countryside ceases to be a simple theater for combat and becomes a setting for the building of local power.

The Latin American security dialogue does not generally refer to the narco-insurgent-paramilitary nexus in terms of each group's individual identities—at least in the sense of a business organization striving to control the price of drugs, weapons, or general protection. Rather, it tends to refer to the whole entity as greater than the sum of its parts. The security dialogue is therefore concerned about a political-economic-military force that has become a major national and transnational non-state actor. That actor threatens national stability, development, and the future of the democratic system not only in Colombia but in the entire Western Hemisphere.[31] To be sure, this is a loose and dynamic merger subject to many vicissitudes, but the "marriage of convenience" has lasted and in some ways appears to be getting stronger.

External Objectives

In addition, the narco-insurgent-paramilitary alliance appears to have developed a political agenda for exerting leverage in the international as well as the Colombian national arena. The perceived goal of a given national agenda is to promote an "egalitarian social revolution" that will open up opportunities for "everybody"—and give the organization the legitimate basis for controlling some sort of nationalistic "narcocracy." The objectives of the international political agenda are to establish acceptance, credibility, and legitimacy among the sovereign states with which the general organization must negotiate.[32]

In that connection, the spillover effects of the illegal drug and arms trafficking industry have inspired criminal violence, corruption, and instability throughout Latin America in general, and Caribbean transit countries in particular. For some time, the illegal drug industry has operated back and forth across Colombia's borders and adjacent seas. Colombian insurgents and paramilitary groups have also made frequent incursions into the neighboring countries of Brazil, Ecuador, Panama, Peru, and Venezuela. The resulting destabilization undermines the security, well-being, and sovereignty of these countries.[33] A 1992 report by the West Indian Commission captures the essence of the scope and gravity of this "equal opportunity" phenomenon:

> Nothing poses greater threats to civil society in [Caribbean] countries than the drug problem, and nothing exemplifies the powerlessness of regional governments more. That is the magnitude of the damage that drug abuse and trafficking hold for our Community. It is a many-layered danger. At base is the human destruction implicit in drug addiction; but implicit also is the corruption of individuals and systems by the sheer enormity of the inducements of the illegal drug trade in relatively poor societies. On top of all this lie the implications for governance itself—at the hands of both external agencies engaged in international interdicting, and the drug barons themselves—the "dons" of the modern Caribbean—who threaten governance from within.[34]

Colombia is of particular importance in this situation because the narco-insurgent-paramilitary alliance represents a dual threat to the authority of that government—and to those of Colombia's hemispheric neighbors. It challenges the central governance of countries affected, and it undermines the vital institutional pillars of regime legitimacy and stability.[35]

The Internal and External Responses

Colombia, the United States, and other countries that might ultimately be affected by the destabilizing consequences of the narco-insurgent-paramilitary nexus in Colombia have tended to deal with the problem in a piecemeal fashion or even ignore it. For forty years the various Colombian governments dealt with the problem on an ad hoc basis—without a strategic-level plan, without adequate or timely intelligence, without a consensus among the political, economic, and military elites about how to deal with the armed opposition, and within an environment of mutual enmity between the civil government and the armed forces.[36] With the promulgation of Plan Colombia in 2000, there is at least the basis of a coherent political program—but not much else.[37]

For a number of years the United States tended to ignore the insurgent and paramilitary problems in Colombia, except for making rhetorical statements regarding the peace process, terrorist activities, and human rights violations. The United States focused its money, training, and attention almost entirely on the counterdrug campaign. Policy and decision makers saw the Colombian crisis in limited terms—the number of hectares of coca eradicated and the number of kilograms of coca detected and destroyed. And, even though the United States and Colombia have achieved a series of tactical "successes" in the coca fields, in the laboratories, and on the streets, the violent nonstate actors remain strong and become ever more wealthy. In the meantime, the nation-state of Colombia has continued to deteriorate and has become ever more fragile.[38]

In the post–September 11 world, the administration of President George W. Bush shifted its focus from one exclusively on drugs to one that addresses the problem of the narco-insurgent-paramilitary nexus. In practical terms, this meant support to Colombia's police and armed forces for counterinsurgency as well as counternarcotics operations. With the arrival of President Uribe on the scene, the United States has an ally who sees the problem in a similar way. Even the issue of Plan Colombia, initiated under the previous administrations of both governments, is seen as an important part of an overall Colombian strategy to resolve the crisis. A particularly significant problem is that the international funding promised by the European Union for development projects has not been forthcoming in anywhere near the amounts pledged. The result has been a major gap in the effectiveness of the strategy as a whole.

Finally, the other countries that are affected by the nefarious activities of the narco-insurgent-paramilitary nexus tend to do little more than watch, debate, and wrangle about what (if anything) to do about the seemingly new and unknown phenomenon.[39] As a consequence, positive political sovereignty, territory, infrastructure, stability, and security are quietly and slowly destroyed—along with tens of thousands of innocents.

◆ ◆ ◆

These are the realities of power operating in the Colombian crisis. Several years ago, Abimael Guzmán, leader of Peru's Sendero Luminoso and self-proclaimed "fourth sword of Marxism," made the assertion, "Except for power, everything else is illusion."[40] His words are aptly applied not only to the Sendero Luminoso and the Colombian narco-insurgent-paramilitary nexus, but also to the virtually infinite universe of gray area phenomena that exists in our current global security environment.

WHERE THE HOBBESIAN TRINITY LEADS: THE OTHER WAR

Nonstate criminal-terrorist organizations such as those that constitute the Colombian narco-insurgent-paramilitary nexus are significant political actors with the ability to compromise the integrity and sovereignty of individual nation-states. Yet neither the public policy nor the academic international relations community has completely grasped that fact—despite the terrorist attacks of September 11, 2001. Many political and military leaders see the violent nonstate actor as a low-level law enforcement issue that does not require sustained policy attention. Many academicians are accustomed to thinking of nonstate actors as bit players on a local stage. That may have been the case in the early stages of their development, but it is certainly not the case in Colombia today.[41]

Threats from the "Hobbesian Trinity" at work in Colombia today come in many forms and in a matrix of different kinds of challenges, varying in scope and scale. If they have a single feature in common, however, it is that they are systemic and well-calculated attempts to achieve political ends.[42] While the narco-insurgent-paramilitary union has generated many consequences, two are most pertinent in relation to that political objective: the erosion of Colombian democracy and the partial collapse of the state.

The Erosion of Colombian Democracy

The policy-oriented definition of democracy that has been generally accepted and used in U.S. foreign policy over the past several years is probably best described as "procedural democracy." This definition tends to focus on the election of civilian political leadership and—perhaps—on a relatively high level of participation on the part of the electorate. Thus, as long as a country is able to hold elections, it is still considered a democracy—regardless of the level of accountability, transparency, corruption, and ability to extract and distribute resources for national development and protection of human rights and liberties.[43]

In Colombia, several important paradoxes are evident in the democratic process. Elections are held on a regular basis, but leaders, candidates, and elected politicians are regularly assassinated. As an example, numerous governmental officials have been assassinated following their election—138 mayors and 569 members of parliament, deputies, and city council members were murdered between 1989 and 1999, along with 174 public officials in other positions. These numbers do not reflect the role played by intimidation, direct threats, and the use of violence on a given person and his family prior to elections. Nor do the numbers include the judiciary: in 1987 alone, 53 members of the judiciary were assassinated.[44] Additionally, although the media is free from state censorship, journalists and academicians who make their opinions known through the press are systematically assassinated.[45]

It is thus hard to credit Colombian elections as being either "democratic" or "free." Neither competition nor participation in elections can be complete in an environment where armed and unscrupulous nonstate actors compete violently to control government—before and after elections. Moreover, it is hard to consider Colombia a democratic state as long as elected leaders are subject to controls or vetoes imposed by vicious nonstate actors. As a consequence, Ambassador David Jordan argues that Colombia is an "anocratic democracy"; that is, Colombia has the procedural features of democracy but retains the features of an autocracy, in which the ruling elite faces no accountability.[46] Similarly, professor Eduardo Pizarro describes Colombia as a "besieged democracy" and writes about the "partial collapse" of the state.[47] In either case, the actions of the narco-insurgent-paramilitary alliance have pernicious effects on democracy and tend to erode the ability of the state to carry out its legitimizing functions.

The Partial Collapse of the State

The Colombian state underwent severe erosion on two general levels in the final decades of the past century. First, the state's presence and authority was physically diminished over large geographical portions of the country. This tendency is epitomized by the area known as the *despegue,* which President Andres Pastrana conceded to the FARC in his effort to reach a peace agreement. At the end of his term, Pastrana recognized that his policy had failed and terminated the official sanctuary. President Uribe has begun a concerted effort to recover the territory. Although the outcome remains in doubt, the new effort has achieved significant successes. Second, the idea of the partial collapse of the state is closely related to the nonphysical erosion of democracy. Jordan argues that corruption is key in this regard and is a prime-mover toward "narcosocialism."[48]

At the first level, the notion of "partial collapse" refers to the fact that there is an absence or only partial presence of state institutions in more than 60 percent of the rural municipalities of the country. Also, even in those areas that are not under the direct control of narco, insurgent, or paramilitary organizations, institutions responsible for protecting citizens—notably, the police and judiciary—have eroded to the point that they are unable to carry out their basic individual and collective security functions. The ramifications of this problem can be seen in two statistics: the murder rate in Colombia is the highest per capita in the world, at 41,564 in 1999;[49] yet the proportion of homicides that end with a conviction is less than 4 percent.[50] These alarming indicators of impunity strongly confirm that the state is not exercising adequate control of its territory or its people.

At the second level, nonphysical erosion of the state centers on the widespread and deeply entrenched issue of corruption. As an example, in 1993 and 1994 the U.S. government alluded to the fact that former president Ernesto Samper had received money from narcotics traffickers. On the basis of that information, in 1996 the United States withdrew Samper's visa and decertified Colombia for not cooperating in combating illegal drug trafficking. Subsequently, the Colombian Congress absolved Samper of all drug charges by a vote of 111–43.[51] Not surprisingly, another indicator of government corruption at the highest levels is found in the Colombian Congress. The Colombian Senate decriminalized the issue of "illicit enrichment" by making it a misdemeanor that could be prosecuted only after the commission of a felony.[52] Moreover, a former U.S. ambassador to Colombia asserted (in public and without fear of contradiction) that about 70 percent of the Colombian Congress "is bent."[53] Clearly, the reality of corruption in government favoring the illegal drug industry in Colombia is inimical to the public good.

Nonstate actors using asymmetric terrorist political-psychological strategies are pervasive in the world today. The general threat to regime stability and existence generated by the Colombian narco-insurgent-paramilitary nexus is only one case in point. In light of the dynamics of violent stateless actors, there is ample reason for worldwide concern—and action.

WHERE TO FROM HERE?

The type of conflict that has come to characterize the post–cold war era now involves entire civil populations—not just "enemy" military formations. In a conflict such as that in Colombia, the relative ability of all parties to shift the proverbial "hearts and minds"—and thus the support—of the people in their respective favor is what makes the difference between success and failure. As Carl von Clausewitz has pointed out, in this type of conflict, two nontraditional centers of gravity exist: public opinion, and the leadership that organizes and directs that opinion (see chapters 3 and 5).[54] For a targeted government such as Colombia to regain the allegiance of the populace, it must pursue several clusters of closely related political, economic, social, and security activities at the strategic (or macro) level. Much of the work entails very little glamour, excitement, or sound-bite material. But three basic elements are the proven keys to a stable, peaceful, and prosperous world: establishing security, capability building, and nurturing legitimate governance (see chapter 2).[55]

Establishing Security

Strategic planners must understand that once an illegal internal enemy— such as Colombia's "Hobbesian Trinity" of insurgents, narco-barons, and paramilitary "vigilante" groups—becomes firmly established, reform and development efforts are insufficient to deal with the entire security problem. The illegal violent adversaries finally will be defeated only by a superior organization and a political-military strategy designed to neutralize or eliminate it. The sum of the parts of a desired countereffort to deal with a major internal security threat requires not only a certain political competence to coordinate a wide-scale political-economic-psychological-military security effort, but also the ability and willingness to exert effective, discrete, and deadly force.[56] For ultimate effectiveness, political and security forces must also be able to deal with the illegal non-state opposition on the basis of the rule of law.[57]

Under President Uribe, the Colombian government has organized itself to achieve these ends through the creation of the Coordinating Center for Integrated Action. This organization exists to coordinate interagency actions in zones recently liberated by the military and involves effective cooperation among civilian agencies, the military, and the police.

In addition to the need to establish and maintain the rule of law, personal and collective freedom from intimidation and violence includes two other elements. First, there is a need to politically, psychologically, economically, and militarily isolate the warring political and criminal factions from all sources of internal and external support. Second, security implicitly requires sustaining life, relieving suffering, and regenerating a distressed economy. At its most basic level, however, enforcing and maintaining the rule of law takes us back to fair but effective control of the national territory and the people in it.[58]

Capability-Building

Another societal requirement for popular support of government and the state is that of political, economic, and social development both to maintain the internal strength of the state and to demonstrate that the government is responsive to the needs of the people. Underdevelopment and resultant individual and collective poverty are being recognized in the international security dialogue as the world's most overwhelming threats. To generate a viable political competence that can and will manage, coordinate, and sustain economic development in troubled regions such as Colombia, three additional goals must be accomplished: eliminate (or at least control) corruption; foster political consent on the part of the various components of the national population; and establish and maintain popularly accepted peaceful societal conflict resolution processes. Only with these building blocks in place do a legitimate civil society and sustainable peace become real possibilities.[59]

Nurturing a Civil Society and Legitimate Governance

Finally, in nurturing a sustainable civil society and a durable internal peace, policy makers also must develop the aggressive unified political-diplomatic, social-economic, psychological-moral, and military-police engagement in society that can and will deal effectively with the multidimensional root causes of instability and violence in places such as Colombia. Generally, such a stance requires a concerted anticorruption and public diplomacy effort. This is essential, as no policy, no strategy, and no internal or foreign engagement can be sustained for any length of time without the support of the people involved—a point first made in the modern era by Niccolò Machiavelli.[60] This takes us directly to the issue of legitimate governance, which cannot be legislated or decreed into existence but must be developed, sustained, and enhanced through concrete micro-level actions over time. Experience and theory alike support the premise that a decision that the political, psychological, economic, and security actions necessary to address this societal requirement are "too hard" will result in a final decision for failure.

Keys to Success

The common denominator of the security dialogue in Colombia and the Western Hemisphere is the underlying issue of national, regional, and international instability. Solutions to the instability exploited by Colombia's violent Hobbesian Trinity of nonstate actors are based on the fundamental requirement that the armed forces, police, and civilian elements of society develop a working relationship that will facilitate the achievement of legitimate national security.

The accomplishment of this most formidable task within the context of illegal insurgent, narco-trafficker, and paramilitary violence requires two fundamental strategic efforts: doctrinal and organizational change to achieve strategic clarity and greater effectiveness in any conflict situation, and the development of professional civil-military leadership to bring about unity of effort.[61] The first, strategic clarity, is developed at length in chapter 4. Fundamentally, however, strategic clarity depends on developing a holistic view of the end-state, in which partnership requirements are factored in. Within the current global security arena, a multiplicity of civilian and military agencies, organizations, and individual governments respond to complex emergencies such as that in Colombia. Duplication of effort and other immediate consequences of the absence of strategic clarity in such situations prove costly in political, personnel, and financial terms. These lessons have been abundantly demonstrated in such diverse cases as the natural disaster relief operation in Central America in the wake of Hurricane Mitch and the various man-made disaster relief, reconstruction, and occupation operations in the former Yugoslavia, Somalia, Afghanistan, and Iraq.[62]

At a base level, however, education—as well as organizational solutions—is needed. Effective partnership ultimately entails the type of professional civilian and military education and leader development that leads to effective diplomacy, as well as to professional competence.[63] Leader development and professionalization involves several educational and cultural imperatives. First, there is the need to attune military and police minds to cope with the many ways in which political and psychological considerations affect the use—and nonuse—of force. Second, there is a requirement to attune military, police, and civilian minds to understand that the number of battlefield victories or the number of "enemies" arrested or killed has meaning only to the extent that such achievements contribute directly to the legitimate strengthening of the state. Third, there is a need to teach military, police, and civilian participants in "our savage wars of peace" how to communicate and deal with a diversity of civil-military cultures. Fourth, there is a requirement to teach military and civilian officials at all levels how to cooperatively plan and implement interagency, international organization, nongovernmental organization, and coalition/partnership civil-military operations. And fifth, nonstate actors in an unstable situation such as that in Colombia are likely to have at their disposal both conventional and unconventional weaponry and tactics. Thus, education and training programs for stability operations must prepare peace forces to be effective warfighters[64] and to know when this is what they must be, as well as knowing when they must be something else.

These professionalization and leader development imperatives provide the bases of the understanding and judgment that civilian and military leaders must have to be successful in a contemporary conflict like that in Colombia. The ultimate requirement is to generate and encourage both a thinking process and an understanding of grand strategy that will allow one to be clear on what the situation in Colombia *is* and what it *is not*.[65]

PART IV

Where To from Here?

CHAPTER 14

REFLECTIONS ON THE SWORD MODEL OVER TWO DECADES

The SWORD Model makes no claim to the theoretical originality of any of its dimensions. It is original only in the way that the dimensions were combined and in how they were derived and tested. Although the model has been refined over the years, we have not been able to refute it. And we have certainly tried.

APPLYING THE SWORD MODEL TO THE CENTRAL STRATEGIC PROBLEM

From our perspective, the central strategic problem is one of legitimate governance. The admonition that the first task of the strategist is to understand the kind of war he must fight and not mistake it for something it is not remains as true today as when Clausewitz first wrote it. Indeed, the failure to heed it was reflected in the terrorist attacks of September 11, 2001.

To say that we had no warning of those attacks—even if we had no specific warning—is not an appropriate defense. Osama bin Laden's declaration of war against the United States was made in 1996, and again in 1998, and was part of the public domain. And he had conducted attacks against Americans and American interests both at home

and abroad since 1993. All of this was well known in the intelligence
and policy communities.

Even the academic world was aware of and had considered the
strategic implications of such attacks on the legitimacy of Western civilization (or the United States, if the focus is narrowed). In 1993 Samuel P.
Huntington published his seminal article "The Clash of Civilizations,"
which he later expanded into a book.[1] In both the article and the book,
Huntington argues the existence of wars of civilizations and predicts a
trend toward their expansion and dominance. Although Huntington does
not focus specifically on asymmetric threats, the inescapable conclusion to
be drawn from his analysis is that any near-term challengers of the West
will have to operate asymmetrically to have any chance of success.

Thus, without even taking into account our previous work (which
does address asymmetric warfare), there was every reason to expect
the kinds of challenges that the United States has since faced. Nor can it
be said that the U.S. military was oblivious to these challenges and
threats. A perusal of both joint doctrine and army doctrine throughout
the last decade of the twentieth century clearly shows such awareness.[2]

Our view of legitimate governance lies clearly within the Western
tradition in that the consent of the governed is essential to any perceived
government legitimacy. In addition, the performance of the governing
body is critical to such perception, along with the right and duty of the
citizen to hold leaders accountable through the mechanism of elections.
Many of the challenges to legitimate governance in the Western tradition come from outside that tradition. Neither the drug lords nor the
militant Islamists are from within that tradition (although for different
reasons). The drug lords are an old adversary in new dress coming
from among the tradition's outlaws. Like other criminals and tyrants of
all kinds, these have grown up within Western civilization but have
rejected its political and social ideals. Their goal is to control and prosper
without regard to the damage they may do to the body politic and civic.
By contrast, the militant Islamists have developed from within another
civilization, in Huntington's terms. Although they may well be outlaws in relation to that tradition, they—like the communists of Western
civilization—claim to be the true keepers of the flame. And their goal is
to establish their own legitimacy on their terms, at our expense.

Thus, whether the challenge comes from drug lords, political insurgents of the Left and Right, or Islamist jihadists, the result is a war for legitimacy. This was true in Central America in the 1980s, it was true in the Balkans and central Africa in the 1990s, and it has been true since the early 1990s in the Middle East, South Asia, and Southeast Asia. And in a peculiarly complex and continuously evolving way, it remains true in Colombia today.

APPLYING THE MODEL IN INSTRUMENTAL WAYS

The SWORD Model clearly reflects the values of Western civilization. However, it is not normative in and of itself. Rather, it is an instrumental model that makes the following basic claim: if a challenged government wishes to achieve success against an asymmetric adversary, it will have to address the seven dimensions of the model. Moreover, evidence points in the direction that failing to address those dimensions will result in failure against the adversary.

Among the more interesting aspects of our analysis over time is the changing emphasis on the importance of the individual dimensions of the model (see chapter 5). The quantitative test of the model demonstrated that the individual dimensions with the greatest predictive power were "support actions of the intervening power" and "legitimacy." Yet as we considered additional case studies, and particularly when we specifically addressed peace operations, we found that the importance of "unity of effort," in particular, had increased so that it rivaled that of "legitimacy."

Our contention, however, had never been that any one dimension was dominant but rather that a challenged government and its allies had to address all seven dimensions to ensure success. Our approach was and remains holistic, but it does not suggest that failure in any one dimension guarantees failure in all of them. Indeed, the world is far more complex than that. In many cases, the issue is one of the relative focuses of the adversaries on the dimensions. Thus, the government may well have problems with its unity of effort, but they may be less serious than those of its adversary. Similarly, both the government and the insurgents may want for legitimacy, with the government's lack in that area putting it at greater risk. Thus, as Sun Tzu observed, albeit in a different context, "When ten to the enemy's one, surround him; . . . When five times his strength, attack him; . . . If double his strength, divide him. . . . If equally matched, you may engage him. . . . If weaker numerically, be capable of withdrawing; . . . And if in all respects unequal, be capable of eluding him, for a small force is but booty for one more powerful."[3]

A BROAD FOCUS ON SPECIFIC
TYPES OF CONFLICT

The SWORD Model was developed to explain success (and failure) in counterinsurgency. It accomplished that extremely well, as we showed in our original article and subsequent studies. As our discussion of El Salvador illustrates, the government, its armed forces, and its allies successfully addressed all seven dimensions of the model. The resulting outcome clearly matched the description given by the late president José Napoleón Duarte of his desired end-state. Because the Salvadoran government and armed forces and the United States focused so strongly on the legitimacy dimension (without neglecting the other six), a negotiated peace was possible. The leaders of the Farabundo Martí National Liberation Front (FMLN) were able to claim that they, too, had achieved their goals and that the nation they were rejoining was much more humane, democratic, and legitimate. In fact, the FMLN might win the next elections and have to demonstrate that they can rule legitimately and more effectively than the current regime.

Peru's fight against Sendero Luminoso generally confirms what we found in El Salvador, but two critical differences are evident. First, although the Peruvian government's military victory over Sendero Luminoso was more complete than the Salvadoran victory over the FMLN, it left the Huallaga Regional Command more or less intact and remnants of the insurgent organization still at large in the Ayacucho region. Whereas El Salvador, by negotiation, had incorporated the

FMLN into the political process, Peru made no effort to do the same with the remaining Senderistas. Second, although the government won the legitimacy war, that victory not only was incomplete, but it was also thrown away. The Fujimori regime's *autogolpe* (self-coup) began a process of delegitimization that ended with the ouster of President Alberto Fujimori and his éminence grise, Vladimiro Montesinos, nearly a decade after the war was over. The fact that the new democratic government failed to deliver on performance—coupled with the survival of Senderista remnants—reignited the insurgency at a low level in 2003. By that time, the professionalism of the armed forces, police, and intelligence services had been seriously degraded, if not shattered, by the corruption of Fujimori and Montesinos and the relative incompetence of President Toledo. Once again, the holistic nature of the explanation given by the SWORD Model is manifest, this time with a negative outcome.

Colombia is simultaneously the third example of the application of the model to insurgency, an example of its application to the "war on drugs," and an example of its application to an ongoing situation. Although drugs played a part in the history of Sendero Luminoso, they were always more of a possible complication than an actual one. By contrast, in Colombia, cocaine is totally intertwined with the insurgency as well as the counterinsurgency. We adopted the term "Hobbesian Trinity" to describe the linkage among the insurgents, the "counter-insurgent" paramilitaries, and the narco-traffickers. Again, the seven dimensions of the SWORD Model provide an effective explanation of how well and how badly the Colombian government is doing in its war against the three kinds of adversaries in their various permutations.

Although Colombia's wars are far from over, the analysis to date suggests that the government has never really been challenged on the legitimacy dimension. This is not to say that it has overwhelmed its opponents with respect to legitimacy but rather that in recent years none of them has even contested the issue. The result has been a significant strength for the government by default. Yet its dominance of legitimacy has done nothing to bring the war to a swift and successful conclusion. Part of the reason for this stagnation is that the "Hobbesian

Trinity" has substituted the resources of the cocaine industry for legitimacy (the "external support to the insurgents" dimension). This strength of the adversaries has been compounded by weaknesses of the government in the dimensions of unity of effort, host country military actions, and actions against subversion. Recent efforts by the government to directly enhance its legitimacy, its military and police capabilities, its strategic planning, and consequently its unity of both command and effort have apparently begun to bear fruit. Combined with expanded U.S. military and nonmilitary support—of the right kind—the odds now are beginning to favor long-term government success.

The SWORD Model's applicability is not limited to insurgencies, however. With an adjustment in terminology, the model also applies to peace operations, such as in Somalia. Somalia is a complicated case of peace enforcement, demonstrating the links between some complex emergencies that require peacekeepers and other kinds of conflict. In the case of Somalia, data became available after September 11, 2001, that associated the conflict with international terrorism—and specifically with Al Qaeda. As a result, the situation in Somalia bears a very strong resemblance to classical counterinsurgency. Indeed, as our analysis demonstrates, the failure to adequately address all the dimensions of the SWORD Model led directly to the failure of the operation. The single most critical dimension was the lack of unity of effort—both within the UNOSOM II command structure and among the force providers, as well as *within* the American component of the operation.

The Somalia case illustrates one additional factor, which is likewise evident in one of the few exceptions to the model as originally drawn: the British loss in Aden. The SWORD Model predicted only a very low chance of a loss in Aden, but the British determination to withdraw by a specific date superseded the predictive value of the seven dimensions of the model. Similarly, in Somalia, the U.S. president lost his nerve and decided to cut his losses despite the fact that Mohammed Farrah Hassan Aideed's defeat was so complete that he was contemplating abandoning Mogadishu and Somalia altogether. The lesson is that the model presumes rational calculation of state interest by state actors. If they misread their interest or fail to act rationally, they can turn a winning hand into a losing one (Aden and Somalia) or vice versa (Cyprus).

Terrorism and homeland security are also addressed by the SWORD Model. The Italian case clearly supports the conclusions of the model while offering both cautionary and positive lessons for the United States. Although Italian terrorism was homegrown, many aspects of the threat are similar to those of international terrorism of the kind we currently face. The Italian case also makes very clear the relationship between terrorism and insurgency; from the point of view of the counter-terrorist, the differences are for the most part insignificant. Nevertheless, the terrorist exhibits a vulnerability that is less apparent among the more successful insurgents: the regular loss of legitimacy with every act of terror. The Italian terrorists never had any degree of legitimacy, and their actions worked against what little legitimacy their cause may have had.

Nevertheless, the failure of the Italian government to successfully deal with terrorist acts in the first days after the threat appeared gave the impression that the government was weak and could not protect its citizens or leaders from the threat. Its failure to provide security thus threatened its own legitimacy.

When we apply the lessons of the Italian case to international terrorism and homeland security, certain dimensions become especially visible. The most obvious of these is unity of effort. At first, the task of achieving unity of effort seems especially daunting. Not only does the United States have to achieve the same kind of unity that the Italians achieved at the national level—with all its attendant problems of inter-agency coordination and responsibility—but this must be accomplished in a federal system among governments at the local, state, and federal levels. As a single glimpse into just one problem, how much intelligence from national systems (particularly the Central Intelligence Agency and National Security Agency) can and should be shared with, for example, the sheriff of La Crosse County, Wisconsin? And how does one go about safeguarding the shared intelligence?

This question leads to a lesson that was not readily apparent in the Italian case. The terrorism threatening the United States today is worldwide in scope. At the moment, however, it is fairly focused on radical Islamist groups that are supported by state sponsors or elements within the governments that can manipulate governmental resources.

What this means is that the international dimension of homeland security and defense must take the fight to other countries, where all the instruments of power must be mobilized to deter would-be terrorists from becoming terrorists in reality, to apprehend or kill those who already are part of the terror network, and to break up networks so that they cannot threaten either the countries where they are located or any other. In other words, addressing terrorism both domestically and on an international scale requires that action be taken with respect to all seven dimensions of the model.

APPLICABILITY OF THE SWORD MODEL

Although the SWORD Model was developed to explain success or failure against insurgency, the fact that it has been applied over the past twenty years to a wide variety of contemporary conflicts suggests that its utility is much greater. The model set the focus of counterinsurgency squarely within the field of international relations rather than the comparative politics subfield of political science. Certainly, internal war and revolution were part and parcel of every insurgency, but our original focus was on how the United States could assist a threatened government to overcome the insurgents, and the names of the dimensions reflect this international bent.

A second feature of the SWORD Model is that its dimensions fully integrate all the instruments of power. We explicitly do not make Joseph Nye's distinction between hard and soft power but rather see what he calls hard and soft power in all the instruments. When an American four-star combatant commander (formerly called a commander in chief) stands beside an American ambassador trying to persuade a reluctant ally to do something he does not want to do, the visible threat of coercion exists alongside the persuasion. This was made clear to John Fishel in El Salvador in 1988 when U.S. ambassador Edwin Corr told the assembled Salvadoran high command that they needed to remember that they served the current elected government until that government was replaced by a newly elected one. The message was significantly reinforced by the presence of the commander in chief of U.S. Southern

Command, General Fred Woerner, in full uniform seated in the front row beside the Salvadoran chief of staff.

This integration of the instruments of power is found among the variables of all seven dimensions of the model. We should point out here that the "traditional" view of the instruments of power sees them as political, economic, psychosocial, and military. Other names have been introduced as substitutes (e.g., "diplomatic" for "political," and "informational" for "psychosocial"). The substitution of names is not particularly significant; however, the four main instruments comprise what we will call here "assets." Thus we can disaggregate the instruments of power to the degree that the terminology appears useful. Below are examples of the kind of disaggregation we have in mind:

- Political instrument assets: head of government summits, diplomats, Central Intelligence Agency, Drug Enforcement Administration, special envoys, former presidents and other high officials (official or unofficial capacity), journalists, private citizens
- Economic instrument assets: Treasury Department, Agency for International Development, Federal Reserve Bank, Export/Import Bank, Overseas Private Investment Corporation, Peace Corps, international financial institutions, UN Development Programme, allied development agencies, nongovernmental organizations, private investment, trade
- Psychosocial instrument assets: public diplomacy, government radio and television programming, psychological operations, Internet, communications media, public relations
- Military instrument assets: U.S. Army, U.S. Navy, U.S. Air Force, U.S. Coast Guard, National Guard, unified commands, Defense Security Cooperation Agency, regional centers, IMET program, JCET program, Joint Exercise program

As can be seen in the above list, the economic instrument (more than the others) relies on nongovernmental agencies to carry out actions, and government often acts in an enabling role rather than giving direction. Nevertheless, assets from each instrument of power can be combined with assets from other instruments of power in a variety of ways to address challenges in each one of the seven dimensions. In this way, the SWORD Model can incorporate a discussion of the traditional instruments of power (and the assets that constitute them), both for analysis of a conflict and to apply those instruments to achieve success in each of the dimensions while engaged in a conflict.

IMPLICATIONS

The implications of the research are both interesting and useful. The SWORD Model provides a tool for organizing the analysis of conflict in terms of both its internal and its external components. Thus, one can use the model to isolate the variables that are likely to lead to victory by one side or the other—or to stalemate—in terms of their domestic and international components. In this way, the model allows us to explain the outcome of past conflicts and gives us a tool for predicting not only the outcomes of ongoing conflicts (as with the guarded probability of success suggested for the Colombian government against the "Hobbesian Trinity"), but also the emergence of future fights. Informed by the model, John Fishel had observed previously that Haiti was particularly likely to revert to its preintervention situation as a failed state. In a book published in 1997 he stated, "In short, there is much cause for concern about whether democracy in Haiti ever will be upheld sufficiently to flourish on its own."[4] A year later he published the following assertion: "As the UNMIH mission wound down, the indications were that Haiti would most likely revert to the kind of authoritarian regime it has known since it won its independence—what scholars of Haiti have dubbed 'a predatory regime.'"[5] Even as the current text was being written, ten years after Haiti's last crisis, President Jean Bertrand Aristide's regime in Haiti was fighting for its very life—and losing—owing to its lost legitimacy as a result of a rigged election, political killings, charges of corruption, and a failure to be able to govern, among other issues. This is clearly not at all surprising to anybody who understands the SWORD Model.

Not only does the model provide a tool for explaining and predicting conflict, but it also has instrumental implications. If the United States, its coalition partners, and Iraqi friends wish to achieve a lasting victory, then they must successfully address the seven dimensions of the model. First, America must implement a strategy for achieving and maintaining legitimacy—both de jure and de facto. This means, first, recognizing our legal obligations as an occupying power. Even if we wish to call ourselves liberators, we are, de jure, occupiers and as such have certain legal obligations and certain legal rights in Iraq. The U.S. request for the support of the secretary general of the United Nations with regard to evaluating the possibility of early elections prior to ending the legal occupation was a step toward greater de jure legitimacy. So, too, was the promise to cede sovereignty to an Iraqi government at the end of June 2004. The fact that this was done greatly increased the legitimacy of the coalition, while the actual holding of successful elections in January 2005 may well signal the turning of the tide.

De facto legitimacy for the current governing council and the Coalition Authority and its successor interim Iraqi government, as well as any future Iraqi government, depends on performance. Security first and foremost, other government services, economic recovery, and accountability in general will go a long way toward achieving this goal. Equally important is the perception of these achievements on the part of the various groups that make up Iraq.

This point leads directly to the dimension of unity of effort. The first issue is unity within the coalition. This is not a problem in the military structure, where unity of command has been established. It does appear to be more or less problematic on the civil side and between the civilian leadership and the military. The relationship between civilian administrator Paul Bremer and military commander Lieutenant General Ricardo Sanchez appeared to be strong and positive but dependent on the personal ability of these two leaders to work together. The degree to which the coalition was able to achieve unity of effort among civilian agencies, both within and among the various governments, is simply not clear. No long-term working relationship between the coalition and the intergovernmental organizations, especially the United Nations, has been established. Finally, there is no indication of what, if any, unity exists between the coalition and important nongovernmental organizations. On the other side of the issue, discord is very real between members of the coalition, in particular the United States, and some of its NATO allies— France and Germany, specifically.

In their military actions the coalition members have done most things relatively well. Their initial troop strength, while more than adequate to defeat Saddam Hussein, was not sufficient to establish order at the moment it was needed. Subsequently, force size was adjusted so that it was large enough, but the buildup was not as rapid as necessary, which allowed a resistance movement to establish itself. Generally, coalition troops have done the right kinds of things. They have, as much as possible, operated as trainers and in a train-the-trainer role. They have also been very effective in a civil affairs role. And their combat operations have usually been in response to good intelligence and more and more often have been conducted in concert with the Iraqis.

In the area of support actions the coalition has shown more perseverance than the internal resistance and their external supporters expected. The real question is whether the strength and length of coalition support will be perceived as sufficient and positive by Iraqis who view the coalition in a favorable light and by the neutrals. Thus, the decision to transfer sovereignty to an Iraqi government by June 30, 2004, is a two-edged sword. Public opinion research conducted by the U.S. Department of State indicates a generally positive reaction on the part of Iraqis;[6] however, the decision to transfer sovereignty (thus ending the legal authority of the occupation) has limited the coalition's ability to control the political situation. The efforts by Shiite leader Grand Ayatollah Sistani to manipulate the method by which the government is chosen is a case in point. Setting an absolute date for the transfer is reminiscent of the decision by the British to withdraw from Aden precisely when they were on the verge of victory, and that transfer of sovereignty has seemingly led to a major challenge by Shiite pretender Muqtada al Sadr and his Mahdi Army.

A letter recovered from an Al Qaeda courier in early February 2004 sheds light on the kind of support the Iraqi resistance has received.[7] Clearly, Al Qaeda has been a source of support in terms of tactics, training, personnel, and some logistics. In addition, some evidence indicates the existence of varying degrees of support for the resistance from neighboring states, including Syria and Iran, both before and after the war itself. Most "sanctuary" for the insurgents appears to be internal (in both urban and rural locales). However, most sanctuary is found in the so-called Sunni Triangle north and west of Baghdad. Nevertheless, the letter suggests that external as well as internal support for the insurgents has been less than totally effective, hence the plea to Al Qaeda.[8]

Coalition forces have conducted a large number of operations against the resistance, achieving significant results over time. At the heart has been the effective collection and analysis of intelligence, which has resulted in the capture or death of at least forty-five of the fifty-five top leaders of the former regime and the resistance—including Saddam Hussein and his two sons. Nevertheless, key leaders of the resistance remain at large. Not so effective have been the coalition's use of psychological operations (including public diplomacy) and population and resource-control measures. The result has been the continuance of the war for legitimacy.

Finally, the coalition has been having some success in building Iraqi security forces. The regular forces appear to be getting good training and are showing high degrees of discipline. Similar results are apparently being achieved with the police and the civil defense forces as well. Despite the fact that members of various security forces are targets of suicide terror attacks, morale appears to be holding up—as seen in the continued desire of people to join the security forces, which are now beginning to lead raids on insurgent targets. Yet the willingness to work toward the collective security of the country may not be enough; Iraqi security forces fell apart when challenged in the Sunni Triangle by Baathist diehards and Al Qaeda and in the Shia south by the Mahdi Army. Lately, in the operation against the insurgent stronghold, Fallujah, Iraqi forces have acquitted themselves well.

Applied to the situation in Iraq, the model suggests that over the intermediate term, the coalition is likely to achieve success as long as it continues to do what it is doing and takes steps to improve upon its current actions. One major lesson from Iraq and all the other conflicts studied is that modern war is built around civil-military operations. Table 1 illustrates a matrix that could be used as a tool to assign assets against objectives in each of the dimensions. It could also be used to

TABLE 1.
Civil-Military Operations and the SWORD Model

Dimension	Asset						
	Political	Diplomatic	Agency for International Development	Department of Justice	Peace Corps	Central Intelligence Agency	Special Operations Forces
Military Actions of the Intervening Power	U.S. regional military commander	U.S. regional military commander	N/A	N/A	N/A	contract agents	army spcial forces battalion
Support Actions of the Intervening Power	president of United States	U.S. ambassador	USAID mission	legal attaché	Peace Corps volunteers	station chief	expanded security assistance office
Legitimacy	political support in United Nations	U.S. country team	USAID mission	U.S. International Criminal Investigative Training Assistance Program	Peace Corps volunteers	psychological operations	psychological operations
External Support to the Insurgents	foreign government rhetorical support	foreign government recognition	N/A	N/A	N/A	N/A	foreign terrorists
Actions versus Subversion	embassy public affairs officer	political section	AID small projects	legal attaché	volunteers in community development	station	psychological operations trainers
Host Country Military Actions	defense leadership	military liaison to United States	N/A	N/A	N/A	intelligence cooperation	host country psychological operations
Unity of Effort	presidential summits	foreign minister-level meetings	donor collaboration	Interpol	volunteer collaboration with local government	intelligence sharing	special forces trainers

Asset

Dimension	Combat Forces	Combat Support Forces	Combat Service Support Forces	Nongovernmental Organizations	Business Firms	Host Country
Military Action of the Intervening Power	attack helicopter company	military police trainer	civil affairs unit	N/A	Halliburton	host country military liaison
Support Actions of the Intervening Power	N/A	expanded security assistance office	expanded security assistance office	AID contracts with NGOs such as World Vision	Bechtel, local hires	host country foreign ministry
Legitimacy	N/A	N/A	civil affairs ministry support team	National Endowment for Democracy	N/A	electoral commission
External Support to the Insurgents	foreign terrorists	foreign intelligence support	foreign logistical support	terrorist organizations	terrorist business fronts	disaffected members of government
	N/A	military intelligence trainer	military engineer training team	N/A	private security c ompanies	host country special operations forces
Host Country Military Actions	infantry unit	military police	logistics command	N/A	contract logistical support	air force
Unity of Effort	infantry mobile training team	military police mobile training team	medical subject matter expert exchange	civil-military operations center	government contracting	host country interagency process

Note: Combat support forces include such task units as military intelligence; combat service support forces include medical, civil affairs, and logistics; nongovernmental organizations include such organizations as CARE.

Abbreviations: AID = Agency for International Development; N/A = not applicable; NGO = nongovernmental organizations; USAID = United States Agency for International Development.

identify what organization should have the lead in achieving each objective. If, for example, one could assume that the most effective form of unity of effort is unity of command, then command should be given to the agency with the preponderance of assets committed (unless there were compelling reasons not to do so).[9]

At the tactical level we see similar principles being applied in Afghanistan and to a lesser extent in Iraq, with the deployment of provincial reconstruction teams. These composite units combine special forces to provide security with civil affairs, psychological operations, engineers, military police, medical units, and sometimes regular infantry, which bring a multitude of capabilities to bear on a particular environment. In this, they are doctrinally similar to the concept of a security assistance force (now called the foreign internal defense augmentation force), which long has been part of American doctrine for low-intensity conflict. They do not, however, include civilian government and nongovernmental organizations, as contemplated in the civil-military operations matrix. One result has been an effort by the intergovernmental-nongovernmental organizations community in Afghanistan to, at a minimum, redirect the provincial reconstruction teams away from their war-winning mission and, at worst, to discredit them as illegitimate intelligence collectors.[10] Thus, the wars for legitimacy and unity of effort continue, with the problem found as much among allies as between adversaries.

CONCLUDING THOUGHTS

After two decades of application, we still find that the SWORD Model has great utility for scholars and analysts as well as practitioners. We have attempted here to show its broad applicability to the variety of "uncomfortable wars" that our nation and its allies face in the twenty-first century. In the current cliché, we find the glass not half-empty but rather half-full. The United States is far better equipped to fight the uncomfortable wars today than when we began this effort twenty years ago. The dimensions of the model have found their way into U.S. service and joint doctrine and have been and are being applied on the battlefields of the uncomfortable wars—with some degree of success.

AFTERWORD

Making and Implementing Policy Based on the SWORD Model

EDWIN G. CORR

In the early twenty-first century it is highly desirable, if not essential, for a superpower such as the United States to have a sound and well-understood paradigm for the conduct of its foreign policy and the protection of national interests. The national security community of the United States is gradually accepting the Manwaring Paradigm, and I think it imperative that the highest leaders of the country understand and endorse the model. However, leaders, scholars, and media pundits continuously discussed and debated the policy of containment during the period it served them, and such discussion can only benefit the effectiveness of any paradigm.

A national security paradigm does not permit practitioners to escape the challenging tasks of constantly educating themselves to know and understand the world. They must determine their nation's vital and important interests in the various regions of the world and how these relate to the overall national interests. They must be able to communicate and negotiate with other power contenders (state and nonstate) and make judgments about what actions to take *or not take* to protect and advance their nation's interests. The policy of containment did not keep our leadership from escalating the Vietnam intervention into a long and costly regional war. Indeed, containment toward the end of the cold war led us to support Islamist "freedom fighters" in Afghanistan, which had the unforeseen and unintended consequences of creating a pool of mujahedin, who later became Al Qaeda terrorists and suicide bombers on a persistent and violent anti-American jihad.

A national security paradigm provides a conceptual framework that aids decision makers and implementers in pointing out what they need to know about the world, in setting goals and programs, and in judging performance. It aids them in choosing ends, ways, and means. However, it is not a panacea, and it does not relieve policy makers from preparation and tough decisions. It essentially provides the necessary overarching framework within which decision makers can study, question, and act, and without which drift and uncalculated incoherence in foreign policy and national security are almost certain. Use of the Manwaring Paradigm in advance to analyze the invasion and occupation of Iraq by the United States would have avoided many of the pitfalls and problems encountered in that country.

THE SEVEN DIMENSIONS OF
THE MANWARING PARADIGM

Manwaring and Fishel stress that the seven dimensions of the paradigm form an integrated whole. However, legitimacy is the most significant dimension, and in later testing, unity of effort appears to be more important in most cases than the other five dimensions. Because of their relatively greater importance, I will later comment specifically on the dimensions of legitimacy and unity of effort.

Even though the seven dimensions should be considered as a whole for analysis or in the planning of operations, individual dimensions will at times be in contradiction or conflict. Moreover, the relationships of one dimension to others may vary according to the time period analyzed. Economists often usefully analyze matters in terms of the short, medium, and long term, and the same approach may be applied to this model. Ideally, we expect that in the long term all seven dimensions of the paradigm should be in harmony. However, this certainly is not true in the short term and sometimes not in the medium term. When the dimensions are not in accord, implementers of policy must make difficult decisions based on the projected impact on the long-term success of the endeavor. The Manwaring Paradigm provides the intellectual framework for making these judgments.

For instance, in the pursuit of legitimacy in El Salvador while I was the U.S. ambassador there, the embassy rightly placed tremendous emphasis on democratization and improving human rights. At the same time we urged the Salvadoran armed forces to be more aggressive in the execution of the war—in carrying out actions against the insurgents. We argued that there was not a conflict between these goals, but in the minds of some Salvadoran military officers, one seemed to exist. During the 1981 and 1989 insurgent "final offensives," when the very survival of the state was at stake, the Salvadoran armed forces executing the war resorted in the short term to violations of human rights, which in the medium and long term undercut the Salvadoran government's vital external support.

Similarly, U.S. armed forces' violations of prisoners' rights in Iraq in an effort to gain intelligence in 2004 undercut U.S. government legitimacy in occupying Iraq (which was based on helping to create a legitimate liberal governance) as well as the legitimacy of the Iraqi Governing Council being supported by the U.S. government. In this case the short-term advantages that were expected to be gained from intelligence (derived through coercion) threatened the long-term goal of stabilizing the state and turning it into a regional ally.

Having information and intelligence about the plans and actions of the enemy is a critical element in the effective execution of a counterterrorist or counterinsurgency strategy. In many countries of the world, intelligence is collected and used for partisan political interests or for personal gain, as well as to vanquish or contain enemies of the state. Thus, the goal of building effective intelligence agencies or concentrating all intelligence functions into a single agency can sometimes have negative political effects by giving undue advantages to the political group in power—and, as a consequence, can adversely affect legitimacy. There is a delicate balance.

Conflicts and contradictions frequently emerge among complementary yet competing goals. Choices in complex, violent environments usually are not between good and bad but between good and better or bad and worse. Policy makers and implementers are forced to make tough decisions, often with too little information and seldom with the ability to forecast confidently the future. Keeping in mind all the dimensions of the Manwaring Paradigm helps the decision makers gain clarity in these situations.

One of the seven dimensions of the paradigm is external support for the government that is the target of terrorist or insurgent aggression. The external power(s) want the targeted government to survive, consolidate governance, and move socially in directions compatible with the supporting powers' national interests. In all of my assignments one of the most frequent complaints by host governments (and especially by host country military) was their inability to plan and purchase needed equipment rationally because of the lack of certainty about the amount and availability of U.S. support and aid. The assumption is that the government under siege can do a better job on the battlefield and in economic development if foreign assistance is steady and certain. However, the reward or denial of aid is one of the essential tools for the American ambassador to influence targeted governments to improve in democratization, human rights, and economic reform—all of which relate to the most critical dimension of the paradigm, legitimacy.

Legitimacy, or a Populace-Based Governance Model

Legitimacy is statistically the most important dimension of the paradigm. In the literature derived from the SWORD Model, the emphasis is on populace-based governance as a means to legitimacy. One might assume that populace-based governance is identical with Western democracy, but it is not. Throughout history and still today, rulers and governments have derived legitimacy—the acceptance by those they govern—from different sources. Religion and the divine right of kings, the mandate of heaven, ideologies, dynastic inheritance, and different forms of accountability and democracy have all bestowed upon rulers the "right" to govern.

In a sense, all governments—even the most authoritarian ones—ultimately must be to some degree accountable to the people. The American value system makes us advocates for democracy, and the promotion of freedom has been an ideal of the people of the United States since the founding of our republic. Among the questions we must ask ourselves are how actively, in what conditions, and with what expectations (including time frames) our government should try to advance the spread of democracy abroad.

Most citizens of our nation suppose that in a democracy rulers are civilians who owe no higher allegiance to any subgroup of the citizenry—or to any single organization or institution within the society, or to any ideology or religion—than they do to the citizenry of the country as a whole. At the same time they are concerned with safeguarding the rights of individuals and minority groups. In many parts of the world this assumption has meant that leaders (and their supporters) backed by the U.S. government have had to compete with or wrest power from military regimes or civilian authoritarians supported by the national security services or private militias. As an additionally complicating factor, since the 1979 Iranian Revolution, authoritarianism has increasingly involved theocratic-based rulers.

A truism is that an external power, no matter how strong and rich, cannot impose on another country either national leaders or a form of government unless some critical mass of citizens of that country (not necessarily a majority) accepts that leadership or form of government. As one of these external powers, the United States can sometimes deter developments in another country, but it is much harder to make something happen. The key for the United States in seeking its foreign policy goals is to find and support (directly or indirectly, depending on the situation) capable and acceptable leaders and groups within a country who share to a great degree a similar vision for their country as does the United States. This generally means a government moving toward a more liberal and open society.

When providing external support to a government under siege or to a group that is trying to win power and the government, an external power must have a deep and thorough understanding of the cultures and languages of the country with which it is dealing. The directors of U.S. policy should consider every action taken in terms of how those actions impact on legitimacy and should maximize their efforts not to make the host government or leadership appear to be weak or ineffective.

When the United States is engaged directly in conventional war or the initial legal occupation of a country (for which the Manwaring Paradigm variables are also pertinent), the Powell Doctrine of employing directly overwhelming military force remains valid. The failure of the Coalition Provisional Authority and the United States to observe this doctrine in the 2003 invasion and initial occupation of Iraq resulted in the loss of social order and allowed an environment of looting, chaos, and anarchy in which an active, strong insurgency could emerge. Had the coalition forces invaded in larger numbers and not disbanded the Iraqi public security and armed forces, much of this turmoil might have been avoided. Nevertheless, except in conventional warfare and times of dire crises and likelihood of imminent failure, the American presence, especially military, should be kept as small as possible. Helping the host government gain legitimacy means that the U.S. government should avoid overt intervention and governance and that the U.S. ambassador and other highly placed U.S. government officials should be careful about making public statements about what the United States does or does not like. There are times when expressions of outrage or offense are appropriate, such as in cases of human rights violations and obvious election fraud.

To ensure that U.S. government actions contribute to the supported government's legitimacy, the American ambassador must at times restrain U.S. armed forces that often are eager to exercise their strength and to test new equipment and tactics. For instance, in El Salvador, Ambassador Thomas Pickering and Charge d'Affaires David Passage stopped the U.S. armed forces from retaliating directly with U.S. military strikes after the guerrillas' assassination of U.S. Marine Corps security guards in 1985. Similarly, in 1986, I refused landing to a U.S. Special Forces team flying to El Salvador to stage raids against insurgents after a guerrilla band kidnapped the daughter of President José Napoleón Duarte. Direct military action by the United States would have made the Salvadoran government appear weaker. It was better for the retaliation to be executed later by Salvadoran military forces, thus enhancing the legitimacy and sovereignty of the Duarte government. In keeping with these principles, I told my U.S. civilian and military staff in El Salvador that there were no American programs in El Salvador, only Salvadoran programs that we supported. We stressed the acronym KISSS, suggested by my military group commander, Brigadier General John Ellerson: "Keep It Simple and Salvadoran, Stupid."

Unity of Effort

A significant contribution to the Manwaring Paradigm body of literature was a speech by Ambassador David C. Miller in which he identified the pillars of success for any conflict to be "a sound theory of engagement; the development and use of appropriate instruments of national power to support the theories of engagement; and the promulgation of an executive branch management structure to ensure the effective implementation of the theories of engagement and the coordination of the various civil and military instruments of power."[1]

The last point, of course, refers to unity of effort. There are horizontal and vertical areas for coordination and support to achieve unity of effort. Those of us who have directed U.S. efforts in conflict situations abroad know that often a great gap exists between U.S. leaders in the implementation zone and policy makers at the highest levels (as well as with decision makers on equipment and training) in Washington.

Coordination, command, and control are usually good in the area of conflict when the effort is directed by the U.S. ambassador, as the personal representative of the U.S. president in the country to which the ambassador is accredited, and under the authority given to him or her by U.S. statute. The ambassador effects coordination and command through the "country team," which comprises the in-country heads of all U.S. government departments and agencies, including the Department of Defense. Coordination, command, and control can also be good in an area of conflict in those instances where the U.S. president has appointed a U.S. military commander to be in charge because of the level of violence and the direct engagement of U.S. forces. The Department of Defense also has the lead in situations of occupation under international law, as in the case of Iraq, although a civilian might be designated as the supreme executive in the conflict area.

Experience reveals that under military and Department of Defense command—even though U.S. military officers are well educated that the ultimate objectives of combat are to achieve political ends and goals—the political aspects of the conflict are too often relegated to lesser importance. This is true both in preparation stages and in implementation. Cases such as Vietnam, Panama, Somalia, and now Iraq show this tendency of the military, which occurs in part because of the immediacy of battle and the drive for military victory. This tendency gives rise to such oft-heard clichés as "win the battles, lose the war" and "win the war, lose the peace."

More important to the imbalance between use of military and civilian instruments is that civilian agencies lack the organization, human and material resources, and statutory mandates to play the roles they should. Equally important, to cope with post–cold war challenges, the national command organization and coordination mechanisms in Washington require further restructuring from their cold war edifice to facilitate effective coordination between the relatively scrawny U.S. civilian departments and the immense Department of Defense and the armed forces. Manwaring and Fishel constructively recommend sound reforms to remedy deficiencies in coordination within the executive branch for national security.

They also clearly emphasize that for better unity of effort to cope with political disorder and conflict abroad, there is need for better U.S. government coordination with nongovernmental organizations (NGOs), international governmental organizations (IGOs), and alliance and coalition partner states. Attention is also urgently needed to effect U.S. control over and coordination of private contractors. The revelation in 2004 that employees of U.S. government–contracted companies were involved in the torture of Iraqi and Afghani prisoners in U.S. military custody shocked the American public and the world. In addition, the implementation of urgently needed development projects in Iraq was greatly slowed by the contracting process of the U.S. government with private American companies. Perhaps the interrogation fiasco was an aberration, but the problem of controlling contracted private companies to ensure that they are working in harmony with U.S. efforts has become increasingly challenging since the great push to outsource everything possible from the government to private companies that began with the Reagan administration. The functions for which private companies are now contracted range from routine administrative matters to development projects to national security and intelligence. Private companies have moved into sensitive areas that were once considered to be reserved for government—functions that are best performed by people who are motivated primarily by serving the public interest rather than by profit.

Manwaring and Fishel's treatment of NGOs and IGOs highlights the problems, but they and the world are still short on solutions. A very high percentage of the U.S. resources for relief and economic development is now channeled through such organizations. However, the fact that NGOs espouse humane causes does not exempt them from error. For example, the actions of some NGOs are generally held to have exacerbated the number of persons massacred in the conflict between the Hutus and the Tutsis in Rwanda. Similarly, in El Salvador there was one Sister Cities organization from the United States that supported towns in the government-controlled areas and another that supported towns in areas under insurgent influence. As the U.S. ambassador I had to try to protect Americans working for both, even though our policy was against the guerrillas and even though the Americans helping towns in the guerrilla areas were entering zones where the Salvadoran armed forces prohibited entry to foreigners. Reconciling differences among NGOs, IGOs, and the U.S. government thus requires constant and great attention.

As the examples of NGOs and private contractors illustrate, a growing and pressing issue in the United States is the hybridization of our institutions. Many of our most important institutions are increasingly a mixture of public and private. Public institutions, such as state universities, more and more receive large parts of their budgets from the private sector; and increasingly, private companies get revenues from the taxpayers through government contracts. Clear lines between the public and the private sector are breaking down. Holding leaders and

their organizations accountable thus becomes difficult, and the repercussions spill over into the international arena and national security.
NGOs are aware of the problem, and their associations are attempting
to set standards and carry out self-policing, but these efforts remain
insufficient. Overcoming this quandary will require years of attention.

Manwaring and Fishel's emphasis on the essentiality of the civilian
factor in the equation for coping successfully with threats such as terrorism and insurgency is one of their greatest contributions. In the U.S.
civilian and military bureaucracies dealing with international relations
and national security, the preponderance of human and material
resources is so greatly weighted toward the Department of Defense, the
intelligence services, and the armed forces that our leaders and the
public invariably turn to them for solutions. The civilian bureaucracies
of the Department of State and the U.S. Agency for International Development (USAID) are too often ignored, even when logic might suggest
that a civilian agency would be more appropriate. The budget for the
Defense Department and armed forces for fiscal year 2005, with sup-
plements, will probably reach around $480 billion. By contrast, the
combined budgets for the State Department and USAID for economic
assistance will be about $30 billion. The U.S. defense budget will be as
large as the defense budgets of the top half of all the other countries of
the world combined. The State Department budget has for decades been
stretched very thin, and the USAID budget for economic development
assistance has for thirty years ranked about twenty-ninth in terms of
the percentage of gross domestic product (GDP) among the top donor
countries of the world. For decades, the Department of State has not had
enough personnel to perform well the tasks assigned to it by statute.
There is little or no slack in its budget.

The Department of Defense has seldom been fully engaged, because
its major responsibilities are to prepare for and to fight wars of small
and major magnitude, and because our nation, as a superpower, must
maintain excess war-fighting capacity. This situation has given the
Defense Department and the armed forces time to train people and to
think about the future. The State Department—lacking in personnel
and resources and constantly fully engaged throughout the globe—has
not enjoyed this luxury. Moreover, because the Department of Defense

budget is so large, that is the organization our top leadership must look to in times of national crises. Thus, one finds civil-military activities, psychological operations, and local and regional economic and social development programs in conflict zones abroad being carried out by U.S. military personnel in conjunction with foreign civilians to promote legitimate and needed governance. Such collaboration with civilians might be more effective if delivered by American civilians, especially from the viewpoint of building strong civilian governments to replace military governments and dictators propped up by armed forces.

Shifting some of the U.S. defense budget to the civilian side and remedying structural and organizational defects in our national security structure would require legislated reorganization and budget changes. Legislation is needed to do for the civilian side of the government what the Goldwater-Nichols Act of 1986 did for the military side. The legislation for homeland security is closing some gaps, but the foreign affairs civilian bureaucracy needs similar attention.

A similar imbalance exists in the allocation of resources within the Department of Defense and the armed forces. Force structure and resources are theoretically created and allocated against the seriousness and urgency of the threats confronting our country and on the basis of the costs of personnel and equipment required to counter the threats. Armed forces are sometimes accused of fighting the last war. They are equipped and organized in the manner that was successful in the last major war, rather than being allocated resources and being organized for the next. This sort of preparedness poses a serious problem in our current geopolitical environment, in which shifts and changes occur suddenly and dramatically.

An additional factor that slows U.S. military adjustment to such changes through the modification of force structure, equipment, and strategy is purely human. Armed forces officers are no less susceptible to the Weberian-described bureaucratic behavior of "empire building" than are civilians. Top military officers must fight to protect and increase their budgets and the continuance and growth of their units. In addition, some parts of the armed forces have powerful political allies in Congress, often reflecting economic interests from their constituents in the form of military installations or manufacturing facilities that profit from the existence of certain types of units, equipment, and weapons. Thus, at the end of the cold war, part of America's reluctance and slowness in revising strategy to accord with new threats was related to the bureaucratic drive of some U.S. military commands and political and economic groups to preserve existing forces and weaponry.

Understanding intramilitary politics of foreign forces supported by the United States is also essential in applying the Manwaring Paradigm. For instance, during El Salvador's civil war, the "campaign plan" for the Salvadoran government's distribution of development aid initially derived more from Salvadoran intramilitary politics than from civilian. The regional and departmental military commanders were insistent that resources and construction contracts go to all fourteen departments (states) rather than being concentrated where conflict and the need to win over the civilian populace were greatest. To bypass the military and departmental bureaucracies, President Duarte implemented a program of providing aid directly to mayors.

Another example of armed forces politics, which frequently appears in developing countries under attack by insurgents, is the almost universal resistance of the regular armed forces to the creation of civil defense (or militia) military organizations. This resistance arises not from concern that undisciplined units are more prone to human rights violations (as some might argue) but mainly because the regular army does not want a rival military force. For similar institutional political reasons, the armed forces of El Salvador fought against Colonel Renaldo Lopez Nuila's initiative to separate the police from the military in 1986. I secured funds to create a separate police academy and to separate graduates from the El Salvadoran armed forces of which they had formed an integral part.

As a final comment about the unity of effort dimension of the Manwaring Paradigm, the idea of trying to establish objectives and a common "vision" of the desired outcome among the various actors at the highest level is a necessary step. However, achieving a common vision among alliance and/or coalition partners; among cooperating NGOs, IGOs, and contractors; among and within the various civilian and defense departments and agencies of the U.S. government; and with the host country that is targeted by guerrillas or insurgents is extremely difficult. It seldom, if ever, can be fully achieved.

The partners in such endeavors are often strange bedfellows with a certain degree of common purpose but too diverse for complete overlap. Examples of such uncomfortable partnerships are clear from observations of Europe, the United States, and Russia in the Balkans; governments and NGOs in Africa; and Western and Arab partners in the first Gulf War. The partners involved must strive for as much agreement on goals and vision as possible, but they cannot neglect their states' basic or vital interests. They must proceed with the greatest shared vision possible. The military officers' continuous search for precision and clarity must often be set aside. Leaders cannot allow the quest for perfection to become the enemy of the higher good.

THE DIFFICULTY OF CHANGING PARADIGMS AND ORGANIZATION

Change is often difficult and painful. Change of an overarching, long-accepted strategy is particularly challenging. Though Franklin Delano Roosevelt began early to try to shift American opinion on U.S. involvement in the Second World War, it took the Japanese attack on Pearl Harbor to shock the nation into a declaration of war. Altering the U.S. policy and action on Vietnam was a long and nation-wrenching process. Shifting from the policy of containment toward the end of the cold war and after has been slow. National leaders who matured during the cold war era are still influenced by patterns of decisions and actions of that period even while attempting to deal with the new security situation. Although the U.S. government became engaged in a "war on terrorism" in the late 1960s in response to violent acts perpetrated by the Palestinian Liberation Organization, the nation as a whole did not give import to this struggle until Al Qaeda attacked the United States on September 11, 2001.

The Manwaring Paradigm has slowly and steadily gained acceptance among the U.S. national security community since its introduction in the mid 1980s by U.S. officials engaged in "uncomfortable wars." It was presented to the American public in Manwaring's 1991 *Uncomfortable Wars*. A quarter of a century later, it is hoped that this book will create a greater understanding of the Manwaring Paradigm. Familiarity with the model, and acceptance of it, by the American people, could only aid in completing the needed paradigm shift.

PERSISTENCE AND STEADFASTNESS

Success in applying the Manwaring Paradigm requires persistence and patience. Historical experience suggests that this is nothing new. After World War II it took Americans and their allies seven years in Japan and ten years in West Germany to achieve success.[2] South Korea required at least ten years. The United States gave up on Vietnam after only seven years. In terms of success stories against insurgents and terrorists, to name only two, the British needed fourteen years in Malaya, and the United States needed about twelve years in El Salvador.

Manwaring and Fishel have provided the United States the components of a new successful national security strategy. By applying it with persistence and patience we can protect our people and our country and protect and advance our interests for many years to come. May our top national leaders and our people collectively decide to do so.

NOTES

FOREWORD

1. Field Manual 100-20, *Military Operations in Low Intensity Conflict* (Washington, D.C.: Headquarters, Department of the Army, 1993); Field Manual 90-8, *Counterguerrilla Operations* (Washington, D.C.: Headquarters, Department of the Army, 1986); Field Manual 100-5, *Operations* (Washington, D.C.: Headquarters, Department of the Army, 1993); Joint Pub 3-0, *Operations* (Washington, D.C., 1993).

2. See also Phillip Chase Bobbitt, *A Shield of Achilles* (New York: Alfred A. Knopf, 2002).

3. John Galvin, "Uncomfortable Wars: Toward a New Paradigm," *Parameters* (December 1986): 2–8.

4. For the development of the SWORD Model see John Fishel, ed., *"The Savage Wars of Peace": Toward a New Paradigm of Peace Operations* (Boulder, Colo.: Westview, 1998), chapter 1.

5. Edwin G. Corr and David C. Miller Jr., "United States Government Organization and Capability to Deal with Low-Intensity Conflict," in Edwin G. Corr and Stephen Sloan, eds., *Low-Intensity Conflict: Old Threats in a New World* (Boulder, Colo.: Westview Press, 1992), p. 16, and idem, "Organizing for Operations Other Than War (OOTW) in the Post–Cold War Era," in Max G. Manwaring and Wm. J. Olson, eds., *Managing Contemporary Conflict: Pillars of Success* (Boulder, Colo.: Westview Press, 1996).

CHAPTER 1. INTRODUCTION TO THE SWORD MODEL

1. Morton Halperin, *Arms Control and Inadvertent General War* (Washington, D.C.: Special Studies Group, Institute for Defense Analyses, 1962); Harry Eckstein, ed., *Internal War: Problems and Approaches* (Westport, Conn.: Greenwood Press, 1980; originally published 1964); B. H. Liddell-Hart, *Strategy*, 2nd rev. ed. (New York: Signet, 1967); Harry G. Summers Jr., *On Strategy: The Vietnam War in Context* (Carlisle Barracks, Penn.: Strategic Studies Institute, 1981); General G. R. Galvin, "Uncomfortable Wars: Toward a New Paradigm," *Parameters* (December 1986): 2–8; Sam C. Sarkesian, *U.S. National Security: Policymakers, Processes, and Politics* (Boulder, Colo.: Lynne Rienner Publishers, 1989).

2. Suffice it to say here that six similar theoretical approaches were tested against each other. The second SWORD Model predicted at an adjusted $R^2=.90$. That is, that model predicted at about 90 percent and was the best performer of the various models tested. The second model by General Paul Gorman (a former commander of U.S. Southern Command) tested next best at an adjusted $R^2=.73$. Additionally, the SWORD Model was statistically significant at the .001 level. In these terms, there is only one chance in a thousand that the result came about by accident. Thus, the model is more powerful than any of its component parts (dependent variables), indicating that victory or success is achieved as a result of the balanced application of all seven of the dependent variables. Finally, the real value of the model may be found in its utility as a conceptual framework within which data from specific conflict situations might be placed and understood. See John Fishel's account of the process in *"The Savage Wars of Peace": Toward a New Paradigm of Peace Operations* (Boulder, Colo.: Westview Press, 1998), 3–17.

3. Max G. Manwaring and John T. Fishel, "Insurgency and Counter-Insurgency: Toward a New Analytical Approach," *Small Wars and Insurgencies* (Winter 1992): 272–310.

4. Frank Kitson, *Warfare as a Whole* (London: Faber and Faber, 1987).

5. Interview conducted by Max Manwaring in the course of developing the SWORD Model.

6. Max G. Manwaring, *Internal Wars: Rethinking Problem and Response* (Carlisle Barracks, Penn.: Strategic Studies Institute, 2001).

7. Ralph Peters, "Constant Conflict," *Parameters* (Summer 1997): 10. See also idem, "The Culture of Future Conflict," *Parameters* (Winter 1995–96): 18–27.

8. Summers, *On Strategy*, 121.

9. Sun Tzu, *The Art of War*, trans. Samuel B. Griffith (London: Oxford University Press, 1971), 122.

10. Manwaring and Fishel, "Insurgency and Counter-Insurgency," 281–82.

11. Michael Howard, "The Forgotten Dimensions of Strategy," *The Causes of War* (London: Temple-Smith, 1981), 109.

12. Manwaring and Fishel, "Insurgency and Counter-Insurgency," 282.

13. Robert Thompson, *Defeating Communist Insurgency: The Lessons of Malaya and Vietnam* (New York: Praeger, 1996), and *Revolutionary War in World Strategy, 1945–69* (New York: Taplinger, 1970).

14. Manwaring interviews, 1984–present.

15. Ibid.

16. Niccolò Machiavelli, *The Art of War* (New York: Da Capo Press, 1965), 7–8, 84–85, 122–23.

17. Winston S. Churchill, *The Birth of Britain* (New York: Dodd, Mead, 1956), 160–65; David Howarth, *1066: The Year of the Conquest* (New York: Penguin Press, 1977), 156–65.

18. Churchill, *Birth of Britain*; Howarth, *1066*.

19. Sun Tzu, *Art of War*, 63.

20. Carl von Clausewitz, *On War*, ed. and trans. Michael Howard and Peter Paret (Princeton, N.J.: Princeton University Press, 1976), 88.

21. Ibid., 88–89.

22. Summers, *On Strategy*, 1.

23. Manwaring interviews, 1984; Eric M. Bergerud, *The Dynamics of Defeat: The Viet Nam War in Hau Nghia Province* (Boulder, Colo.: Westview Press, 1991); Phillip B. Davidson, *Viet Nam at War: The History, 1946–1975* (Norton, Okla.: Providio Press, 1988); Bernard B. Fall, "Indochina, 1946–1954" and "South Viet-Nam, 1956 to November 1963," in D. M. Condit, et al., eds., *Challenge and Response in Internal Conflict: The Experience in Asia*, vol. 1 (Washington, D.C.: American University Center for Research in Social Systems, 1968), 237–66, 333–68; Michael A. Hennessy, *Strategy in Viet Nam: The Marines and Revolutionary Warfare in I Corps, 1965–1972* (Westport, Conn.: Praeger, 1997); Richard A. Hunt, *Pacification: The American Struggle for Viet Nam's Hearts and Minds* (Boulder, Colo.: Westview Press, 1995); Andrew F. Krepinevich Jr., *The Army and Viet Nam* (Baltimore, Md.: Johns Hopkins University Press, 1986); Bruce Palmer Jr., *The Twenty-Five-Year War: America's Military Role in Vietnam* (Lexington: University Press of Kentucky, 1984); Dave Richard Palmer, *Summons of the Trumpet* (San Rafael, Calif.: Presidio Press, 1978); Jeffrey Race, *War Comes to Long An: Revolutionary Conflict in a Vietnamese Province* (Berkeley: University of California Press, 1972); U. S. Grant Sharp, *Strategy for Defeat: Viet Nam in Retrospect* (San Rafael, Calif.: Presidio Press, 1978); Summers, *On Strategy*.

24. Manwaring interviews, 1984.

25. Quotation attributed to Secretary McNamara in David K. Shipler, "Robert McNamara Meets the Enemy," *New York Times Magazine*, August 10, 1997, p. 50.

26. Vo Nguyen Giap, *People's War, Peoples' Army* (New York: Frederick A. Praeger, 1962), 34.

27. Howard, "Forgotten Dimensions of Strategy," 101–15.

28. Sun Tzu, *Art of War*, 63–64, 77–79.

29. Clausewitz, *On War*, 92–93.

30. See note 23 above.

31. Ibid.

32. Ibid.

33. Ibid.

34. Giap, *People's War, Peoples' Army*, 36.

35. Manwaring interviews, 1984–1985.

36. Ibid.; Race, *War Comes to Long An*; Edward G. Lansdale, *In the Midst of Wars: An American's Mission to Southeast Asia* (New York: Harper and Row, 1972); John J. McCuen, *The Art of Counter-Revolutionary War* (Harrisburg, Penn.: Stackpole Books, 1966); Robert W. Komer, *Bureaucracy Does Its Thing: Institutional Constraints on US-GVN Performance in Vietnam* (Santa Monica, Calif.: Rand Corporation, 1972).

37. See note 36.

38. Clausewitz, *On War*, 80–81, 89.

39. Manwaring interviews, 1984–1985.

40. Maxwell D. Taylor, *Swords and Plowshares* (New York: Norton, 1972), 247; see also Norman B. Hannah, *The Key to Failure: Laos and the Viet Nam War* (Lanham, Md.: Madison Books, 1987).

41. Anthony James Joes, "Isolating the Belligerents: A Key to Success in the Post-counterinsurgency Era," in Max G. Manwaring and Anthony James Joes, eds., *Beyond Declaring Victory and Coming Home: The Challenges of Peace and Stability Operations* (Westport, Conn.: Praeger, 2000), 241–42.

42. Manwaring interviews, 1984–present; Summers, *On Strategy*, 1.

43. Manwaring interviews, 1984–present.

44. Clausewitz, *On War*, 596.

45. Manwaring interviews, 1984–present.

46. Clausewitz, *On War*.

47. Summers, *On Strategy*, 83.

48. Sun Tzu, *Art of War*, 73.

49. Manwaring interviews, 1984–present.

50. Ibid.

51. General John R. Galvin, "Uncomfortable Wars: Toward a New Paradigm," *Parameters* (December 1986): 2–8.

52. Manwaring interviews, 1984–present.

53. Sun Tzu, *Art of War*, 88.

54. This mandate was the impetus behind the SWORD Model. See Fishel, *"Savage Wars of Peace."*

55. Ibid.

56. Guillermo M. Ungo, "The People's Struggle," *Foreign Policy* (Fall 1983): 51–63. Manwaring interviews with Ungo (1986–1987) and José Napoleón Duarte (1986).

57. José Napoleón Duarte, *Duarte: My Story* (New York: G. P. Putman's Sons, 1986), 279.

58. SWORD Papers (out of print), archived by a private research organization, the National Security Archives, in Washington, D.C.

59. Ibid.

60. Ibid.

61. Ibid.

62. This and the subsequent statement regarding the Italian case are consensus statements based on author interviews with senior Italian Caribinieri officials. Manwaring is particularly indebted to General Carlo Alfiero for his guiding remarks. However, the intent is to allow anonymity for those who object to their names being made public. Thus, these statements are cited as Carabinieri nonattribution interviews.

63. SWORD Papers.

64. Ibid.

65. Ibid.

66. Ibid.

67. Manwaring interviews, 1984–present.

68. SWORD Papers.

69. Komer, *Bureaucracy Does Its Thing*.

70. SWORD Papers.

71. The reality of this assertion is demonstrated in former president Bill Clinton's speech that opened the summit meeting of world leaders at the United Nations in September 2000. In that speech, he urged the gathering to prepare national and international institutions for a new age in which unilateral and international forces will have to "reach rapidly and regularly inside national boundaries to protect threatened people." *New York Times*, September 7, 2000, p. 1.

72. Leslie H. Gelb, "Quelling the Teacup Wars," *Foreign Affairs* (November–December 1994): 5.

73. Manwaring interviews, 1984–present.

74. Gelb, "Quelling the Teacup Wars."

75. Liddell-Hart, *Strategy*, 367.

76. Qiao Liang and Wang Xiangsui, *Unrestricted Warfare* (Beijing: PLA Literature and Arts Publishing House, 1999), 10–11.

77. Steven Metz, *The Future of Insurgency* (Carlisle Barracks, Penn.: Strategic Studies Institute, 1993).

78. Field Manual 90-8, *Counterguerrilla Operations* (Washington, D.C.: Headquarters, Department of the Army, 1986).

79. Ian Beckett, "Forward to the Past: Insurgency in Our Midst," *Harvard International Review* (Summer 2001): 63.

80. The assertions in this section are derived from Manwaring interviews, 1984–present.

81. Steven Metz and Douglas V. Johnson II, *Asymmetry and U.S. Military Strategy: Definitions, Background, and Strategic Concepts* (Carlisle Barracks, Penn.: Strategic Studies Institute, 2001), pp. 4–12. Also see Metz, *Future of Insurgency,* pp. 13–15.

82. Joint Pub 3-0, *Operations* (Washington, D.C., 1993); Joint Pub 3-07, *Military Operations Other Than War*; Field Manual 100-5, *Operations* (Washington, D.C.: Headquarters, Department of the Army), 1993; Field Manual 100-20, *Military Operations in Low Intensity Conflict* (Washington, D.C.: Headquarters, Department of the Army, 1993).

83. Colonel William G. Hanne, "Doctrine not Dogma," *Military Review* (June 1983): 11–25.

CHAPTER 2. THE REALITY OF THE CONTEMPORARY GLOBAL SECURITY ENVIRONMENT

1. See World Conflict and Human Rights Map, prepared by Berto Jongman with the support of the Goals for Americans Foundation, St. Louis, Missouri, 2000.

2. See David Callahan, *Unwinnable Wars: American Power and Ethnic Conflict* (New York: Twentieth Century Fund, 1997), 57–59, 111–14, 143–45.

3. Leslie H. Gelb, "Quelling the Teacup Wars," *Foreign Affairs* (November–December 1994): 5.

4. Thomas F. Homer-Dixon, "On the Threshold: Environmental Changes as Causes of Acute Conflict," *International Security* (Fall 1991): 76–116, and *Environment, Scarcity, and Violence* (Princeton, N.J.: Princeton University Press, 1999), 133–68. Also see Daniel C. Esty, Jack Goldstone, Ted Robert Gurr, Barbara Harff, Pamela T. Surko, Alan N. Unger, and Robert S. Chen, "The State Failure Project: Early Warning Research for U.S. Foreign Policy Planning," in John L. Davies and Ted Robert Gurr, eds., *Preventive Measures: Building Risk Assessment and Crisis Early Warning Systems* (New York: Rowman and Littlefield, 1998), 27–38.

5. Robert D. Kaplan, "The Coming Anarchy," *Atlantic Monthly* (February 1994): 72–76, and *The Coming Anarchy* (New York: Random House, 2000), pp. 3–57.

6. See, for example, Enrico Fenzi, *Armi e Bagagli: Un Diario dalle Brigate Rosse* (Genoa: Costa and Nolan, 1987), 76.

7. George P. Shultz, "Low-Intensity Warfare: The Challenge of Ambiguity," remarks by the secretary of state at the Low-Intensity Warfare Conference at the National Defense University in Washington, D.C., January 15, 1986. In the context of Afghanistan, also see Saad Mehio, "How Islam and Politics Mixed," *New York Times* op-ed, December 2, 2001; Alan Schwartz, "Getting at the Roots of Arab Poverty," *New York Times* op-ed, December 3, 2001.

8. Michael Howard, "The Forgotten Dimensions of Strategy," *The Causes of War* (London: Temple-Smith, 1981), 101–15. Also see Gregory D. Foster, "America and the World: A Security Agenda for the Twenty-First Century," *Strategic Review* (Spring 1993): 29; Anthony Lake, "From Containment to Enlargement," remarks by the assistant to the president for national security affairs, Johns Hopkins University, Washington, D.C., September 21, 1993; Max G. Manwaring, "Beyond the Cold War," in Max G. Manwaring, ed., *Gray Area Phenomena: Confronting the New World Disorder* (Boulder, Colo.: Westview Press, 1993), 63–76.

9. Frank Kitson, *Warfare as a Whole* (London: Faber and Faber, 1987), 68–71. In the context of the terrorism in Italy in the early 1980s, also see "Testimony of Red Brigadist Roberto Buzzatti," quoted in Richard Drake, *The Aldo Moro Murder Case* (Cambridge, Mass.: Harvard University Press, 1995), 143; "Testimony of Antonio Savasta," quoted in Drake, *Aldo Moro Murder Case,* 51; "Testimony of Patricio Pecil," recorded in Sue Ellen Moran, ed., *A Rand Note: Court Depositions of Three Red Brigadists* (Santa Monica, Calif.: Rand, February 1986), 47.

10. Kitson, *Warfare as a Whole.* Also see Steven Metz and Douglas V. Johnson II, *Asymmetry and U.S. Military Strategy: Definitions, Background, and Strategic Concepts* (Carlisle Barracks, Penn.: Strategic Studies Institute, 2001); Steven Metz, *The Future of Insurgency* (Carlisle Barracks, Penn.: Strategic Studies Institute, 1993).

11. Martha Crenshaw, "The Causes of Terrorism," *Comparative Politics* (July 1981): 379–99. Also see Caleb Carr, "Terrorism as Warfare," *World Policy Journal* (Winter 1996–97): 1–12; Walter Laquer, "Postmodern Terrorism," *Foreign Affairs* (September–October 1996): 24–36; Bernard Lewis, "The Revolt of Islam," *The New Yorker,* November 30, 2001.

12. See note 11.

13. See Anthony Lewis, "The Inescapable World," *New York Times,* October 20, 2001; Thomas L. Friedman, *The Lexus and the Olive Tree* (New York: Anchor Books, 2000), 327–47.

14. See *Patterns of Global Terrorism 2000* (Washington, D.C.: U.S. Department of State, April 2001). Also, for nearly one hundred years, a strong current of Latin American sociopolitical thought has been influenced by Uruguay's foremost literary figure, José Enrique Rodo. He urged the youth of his country and the rest of Spanish America to reject the materialism of the United States and to cling to the spiritual and intellectual values of their Spanish heritage. These sentiments are strongly reflected in Latin American reaction to contemporary U.S. policy. See José Enrique Rodo, *Ariel* (any English or Spanish edition); see also Lars Schoultz, *National Security and United States Policy toward Latin America* (Princeton, N.J.: Princeton University Press, 1987). For more generalized treatment of the problem, see Mehio, "How Islam and Politics Mixed"; Schwartz, "Getting at the Roots of Arab Poverty"; Friedman, *The Lexus and the Olive Tree.* Also see Niall Ferguson, "2001," *New York Times Magazine,* December 2, 2001.

15. The authors are indebted for this observation to Kimbra Fishel. Her ideas on this subject are developed in "Challenging the Hegemon," published in a special edition of *Low Intensity Conflict Law Enforcement* 11, no. 2/3 (Winter 2002) and subsequently in a book to be published by Frank Cass, London.

16. SWORD Papers.

17. See Martha Crenshaw, ed., *Terrorism in Context* (University Park: Pennsylvania State University Press, 1995).

18. Other terms are also frequently applied. "Operations other than war" is a U.S. military term and is elaborated in Field Manual 100-20, *Military Operations in Low Intensity Conflict* (Washington, D.C.: Headquarters, Department of the Army, 1993). "Teapot wars" is Leslie Gelb's term. "Spiritual and commercial insurgencies" are concepts developed by Metz and Johnson, *Asymmetry and U.S. Military Strategy.* "Unrestricted warfare" comes from Qiao Liang and Wang Xiangsui, *Unrestricted Warfare* (Beijing: PLA Literature and Arts Publishing House, 1999).

19. Olson, "International Organized Crime."

20. Jessica Mathews, "Power Shift," *Foreign Affairs* (January–February 1997): 58–60.

21. Michael Radu, *Afghanistan: The Endgame,* Foreign Policy Research Institute, "E-Notes," November 19, 2001. Also see John Mackinlay, "War Lords," *Defense and International Security* (April 1998): 24–32.

22. Two studies that make this point are Angel Rabasa and Peter Chalk, *Colombian Labyrinth: The Synergy of Drugs and Insurgency and Its Implications for Regional Stability* (Santa Monica, Calif.: Rand, 2001); Eduardo Pizarro, "Revolutionary Guerrilla Groups in Colombia," in Charles Bergquist, Ricardo Penaranda, and Gonzalo Sanchez, eds., *Violence in Colombia: The Contemporary Crisis in Historical Perspective* (Wilmington, Del.: SR Books, 1992).

23. General Sir Robert Thompson was one of the first to note this phenomenon, as a result of his experience in Malaysia. Author interview, January 16, 1986, in Washington, D.C. Also see Robert Thompson, *Defeating Communist Insurgency* (New York: Praeger, 1966), 87.

24. Ralph Peters, "Constant Conflict," *Parameters* (Summer 1997): 10. Also see "The Culture of Future Conflict," *Parameters* (Winter 1995–96): 18–27.

25. Lewis, "Inescapable World."

26. Edwin G. Corr and Max G. Manwaring, "Confronting the New World Disorder," in Manwaring and Olson, *Managing Contemporary Conflict,* 40–41. It is heuristically valuable to portray the relationships among these elements in a mathematical formula: S = (MI + E) X PC.

27. The following discussion of elements of a strategic stability equation benefited from author interviews with Lieutenant General William G. Carter III (USA, Ret.), November 30, 1998, and March 2, 1999, Washington, D.C.; author interviews with General Charles E. Wilhelm (USMC, Ret.), February 9, 2001,

and June 22, 2001, Reston, Va.; and author interview with General John R. Galvin (USA, Ret.), August 6, 1997, Boston, Mass.

28. Also see Walter Clarke and Robert Gosende, "The Political Component: The Missing Vital Element in U.S. Intervention Planning," *Parameters* (Autumn 1996): 35–51; Joseph N. McBride, "Coping with Chaos: Democracy and Stability in the Post-counterinsurgency Era," in John N. Petrie, ed., *Essays on Strategy XI* (Washington, D.C.: National Defense University Press, 1994), 299–325.

29. Author interview with Ambassador Edwin G. Corr, April 9, 1992, Washington, D.C.

30. Carter and Galvin interviews.

31. Author interviews with Ambassador Robert Oakley, June 2–3, 1999, Washington, D.C.

32. Carter and Galvin interviews.

33. Ibid.; see also Thomas J. Daze and John T. Fishel, "Peace Enforcement in Somalia: UNOSOM II," in John T. Fishel, ed., *"The Savage Wars of Peace": Toward a New Paradigm of Peace Operations* (Boulder, Colo.: Westview Press, 1998), 156–58.

34. Doctrinal requirements are derived from statements made at the first Bosnia-Herzegovina After Action Review (BHAAR I) Conference, held at Carlisle Barracks, Pennsylvania, on May 19–23, 1996.

CHAPTER 3. THE CENTRAL POLITICAL CHALLENGE IN THE GLOBAL SECURITY ENVIRONMENT

1. For discussions of these phenomena, see Samuel Huntington, *The Clash of Civilizations and the Remaking of World Order* (New York: Simon and Schuster, 1996); Robert D. Kaplan, *The Coming Anarchy* (New York: Random House, 2000).

2. SWORD Papers.

3. See Anthony Lewis, "A Regime of Thugs," *New York Times*, May 5, 2001; Max G. Manwaring, "Italian Terrorism, 1968–1982: Strategic Lessons That Should Have Been Learned," *Low Intensity Conflict and Law Enforcement* (Summer 1998): 121–35.

4. SWORD Papers.

5. See David Callahan, *Unwinnable Wars: American Power and Ethnic Conflict* (New York: Twentieth Century Fund, 1997), 57–59, 111–14, 143–45.

6. Jacques Maritain, *Man and the State* (Chicago: University of Chicago Press, 1963), 19.

7. See Max G. Manwaring and Edwin G. Corr, "Confronting the New World Disorder: A Legitimate Governance Theory of Engagement," in Max G. Manwaring and Wm. J. Olson, eds., *Managing Contemporary Conflict: Pillars of*

Success (Boulder, Colo.: Westview Press, 1996), 31–47; Robert W. Jackman, *Power without Force* (Ann Arbor: University of Michigan Press, 1993), 138–54.

8. As an example, see Larry Diamond, Juan J. Linz, and Seymour Martin Lipset, *Politics in Developing Countries: Comparing Experiences with Democracy* (Boulder, Colo.: Lynne Rienner Publishers, 1990). Also see John Locke, *Of Civil Government* (Chicago: Gateway, n.d.); John Stuart Mill, *Considerations on Representative Government* (Chicago: Gateway, 1962); Jean–Jacques Rousseau, *The Social Contract*, trans. Charles Frankel (New York: Hafner Publishing Company, 1951); George H. Sabine and Thomas L. Thorson, *A History of Political Theory*, 4th ed. (Hinsdale, Ill.: Dryden Press, 1973); Sheldon S. Wolin, *Politics and Vision: Continuity and Innovation in Western Political Thought* (Boston: Little, Brown, 1960); Leo Strauss and Joseph Cropsey, *History of Political Philosophy*, 2nd ed. (Chicago: University of Chicago Press, 1972); J. L. Talmon, *The Origins of Totalitarian Democracy* (New York: Frederick A. Praeger, 1960).

9. See Max G. Manwaring and John T. Fishel, "Insurgency and Counter-Insurgency: Toward a New Analytical Approach," *Small Wars and Insurgencies* (Winter 1992): 272–310.

10. Ibid.

11. Ernest Evans, "Our Savage Wars of Peace," *World Affairs* (Fall 2000): 90–94.

12. Ibid.; also see Max G. Manwaring and Court Prisk, *El Salvador at War: An Oral History* (Washington, D.C.: National Defense University Press, 1988), 186–92.

13. Manwaring and Prisk, El *Salvador at War.* See also multiple author interviews with Dr. Alvaro Magana conducted in San Salvador, El Salvador, over the period 1987–1992.

14. Manwaring, "Italian Terrorism."

15. Brian Freemantle, *The Fix: Inside the World Drug Trade* (New York: Tom Doherty Associates, 1986), 242. Also multiple author interviews with Ambassador Edwin G. Corr over the period 1987–2002.

16. See Gabriel A. Almond and Sidney Verba, *The Civic Culture: Political Attitudes and Democracy in Five Nations* (Newbury Park, Calif.: Sage Publications, 1989; originally published 1963).

17. Ibid.

18. Robert F. Zimmerman, "Thailand: The Domino That Did Not Fall," in Edwin G. Corr and Stephen Sloan, eds., *Low–Intensity Conflict: Old Threats in a New World* (Boulder, Colo.: Westview Press, 1992), 92.

19. SWORD Papers. Also see Max G. Manwaring and Courtney E. Prisk, "The Umbrella of Legitimacy," in Max G. Manwaring, ed., *Gray Area Phenomena: Confronting the New World Disorder* (Boulder, Colo.: Westview Press, 1993), 88–89.

20. Constitution of the United States.

21. Manwaring and Fishel, "Insurgency and Counter-Insurgency." Also author interview with General Sir Robert Thompson, January 1986, Washington, D.C.

22. Manwaring and Fishel, "Insurgency and Counter-Insurgency." Also see David Passage, *The United States and Colombia: Untying the Gordian Knot* (Carlisle Barracks, Penn.: U.S. Army War College, 2000), 21–27.

23. "Strike Two against Wahid," *Economist*, May 5, 2001, p. 34.

24. Joseph N. McBride, "America Coping with Chaos at the Strategic Level: Facilitator for Democratic Stability in the Post–counterinsurgency Era," in Max G. Manwaring and Anthony James Joes, eds., *Beyond Declaring Victory and Coming Home: The Challenges of Peace and Stability Operations* (Westport, Conn.: Praeger, 2000), 214–15.

25. See Manwaring and Fishel, "Insurgency and Counter-Insurgency."

26. McBride, "America Coping with Chaos," 214–15.

27. Author interviews with Lieutenant General William G. Carter III (USA, Ret.) on November 30, 1998, and March 2, 1999, in Washington, D.C.; author interviews with General Charles E. Wilhelm (USMC, Ret.) on February 9, 2001, and June 22, 2001, in Reston, Va.; and author interview with General John R. Galvin (USA, Ret.), August 6, 1997, in Boston, Mass.; also see Walter Clarke and Robert Gosende, "The Political Component: The Missing Vital Element in U.S. Intervention Planning," *Parameters* (Autumn 1996): 35–51.

28. Eugene V. Rostow, *Toward Managed Peace: The National Security Interests of the United States, 1759 to the Present* (New Haven, Conn.: Yale University Press, 1993), 4.

CHAPTER 4. STRATEGIC CLARITY

1. Additionally, this and subsequent assertions in this section are based on the consensus reached in three different after-action reviews (AAR), hereafter cited as AAR author interviews. The first Bosnia-Herzegovina AAR (BHAAR I) conference was held at Carlisle Barracks, Pennsylvania, May 19–23, 1996. The second Bosnia-Herzegovina AAR (BHAAR II) conference was held at Carlisle Barracks, Pennsylvania, April 13–17, 1997. The third AAR, which dealt with the U.S. Army effort in the aftermath of the Hurricane Mitch disaster in Central America, was held at Carlisle Barracks, Pennsylvania, September 20–23, 1999. The BHAAR process provided more than seventy-five recommendations to the chief of staff of the U.S. Army that focused on those strategic and high operational-level lessons learned that related to his Title 10, Joint Chiefs of Staff (JCS), and advisory responsibilities. The Hurricane Mitch AAR provided about fifty recommendations for the U.S. Army deputy chief of staff for operations that also centered on Title 10, JCS, and other advisory functions. Manwaring was

the rapporteur at the three conferences and wrote the subsequent reports. In addition to the BHAAR process, the Bosnia case is well documented by the periodic report of the United Nations Secretary General and by a number of other lessons-learned projects, including "Multidisciplinary Peacekeeping: Lessons from Recent Experience" (UN Lessons Learned Unit, Department of Peacekeeping Operations, December 1996).

2. Carl von Clausewitz, *On War*, ed. and trans. Michael Howard and Peter Paret (Princeton, N.J.: Princeton University Press, 1976), 596.

3. AAR author interviews.

4. A very good illustration of this point is found in Jean Larteguy, *The Centurians* (New York: E. P. Dutton, 1961), 181–82.

5. Clausewitz, *On War*. See also Max G. Manwaring, ed., *Uncomfortable Wars: Toward a New Paradigm of Low Intensity Conflict* (Boulder, Colo.: Westview Press, 1990).

6. AAR author interviews.

7. Author interviews with Lieutenant General William G. Carter III (USA, Ret.), November 30, 1998, and March 2, 1999, Washington, D.C.

8. *New York Times,* May 14, 2000, section 4, p. 1.

9. Carter interview.

10. Author interview with General John R. Galvin (USA, Ret.), August 6, 1997, Boston, Mass. The complete interview is included in the Spring 1998 special issue of *Small Wars and Insurgencies,* p. 9, no. 1.

11. Ibid.

12. Ibid.

13. Boutros Boutros-Ghali, *An Agenda for Peace: Preventive Diplomacy, Peacemaking, and Peacekeeping* (New York: United Nations, 1992), 33.

14. Galvin interview.

15. Interview with General Anthony Zinni (USMC, commander-in-chief, United States Central Command), June 2, 1999, Washington, D.C.

16. The material laying out organizational mechanisms to achieve unity of effort derives from AAR author interviews.

17. Ibid.

18. Ibid.

CHAPTER 5. A POPULACE-ORIENTED MODEL FOR REEXAMINING CONTEMPORARY THREAT AND RESPONSE

1. Max G. Manwaring and John T. Fishel, "Insurgency and Counter-Insurgency: Toward a New Theoretical Approach," *Small Wars and Insurgencies* (Winter 1992): 272–310.

2. See, for example, John T. Fishel, ed., *"The Savage Wars of Peace": Toward a New Paradigm of Peace Operations* (Boulder, Colo.: Westview Press, 1997).

3. We have used some variations in wording for the names of the seven dimensions in our different publications; however, the variables that make up each factor remain the same no matter what we have chosen to call the dimension. See Fishel, *"Savage Wars of Peace,"* 15 n. 18, for a full discussion of this issue.

4. Manwaring and Fishel, "Insurgency and Counter-Insurgency," 281.

5. Ibid., 283.

6. Fishel, *"Savage Wars of Peace."*

7. Max G. Manwaring and Kimbra L. Fishel, "Lessons That Should Have Been Learned: Toward a Theory of Engagement for 'The Savage Wars of Peace,'" in Fishel, *"Savage Wars of Peace,"* 199.

8. Steven R. David, "Saving America from the Coming Civil Wars," *Foreign Affairs* (January–February 1999): 116.

9. The SWORD Model dimensions as applicable to the populace-oriented extension are the strength or weakness of a country's governmental institutions (i.e., the degree of a regime's legitimacy); the ability to reduce internal and external support for an illegal challenger; the type and consistency of outside support for a targeted government; the credibility of objectives and degree of organization for unity of effort; the level of discipline and capabilities of security forces; and the effectiveness of the intelligence apparatus.

10. Kalman H. Silvert, *Expectant Peoples: Nationalism and Development* (New York: Random House, 1963), 32.

11. Manwaring and Fishel, "Insurgency and Counter-Insurgency."

12. Boutros Boutros Ghali, "Global Leadership after the Cold War," *Foreign Affairs* (March–April 1996): 86–98, and *An Agenda for Peace* (New York: United Nations, 1992), 11, 32–34.

CHAPTER 6. THE "ALMOST OBVIOUS" LESSONS OF PEACE OPERATIONS

1. Boutros Boutros-Ghali, *An Agenda for Peace* (New York: United Nations, 1992), 11, 32–34.

2. See John T. Fishel, ed., *"The Savage Wars of Peace": Toward a New Paradigm of Peace Operations* (Boulder, Colo.: Westview Press, 1997), 9.

3. Max G. Manwaring and Edwin G. Corr, "Confronting the New World Disorder: A Legitimate Governance Theory of Engagement," in Max G. Manwaring and Wm. J. Olson, eds., *Managing Contemporary Conflict: Pillars of Success* (Boulder, Colo.: Westview Press, 1996), 31–47.

4. See, for example, Walt W. Rostow, *The Stages of Economic Growth: A Non-Communist Manifesto* (Cambridge: Cambridge University Press, 1960).

5. Gabriel A. Almond and James S. Coleman, eds., *The Politics of the Developing Areas* (Princeton, N.J.: Princeton University Press, 1960), 537.

6. Nancy Birdsall and Richard Sabot, "Inequality as a Constraint in Latin America," *Development Policy* [Inter-American Development Bank] 3, no. 3 (September 1994): 1–5.

7. Ibid., 1.

8. Robert H. Bates, ed., *Toward a Political Economy of Underdevelopment* (Berkeley: University of California Press, 1988), 331–32.

9. This observation appears in one form or another throughout the eight books of Carl von Clausewitz, *On War*, ed. and trans. Michael Howard and Peter Paret (Princeton, N.J.: Princeton University Press, 1976).

10. George F. Kennan, "Morality and Foreign Policy," *Foreign Affairs* (Winter 1985–86): 205–18.

CHAPTER 7. STRATEGIC VISION AND INSURGENCY IN EL SALVADOR AND PERU

1. Carl von Clausewitz, *On War*, ed. and trans. Michael Howard and Peter Paret (Princeton, N.J.: Princeton University Press, 1976), 88.

2. Ibid.

3. B. H. Liddell-Hart, *Strategy*, 2nd rev. ed. (New York: Signet, 1967), 324.

4. See Cynthia McClintock, *Revolutionary Movements in Latin America: El Salvador's FMLN & Peru's Shining Path* (Washington, D.C.: USIP Press, 1998).

5. In 1986, Fishel was on a staff visit to Peru, where he saw evidence of cooperation developing between the United States and the Peruvian National Intelligence Service (SIN). In 1987, he was invited to lecture at the Center for Higher Military Studies (CAEM), at which time he introduced senior Peruvian officers and civilians to the dimensions of the SWORD Model. Later that same year, he led a subject matter expert exchange (SMEE) team from the U.S. Southern Command that addressed many of the problems dealt with in this chapter from the SWORD Model perspective. One of the issues that the SMEE raised was the need for a civil militia kind of program similar to what was then being attempted in El Salvador and Guatemala (with differing degrees of success) and would later be adopted in Peru.

6. "The Role of Unity in the Revolutionary War: An Interview with Juan Chacón," in Marlene Dixon and Suzanne Jonas, eds., *Revolution and Intervention in Central America* (San Francisco, Calif.: Synthesis Publications, 1983), 41, 43. Also see Joaquin Villalobos, "El Estado Actual de la Guerra y Sus Perspectivas," *ECA Estudios Centroamericanos* (March 1986): 169–204.

7. Chacon interview in Dixon and Jonas, *Revolution and Intervention*, 40–46.

8. On October 11, 1980, the Unified Revolutionary Directorate (DRU) announced the founding of the Farabundo Martí National Liberation Front (FMLN). It was made up of the Popular Liberation Forces–Farabundo Martí, the People's Revolutionary Army, and the Armed Forces for National Liberation. On November 11, the Armed Forces of National Resistance were also incorporated into the FMLN.

9. Rafael Menjivar, "The First Phase of the General Offensive," in Dixon and Jonas, *Revolution and Intervention,* 63–69.

10. Max G. Manwaring, interview with Miguel Castellanos, September 25, 1987, San Salvador, El Salvador.

11. Marta Harnecker, "From Insurrection to War: An Interview with Joaquín Villalobos," in Dixon and Jonas, *Revolution and Intervention,* 70–71.

12. Chacón interview, in Dixon and Jonas, *Revolution and Intervention,* 42.

13. José Napoleón Duarte, *Duarte: My Story* (New York: G. P. Putnam's Sons, 1986), 170. President Duarte stated that this was the lowest point in the conflict as far as he was concerned.

14. The assertions made here and below regarding the Salvadoran conflict are the result of interviews with approximately forty senior Salvadoran and U.S. officials (hereafter cited as El Salvador nonattribution interviews) and with Dr. Guillermo M. Ungo of the Democratic Revolutionary Front (FDR) and former FMLN commandant Miguel Castellanos. These interviews were conducted between October 1986 and December 1987 in El Salvador, the United States, and Panama. A complete list of interviews and interviewees may be found in Max G. Manwaring and Court Prisk, *The Conflict in El Salvador: An Oral History* (Washington, D.C.: National Defense University Press), 1988.

15. Max G. Manwaring, interview with Dr. Guillermo M. Ungo, December 11, 1987, Panama City, Panama.

16. Villalobos, "El Estado Actual."

17. Ungo interview.

18. Ibid.

19. Villalobos, "El Estado Actual"; Harneker, "From Insurrection to War," 69–105.

20. Villalobos, "El Estado Actual"; Harneker, "From Insurrection to War," 69–105.

21. El Salvador nonattribution interviews; Villalobos, "El Estado Actual"; Harneker, "From Insurrection to War," 69–105.

22. Clausewitz, *On War,* 619.

23. For example, the peace agreement required the separation of the public security forces from the military and the establishment of a national civil police. Although this was hailed as a great victory for the FMLN, it merely confirmed actions that had been initiated by the Duarte administration in 1987 and

put on the back burner (but not abandoned) by the government of Alfredo Christiani.

24. Robert Thompson, *Revolutionary War in World Strategy* (New York: Taplinger, 1970), 8; cited in Max G. Manwaring and John T. Fishel, "Insurgency and Counter-Insurgency: Toward a New Analytical Approach," *Small Wars and Insurgencies* (Winter 1992): 290.

25. John D. Waghelstein, "Military-to-Military Contacts: Personal Observations—The El Salvador Case," *Low Intensity Conflict and Law Enforcement* (Summer 2001): 22.

26. Ibid., 35.

27. Hugh Byrne, *El Salvador's Civil War: A Study of Revolution* (Boulder, Colo.: Lynne Rienner Publishers, 1996), 95.

28. Fishel discussed this point in a chapter of *Winning the Peace*, ed. John W. De Pauw and George A. Lutz (Westport, Conn.: Praeger, 1992), where he addressed two types of military civic action—mitigating and developmental. What the El Salvador armed forces (ESAF) were doing was mitigating civic action in its purest form. See also John T. Fishel and Edmund S. Cowan, "Civil-Military Operations and the War for Moral Legitimacy in Latin America," *Military Review* (January 1988): 50–52.

29. Civil defense units tended to be more effective in the western departments such as Santa Ana. There, Fishel observed a well-equipped and well-trained unit from Metapan coming in from local patrolling. Clearly, it had high morale and appeared to be very effective. However, the ESAF, particularly early on, was none too keen on the civil defense program, and there was the appearance that the program was related to the repressive ORDEN organization, an appearance that the FMLN was all too ready to exploit. Finally, a reading of the peace accords shows that the civil defense units were, indeed, to be disbanded. The program has been replaced by one of the few effective reserve military forces in Latin America, which showed its mettle in the relief operations in the wake of Hurricane Mitch.

30. In 1986 Fishel observed the operations of one immediate-reaction battalion (BIRI), the Bracamonte, in one of the major conflict zones. The remaining discussion of military strategy is based on his observations as executive officer of the Combined ESAF Assessment Team in 1987 and 1988.

31. This force, which at its peak reached 56,000, comprised about 11,300 volunteers (20 percent of the entire force).

32. As executive officer of the Combined ESAF Assessment Team, Fishel was present at the briefing.

33. The assertions made here and below regarding the Peruvian insurgency are the result of interviews with approximately fifty lieutenant colonels and colonels, and their naval equivalents, conducted May 16–20, 1988, in Lima, Peru, by Max G. Manwaring. While they have no objection to the published use

of the interviews, these officers have asked that a nonattribution policy be applied to them. (Hereafter cited as Peru nonattribution interviews.)

34. "El Discurso del Dr. Guzmán," in Rogger Mercado U., *Los Partidos Politicos en el Peru* (Lima: Ediciones Latinamericanos, 1985), 85–90 (hereafter cited as Guzmán speech); and Abimael Guzmán, *Desarrollar la Guerra Popular Sirviendo a la Revolucion Mundial* (Lima: Comite Central del Partido Comunista del Peru, 1986), 82–88.

35. José Carlos Mariátegui, *Siete Ensayos de Interpretación de la realidad Peruana* (Caracas, Venezuela: Biblioteca Ayacucho, 1979; originally published 1944).

36. Guzmán speech.

37. Guzmán speech and *Desarrollar la Guerra*.

38. Guzmán speech and *Desarrollar la Guerra*.

39. The Sendero cadre was largely made up of Guzmán's students at the University of Huamanga. Most were bilingual in Quechua and Spanish, and many had peasant roots. See David Scott Palmer, "The Sendero Luminoso Rebellion in Rural Peru," in Georges Fauriol, ed., *Latin American Insurgencies* (Washington, D.C.: National Defense University Press, 1985), 69.

40. Peru nonattribution interviews.

41. Gordon H. McCormick, *The Shining Path and Peruvian Terrorism*, Publication No. 7297 (Santa Monica, Calif.: Rand, 1987), 11.

42. Peru nonattribution interviews.

43. Ibid.; see also *Dario la Republica*, April 24, 1988, pp. 15–17; *Expresso*, April 18, 1988, p. 4.

44. See David Scott Palmer, ed., *Shining Path of Peru* (London: Hurst, 1992).

45. Guzmán speech and *Desarrollar la Guerra*; Palmer, *Shining Path*.

46. Peru nonattribution interviews.

47. Ibid.

48. Ibid.

49. Ibid.

50. Discussions by Fishel with Peruvian military and intelligence officers in Lima in 1986 and 1987.

51. For examples, see the *Los Angeles Times*, June 19 and 20, 1986.

52. Peru nonattribution interviews.

53. Ibid.

54. Ibid.

55. Ibid.

56. See Cynthia McClintock and Fabian Vallas, *The United States and Peru: Cooperation at a Cost* (New York: Routledge, 2003), 33–35.

57. As reported in a personal communication by the then–deputy chief of mission at the U.S. embassy in Lima and as witnessed by Fishel as an action officer in U.S. Southern Command's Small Wars Operations Research Directorate and J5.

58. At least one subject matter expert exchange team focused directly on counterinsurgency operations, as it was led by Fishel.

59. These statements are derived from participant observation from 1986 to 1989 and McClintock and Vallas, *United States and Peru,* 70–72.

60. Discussions by Fishel with Peruvian National Intelligence Service analysts in 1986 and 1987.

61. This concept is developed in John T. Fishel and Edmund S. Cowan, "Civil-Military Operations and the War for Legitimacy in Latin America," *Military Review* (January 1988): 327. Also see Barry M. Blechman and Stephen S. Kaplan, *Military Force as a Political Instrument since the Second World War* (Washington, D.C.: Brookings Institution, 1976); Michael Howard, "The Forgotten Dimensions of Strategy," *The Causes of War: And Other Essays* (Cambridge, Mass.: Harvard University Press, 1983), 101–15; Edward G. Lansdale, *In the Midst of Wars: An American's Mission to Southeast Asia* (New York: Harper and Row, 1972); Max G. Manwaring, "Toward an Understanding of Insurgent Warfare," *Military Review* (January 1988): 28–35; Robert Thompson, *Revolutionary War in World Strategy, 1945– 1969* (New York: Taplinger, 1970).

62. General Edgardo Mercado Jarrin, "Insurgency in Latin America: Its Impact on Political and Military Strategy," *Military Review* (March 1969): 10–20. This article was originally published in Peru in 1967.

63. Guzmán speech.

64. Mercado Jarrin, "Insurgency in Latin America," 16.

65. Ungo interview.

66. Duarte, *My Story,* 279.

CHAPTER 8. APPLYING THE "PILLARS OF SUCCESS" TO THE PROBLEM OF HOMELAND DEFENSE

1. See, as examples, Daniel C. Esty, Jack Goldstone, Ted Robert Gurr, Barbara Harff, Pamela T. Surko, Alan N. Unger, and Robert S. Chen, "The State Failure Project: Early Warning Research for U.S. Foreign Policy Planning," in John L. Davies and Ted Robert Gurr, eds., *Preventive Measures: Building Risk Assessment and Crisis Early Warning Systems* (New York: Rowman and Littlefield, 1998), 27–38; World Conflict and Human Rights Map, prepared by Berto Jongman with the support of the Goals for Americans Foundation, St. Louis, Missouri, 2000.

2. Constitution of the United States of America.

3. Michael P. C. Carns, "Reopening the Deterrence Debate: Thinking about a Peaceful and Prosperous Tomorrow," in Max G. Manwaring, ed., *Deterrence in the Twenty-first Century* (London: Frank Cass, 2001), 7–16.

4. John J. Hamre, "A Strategic Perspective on U.S. Homeland Defense: Problem and Response," in Max G. Manwaring, ed., *To Insure Domestic Tranquility,*

Provide for the Common Defense . . . (Carlisle Barracks, Penn.: Strategic Studies Institute, 2000), 11–25.

5. Ibid.

6. Ibid.

7. Edwin G. Corr and Max G. Manwaring, "The Challenge of Preventive Diplomacy and Deterrence in the Global Security Environment," in Manwaring, *Deterrence*, 124–31.

8. Sun Tzu, *The Art of War,* trans. Samuel B. Griffith (London: Oxford University Press, 1971), 63; Carl von Clausewitz, *On War,* ed. and trans. Michael Howard and Peter Paret (Princeton, N.J.: Princeton University Press, 1976), 88–89.

9. George F. Kennan, "The Sources of Soviet Conduct," *Foreign Affairs* (July 1947): 566–82.

10. Ted Robert Gurr and John L. Davies, eds., *Assessment and Crisis: Early Warning Systems* (New York: Rowman and Littlefield, 1998), 27–39; Thomas F. Homer-Dixon, *Environment, Security, and Violence* (Princeton, N.J.: Princeton University Press, 1999), 133–68. Also see Wm. J. Olson, "International Organized Crime: The Silent Threat to Sovereignty," *Fletcher Forum of World Affairs* (Summer–Fall 1997): 66–80; Roy Godson and Wm. J. Olson, "International Organized Crime," *Society* (January–February 1995): 18–29; Wm. J. Olson, "A New World, and New Challenges," in Max G. Manwaring and Wm. J. Olson, eds., *Managing Contemporary Conflict: Pillars of Success* (Boulder, Colo.: Westview Press, 1996), 3–12.

11. Case studies can be found in the SWORD Papers.

12. John LeCarre, *The Constant Gardner* (New York: Scribner, 2001), 137.

13. For key points dealing with the threats posed by the terrorist phenomenon, see Steven Metz and Douglas V. Johnson II, *Asymmetry and U.S. Military Strategy: Definitions, Background, and Strategic Concepts* (Carlisle Barracks, Penn.: Strategic Studies Institute, 2001); Steven Metz, *The Future of Insurgency* (Carlisle Barracks, Penn.: Strategic Studies Institute, 1993); Martha Crenshaw, ed., *Terrorism in Context* (University Park: Pennsylvania State University Press, 1995); Jessica Mathews, "Power Shift," *Foreign Affairs* (January–February 1997): 58–60; Ian Beckett, "Forward to the Past: Insurgency in Our Midst," *Harvard International Review* (Summer 2001): 63.

14. This quotation is from Neville Chamberlain's statement on the eve of the Munich conference, in which he followed the policy of appeasement to its logical conclusion and gave Czechoslovakia up to the Nazi barbarians.

15. White House, *National Strategy for Combating Terrorism* (Washington, D.C.: February 2003), 23.

16. SWORD Papers.

17. Ibid. See also Max G. Manwaring, "Italian Terrorism, 1968–1982: Strategic Lessons That Should Have Been Learned," *Low Intensity Conflict and Law Enforcement* (Summer 1998): 121–35.

300   NOTES TO PAGES 137–50

18. Colin S. Gray, *Explorations in Strategy* (Westport, Conn.: Greenwood Press, 1996), 31–46, *Modern Strategy* (Oxford: Oxford University Press, 1999), and "Deterrence and the Nature of Strategy," in Manwaring, *Deterrence,* 17–26.

19. For interesting discussions of this issue, see Qiao Liang and Wang Xziangsui, *Unrestricted Warfare* (Beijing: PLA Literature and Arts Publishing House, 1999), and Richard Danzig, "Countering Traumatic Attacks," in Manwaring, *Deterrence,* 98–105.

20. Gray, "Deterrence." Also see Edwin G. Corr and Max G. Manwaring, "The Challenge of Preventive Diplomacy and Deterrence in the Global Security Environment," in Manwaring, *Deterrence.*

21. Gray, "Deterrence"; Corr and Manwaring, "Challenge of Preventive Diplomacy."

22. Lewis Carroll, *Alice in Wonderland and Through the Looking Glass* (New York: Grosset and Dunlap, 1982), 66–67.

CHAPTER 9. STRATEGIC LESSONS OF ITALIAN TERRORISM

1. Max G. Manwaring and John T. Fishel, "Insurgency and Counter-Insurgency: Toward a New Analytical Approach," *Small Wars and Insurgencies* 3 (Winter 1993): 272–310.

2. This and subsequent assertions made in the following sections of this paper are consensus statements based on interviews with senior Italian Caribinieri officials. Manwaring is particularly indebted to General Carlo Alfiero for his guiding remarks. However, the intent is to allow anonymity for those who object to their names being made public. Thus, in subsequent notes, these statements are cited as Carabinieri interviews.

3. Testimony of Red Brigadist Roberto Buzzatti, quoted in Richard Drake, *The Aldo Moro Murder Case* (Cambridge, Mass.: Harvard University Press, 1995), 143.

4. Declaration of the Red Brigades sent to *L'Espresso* and published as "Le Due Anime delle BR," March 1, 1987.

5. Carabinieri interviews.

6. Figures reported in Vittorfranco S. Pisano, *The Dynamics of Subversion and Violence in Contemporary Italy* (Stanford, Calif.: Hoover Institution Press, 1987), 37.

7. Passage extracted from Red Brigades documents, quoted in ibid., 39.

8. Carabinieri interviews.

9. Ibid.

10. Testimony of Red Brigadist Antonio Savasta quoted in Drake, *Aldo Moro Murder Case,* 51.

11. Testimony of Red Brigadist Patrizio Peci recorded in Sue Ellen Moran, ed., *A Rand Note: Court Depositions of Three Red Brigadists* (Santa Monica, Calif.: Rand, February 1986), 47.

12. Carabinieri interviews.

13. Ibid.

14. Ibid. See also Robert Thompson, *Defeating Communist Insurgency: The Lessons of Malaya and Vietnam* (New York: Praeger, 1966), 87.

15. Savasta testimony in Drake, *Aldo Moro Murder Case*, 50.

16. Carabinieri interviews. See also Max G. Manwaring and Robert M. Herrick, "A Threat-Oriented Strategy for Conflict Control," *Military Review* (July 1987): 3.

17. Carabinieri interviews.

18. Ibid. See also Pisano, *Dynamics of Subversion*, 144–45.

19. Carabinieri interviews. See also Manwaring and Fishel, "Insurgency and Counter-Insurgency."

20. Carabinieri interviews; Pisano, *Dynamics of Subversion*, 144–51; Donatella della Porta, "Left-Wing Terrorism in Italy," in Martha Crenshaw, ed., *Terrorism in Context* (University Park: Pennsylvania State University Press, 1995), 118–19.

21. See note 20.

22. Carabinieri interviews.

23. Ibid.

24. Manwaring and Fishel, "Insurgency and Counter-Insurgency."

25. Carabinieri interviews.

26. Manwaring and Fishel, "Insurgency and Counter-Insurgency."

27. Carabinieri interviews.

28. Manwaring and Fishel, "Insurgency and Counter-Insurgency."

29. Carabinieri interviews; Pisano, *Dynamics of Subversion*, 146.

30. Manwaring and Fishel, "Insurgency and Counter-Insurgency."

31. Interview with a militant quoted in della Porta, "Left-Wing Terrorism," 150.

32. Quoted in Enrico Fenzi, *Armi e Bagagli: Un Diario dalle Brigate Rosse* (Genoa: Costa and Nolan, 1987), 76.

33. Manwaring and Fishel, "Insurgency and Counter-Insurgency."

34. Carabinieri interviews; della Porta, "Left-Wing Terrorism," 157–59.

35. For only a few examples, see Moran, *Rand Note*, 36, 59–60; Pisano, *Dynamics of Subversion*, 119–43; della Porta, "Left-Wing Terrorism," 120; *Panorama*, September 15, 1980, p. 45; Federico Orlando, ed., *Siamo in Guerra* (Rome: Armando, 1980), 195–96; Vittorfranco S. Pisano, "Libya's Foothold in Italy," *Washington Quarterly* (Spring 1982): 179–82.

36. Ibid.

37. Carabinieri interviews; Pisano, *Dynamics of Subversion*, p. 145.

38. Manwaring and Fishel, "Insurgency and Counter-Insurgency."

39. Carabinieri interviews.

40. Ibid.

41. Alberto Franceschini, *Mara, Renato, e Io: Storia dei Fondatori delle BR* (Milan: Mondadori, 1988), 204.

42. Carabinieri interviews; della Porta, "Left-Wing Terrorism," 129–32.

43. Carabinieri interviews; Drake, *Aldo Moro Murder Case*, 193–94.

44. Carabinieri interviews.

45. Carabinieri interviews and della Porta, "Left-Wing Terrorism," 157–59.

46. Ibid.

47. Carabinieri interviews.

48. Della Porta, "Left-Wing Terrorism," 105.

CHAPTER 10. THE PRINCIPLE OF UNITY OF EFFORT

1. Max G. Manwaring and John T. Fishel, "Insurgency and Counter-Insurgency: Toward a New Analytical Approach," *Small Wars and Insurgencies* (Winter 1992): 281.

2. John T. Fishel, ed., *"The Savage Wars of Peace": Toward a New Paradigm of Peace Operations* (Boulder, Colo.: Westview Press, 1997), especially chapter 11.

3. Sun Tzu, *The Art of War*, trans. Samuel B. Griffith (New York: Oxford University Press, 1963), 69.

4. Ibid., 69.

5. Ibid., 77.

6. Ibid., 77–78.

7. Ibid., 78.

8. Ibid., 83.

9. Carl von Clausewitz, *On War*, ed. and trans. Michael Howard and Peter Paret (New York: Alfred A. Knopf, 1993), 138.

10. Ibid., 138–39.

11. Ibid., 721.

12. Ibid., 731.

13. John T. Fishel, "Achieving the Elusive Unity of Effort," in Max G. Manwaring, ed., *Gray Area Phenomena: Confronting the New World Disorder* (Boulder, Colo.: Westview Press, 1993), 124.

14. See John T. Fishel, *Liberation, Occupation, and Rescue: War Termination and Desert Storm* (Carlisle Barracks, Penn.: Strategic Studies Institute, 1992).

15. See Gary Bryant, "What is COCOM?" MMAS thesis, U.S. Army Command and General Staff College, Fort Leavenworth, Kans., 1993.

16. See Field Manual 100-5, *Operations* (Washington, D.C.: Headquarters, Department of the Army, 1993); Joint Pub 3-0, *Operations* (Washington, D.C., 1993).

17. This is Joint Task Force B, at Soto Cano Air Force Base, Honduras, established in 1983. Although it was scheduled to be stood down in 1994, it has continued with new missions since the U.S. withdrawal from bases in Panama. Current thinking in the Department of Defense is to create permanent standing joint forces as headquarters that can undertake any number of missions.

18. These considerations are not well addressed in doctrine.

19. See John T. Fishel, *The Fog of Peace: Planning and Executing the Restoration of Panama* (Carlisle Barracks, Penn.: Strategic Studies Institute, 1992), especially chapter 4.

20. Various press sources.

21. Field Manual 100-20, *Military Operations in Low Intensity Conflict* (Washington, D.C.: Headquarters, Department of the Army, 1990), Appendix A.

22. Fishel, *Liberation, Occupation, and Rescue,* chapter 6. As stated above, current thinking focuses on the standing joint force. This is an adaptation of the concept of the deployable joint task force, which has been used in U.S. Southern Command and Joint Forces Command since the late 1980s.

23. Ibid., p. 6.

24. Robert Hopkins Miller, *Inside an Embassy* (Washington, D.C.: Institute for the Study of Diplomacy, 1992), 3.

25. Ibid.

26. See Barbara Tuchman, *The Guns of August* (New York: Dell, 1962).

27. Fishel, *Liberation, Occupation, and Rescue,* chapter 6.

28. Rick Atkinson, *Crusade: The Untold Story of the Persian Gulf War* (Boston: Houghton Mifflin, 1993).

29. This discussion derives from multiple sources on Operations JUST CAUSE and PROMOTE LIBERTY, including the participant observation of Fishel (hereafter cited as participant observation) and interviews with participants (hereafter cited as joint operations interviews). See also Fishel, *Fog of Peace.*

30. See Department of Defense Reorganization Act (known as the Goldwater-Nichols Act), 1986, Title 10, USC.

31. Operational Command (OPCOM) is the term that preceded Combatant Command (COCOM). While it did include operational control (UPCON), it did not give directive authority for logistics. Although the term no longer exists in joint terminology, it is still a current NATO command relationship.

32. Interviews with General Fred F. Woerner, May 1991, and Dr. Gabriel Marcella, 1991–1992; also participant observation.

33. Woerner interview.

34. Fishel, *Liberation, Occupation, and Rescue,* chapter 1.

35. Participant observation; Fishel, *Fog of Peace,* passim.

36. Joint operations interviews, 1991; participant observation.

37. Interview with Major General William Hartzog, April 1991.

38. Tacitus, "Few Lessons Were Learned in Panama Invasion," *Armed Forces Journal International* (June 1993): 54.

39. Fishel, *Fog of Peace*, 75.

40. Interview with Colonel (Ret.) Chuck Fry, former commander of Special Operations Command–South, October 1994.

41. Interview with John Maisto, former deputy chief of mission, U.S. Embassy, Panama, October 1992.

42. See Fishel, *Fog of Peace*; participant observation. See also Maisto interview.

43. Fishel, *Liberation, Occupation, and Rescue*.

44. Ibid.; Department of Defense, *Final Report to Congress: Conduct of the Persian Gulf War,* Pursuant to Title V (Public Law 102-25), hereafter cited as Title V, p. 19.

45. Title V.

46. Fishel, *Liberation, Occupation, and Rescue*.

47. Bryant, "What Is COCOM?"; AFSC Pub. 1, *Joint Staff Officers' Guide* (Norfolk, Va.: Armed Forces Staff College, 1993).

48. Interviews with Colonel Douglas Craft, former chief of the Policy and Strategy Division, J5, U.S. Central Command, 1991–1992.

49. Title V.

50. The current secretary of defense, Donald Rumsfeld, has directed that the term "commander in chief" applies only to the president of the United States. The former commanders in chief of the unified commands are now known simply as commanders or combatant commanders.

51. Title V, p. 487; Fishel, *Liberation, Occupation, and Rescue,* passim.

52. Title V, p. 44; Robert H. Scales, *Certain Victory: The U.S. Army in the Gulf War* (Fort Leavenworth, Kans.: U.S. Army Command and General Staff College Press, 1994), 122.

53. Title V. See pages 555–59 for discrepancies between command and control as depicted in the text and the graphics. I have followed the text, as it is more in accordance with both doctrine and common sense.

54. Ibid.

55. See Scales, *Certain Victory*, 103–106.

56. This section is drawn from Fishel, *Liberation, Occupation, and Rescue*.

CHAPTER 11. CONFRONTING THE "WAR ON DRUGS"

1. Peter Lupsha, "Grey Area Phenomenon: New Threats and Policy Dilemmas," unpublished paper presented at the High Intensity Crime/Low Intensity Conflict Conference, Chicago, Illinois, September 27–30, 1992, p. 1.

2. See Max G. Manwaring and John T. Fishel, "Insurgency and Counter-Insurgency: Toward a New Analytical Approach," *Small Wars and Insurgencies* (Winter 1992): 272–310.

3. Using a version of cognitive mapping techniques, Fred Polk, Dave Davis, and Chris Beal developed an integrated causal model of the cocaine problem in the Andean Ridge countries of South America based on an analysis of a sample of the professional literature written in English and Spanish during 1988–1990. The model was developed for Headquarters, U.S. Southern Command, in Panama. It was validated through extensive interviews conducted by Max G. Manwaring and Robert Baratta in the United States, Central America, and South America during April–July 1990 and by Max G. Manwaring in May–June 1992. All citations and assertions that follow are corroborated by these interviews, hereafter cited as drug wars interviews.

4. General John R. Galvin, "Uncomfortable Wars: Toward a New Paradigm," in Max G. Manwaring, ed., *Uncomfortable Wars: Toward a New Paradigm of Low Intensity Conflict* (Boulder, Colo.: Westview Press, 1991), 14.

5. Drug wars interviews; also see Kevin Healy, "Coca, the State, and the Peasantry in Bolivia, 1982–1988," *Journal of Interamerican Studies and World Affairs* (Summer–Fall 1988): 105–106.

6. Drug wars interviews; also see Christopher Able, "The Crisis of Liberalism in Colombia," *Contemporary Review* (July 1989): 1; Merrill Collett, "Cocaine Capitalism," *New Statesman and Society,* August 12, 1988, pp. 14–17.

7. Drug wars interviews.

8. See Courtney E. Prisk, "The Umbrella of Legitimacy," in Manwaring, *Uncomfortable Wars,* 73.

9. Drug wars interviews; also see Rensselaer W. Lee III, "Why the U.S. Cannot Stop South American Cocaine," *Orbis* (Fall 1988): 507–509.

10. Drug wars interviews; also see Tina Rosenberg, "The Kingdom of Cocaine," *New Republic,* November 27, 1989, pp. 27–28; Douglas W. Payne, "The Drug 'Super State' in Latin America," *Freedom at Issue* (March–April 1989): 7; Francis Alexis, "The Politics of Drug Trafficking," paper delivered by the attorney general for Grenada to the Caribbean Studies Association Conference, Ramada Renaissance Hotel, Grand Anse, St. George's, Grenada, May 28, 1992.

11. Drug wars interviews.

12. Ibid.

13. Ibid.; also see Iban de Rementeria, "La Sustitucion de Cultivos como Perspectiva," in Diego Garcia-Sayan, ed., *Coca, Cocaina y Narcotrafico: Laberinto en los Andes* (Lima, Peru: Comision Andina de Juristas, 1990), 361–88.

14. See note 13.

15. Drug wars interviews; also see "Drugs War High in the Andes," *Economist,* February 13–19, 1993, pp. 45–46.

16. Drug wars interviews.

17. Ibid.

18. Ibid.

19. Ibid.

20. Ibid.

21. Ibid.

22. Ibid.; also see Healy, "Coca"; Francisco E. Thoumi, "Some Implications of the Growth of the Underground Economy in Colombia, *Journal of Interamerican Studies and World Affairs* (Summer 1987): 35–53.

23. Drug wars interviews; also see Richard B. Craig, "South American Drug Traffic," *Handbook of Drug Control in the United States* (New York: Greenwood Press, 1990), 207.

24. Drug wars interviews.

25. Ibid.; also see Lee, "Why the U.S.," 514.

26. Drug wars interviews; also see Bruce M. Bagley, "Winning Battles, Losing the War: U.S. Anti-Drug Policies in Latin America," *Hemisphere* (Fall 1988): 31; idem, "U.S. Foreign Policy and the War on Drugs: Analysis of a Policy Failure," *Journal of Interamerican Studies and World Affairs* (Summer–Fall 1988): 189–212; idem, "The New Hundred Years War? U.S. National Security and the War on Drugs in Latin America," *Journal of Interamerican Studies and World Affairs* (Spring 1988): 161–81.

27. Drug wars interviews; also see Frank Kitson, *Warfare as a Whole* (London: Faber and Faber, 1987); Carl von Clausewitz, *On War,* ed. and trans. Michael Howard and Peter Paret (Princeton, N.J.: Princeton University Press, 1976), 89–95, 595–96.

28. See Scott B. Macdonald, "The New 'Bad Guys': Exploring the Parameters of the Violent New World Order," in Max G. Manwaring, ed., *Gray Area Phenomena: Confronting the New World Disorder* (Boulder, Colo.: Westview Press, 1993), 33–60.

CHAPTER 12. THE CHALLENGE
OF PEACE ENFORCEMENT

1. U.S. Forces Somalia, *After Action Report* (Carlisle, Penn.: U.S. Army Peacekeeping Institute, 1994), "Executive Summary."

2. Ibid., 4.

3. See Max G. Manwaring and John T. Fishel, "Insurgency and Counter-Insurgency: Toward a New Analytical Approach," *Small Wars and Insurgencies* (Winter 1992): 272–310.

4. See John T. Fishel, "Achieving the Elusive Unity of Effort," in Max G. Manwaring, ed., *Gray Area Phenomena: Confronting the New World Disorder* (Boulder, Colo.: Westview Press, 1993), 109–27.

5. Field Manual (FM) 100-23, *Peace Operations* (Washington, D.C.: Headquarters, Department of the Army, 1994), 23.

6. This assertion is derived from interviews with officers who have served in UN peacekeeping operations over a number of years.

7. U.S. Forces Somalia, *After Action Report,* 2–3.

8. FM 100-23, *Peace Operations*.

9. "Terms of Reference (TOR) for U.S. Forces in Somalia," April 1993.

10. Ibid.

11. "Legitimacy" differs from "host government legitimacy" only to the degree that it expands the concept from the host government to all the players, including the belligerents (although not in their belligerent roles). The connotative differences in the other dimensions are self-evident.

12. Jennifer Parmelee, "Relaxing in Ethiopia, Unrepentant Aide Finds Time for Envoys," *Washington Post,* December 26, 1993, p. A41; Alex Shoumatoff, "The Warlord Speaks," *The Nation*, April 4, 1994, p. 444.

13. Walter S. Clarke, "Testing the World's Resolve in Somalia," *Parameters* (Winter 1993–94): 53.

14. Ibid.

15. UNOSOM II fax from the under secretary general for peacekeeping operations to the special representative to the secretary general, "Draft Resolution on Somalia, S/25889," June 6, 1993, pp. 2–4.

16. Michael Elliott, "The Making of a Fiasco," *Newsweek,* October 18, 1993, p. 36.

17. UNOSOM II memorandum from Force Command to the special representative to the secretary general, "Trip Report to Italian Brigade," May 27, 1993, p. 2.

18. UNOSOM II code cable from the special representative to the secretary general to the under secretary general for peacekeeping operations, "Additional Concerns of Force Commander," July 18, 1993, p. 1.

19. Terrence Lyons and Ahmed I. Samatar, *Somalia: State Collapse, Multilateral Intervention, and Strategies for Political Reconstruction* (Washington, D.C.: Brookings Institute, 1995), pp. vii–13.

20. Ibid., 44–49.

21. UNOSOM II Force Command special SITREP to UN New York, July 3, 1993, pp. 1–3; UNOSOM II code cable from the SRSG to the under secretary general for peacekeeping operations, "Additional Insights re Situation in Mogadishu," July 16, 1993, p. 2.

22. UNOSOM II code cable from Force Command to the under secretary general for peacekeeping operations, "Security Situation in Mogadishu," July 6, 1993, p. 2.

23. UNOSOM II Force Command SITREP to UN New York, July 7, 1993, p. 9.

24. UNOSOM II Operations Division memorandum for record, "Occupation of Strong Points 19, 42, and 207," September 10, 1993, p. 2.

25. Carl von Clausewitz, *On War,* ed. and trans. Michael Howard and Peter Paret (Princeton, N.J.: Princeton University Press, 1984), 88.

26. F. M. Lorenz, "Law and Anarchy in Somalia," *Parameters* (Winter 1993–94): 37.

27. UNOSOM II memorandum from Force Command to the special representative to the secretary general, "UNOSOM Transition Process," April 18, 1993.

28. Ibid.

29. UNOSOM II fax from commander of Belgian Brigade to the force commander, "Situation in Kismayo," May 7, 1993.

30. UNOSOM II fax from Force Command to commander of Belgian Brigade, "Current Operation within AOR Kismayo," May 11, 1993, p. l.

31. Daze, field notes, June 22, 1993.

32. Letter from the chief of the French Defence Staff to Force Command, June 14, 1993.

33. UNOSOM II Force Command SITREP to UN New York, June 22, 1993.

34. UNOSOM II Force Command SITREP to UN New York, June 28, 1993.

35. See article by former CIA case officer Garrett Jones, "Iraq: We Have Seen This Movie Before," Foreign Policy Research Institute, "E-Notes," *www.fpri.org*, December 15, 2003.

36. Keith B. Richburg, "Criticism Mounts over Somali Raid," *Washington Post*, July 15, 1993, p. A21.

37. Thomas W. Lippman and Barton Gellman, "A Humanitarian Gesture Turns Deadly," *Washington Post*, October 10, 1993, p. 3.

38. This account is taken from UNOSOM II Force Command SITREP to UN New York, October 3, 1993; U.S. Quick Reaction Force, Falcon Brigade, 10th Mountain Division, summary of operations on October 3, 1993.

39. Sun Tzu, *The Art of War*, trans. Samuel B. Griffith (London: Oxford University Press, 1963), 71.

40. Interview with a member of Ambassador Oakley's staff, 1994.

41. U.S Army Forces Somalia, 10th Mountain Division (LI), "After Action Report: Summary," 1994, p. 31.

42. Ibid., p. 30.

43. Sun Tzu, *Art of War*, 145.

44. See Jones, "Iraq."

45. UNOSOM II interdivisional memorandum, "Galcayo as Keystone," May 1993.

CHAPTER 13. TAKING THE "ENEMY" INTO CONSIDERATION

1. The term "Hobbesian Trinity" was coined by Joseph R. Nuñez in *Fighting the Hobbesian Trinity in Colombia: A New Strategy for Peace* (Carlisle Barracks, Penn.: Strategic Studies Institute, 2001).

2. Michael Shifter, *Toward Greater Peace and Security in Colombia* (New York: Council on Foreign Relations and the Inter-American Dialogue, 2000), pp. viii, 1–2, 18.

3. A classic book on this topic is Vernon Lee Fluherty, *Dance of the Millions: Military Rule and the Social Revolution in Colombia, 1930–1956* (Pittsburgh, Penn.: University of Pittsburgh Press, 1957). Also see Dennis M. Hanratty and Sandra W. Meditz, eds., *Colombia: A Country Study* (Washington, D.C.: Federal Research Division, Library of Congress, 1990).

4. See note 3. Also see Luis Alberto Restrepo, "The Crisis of the Current Political Regime and Its Possible Outcomes," in Charles Bergquist, Ricardo Penaranda, and Gonzalo Sanchez, eds., *Violence in Colombia: The Contemporary Crisis in Historical Perspective* (Wilmington, Del.: SR Books, 1992), 273–92.

5. See note 3. Also see Angel Rabassa and Peter Chalk, *Colombian Labyrinth* (Santa Monica, Calif.: Rand, 2001), 39–60; Eduardo Pizarro, "Revolutionary Guerrilla Groups in Colombia," in Bergquist, Penaranda, and Sanchez, *Violence in Colombia*, 169–93; Hal Klepak, "Colombia: Why Doesn't the War End?" *Jane's Intelligence Review* (June 2000): 41–45.

6. These and subsequent assertions are consensus statements based on a series of interviews with more than ninety senior U.S. and Latin American civilian and military officials. These interviews were conducted October 1989–July 1994; September 1996; December 1998; November 2000; and February 2001. To allow anonymity for those who have an objection to their names being made public, these are cited hereafter as Latin America nonattribution interviews.

7. Latin America nonattribution interviews.

8. Ibid.

9. Ibid.; Manwaring interview with Ambassador Curtis Kamman, December 7, 2000, Carlisle Barracks, Penn.

10. Latin America nonattribution interviews; Thomas A. Marks, *Colombian Army Adaptation to FARC Insurgency* (Carlisle Barracks, Penn.: Strategic Studies Institute, 2002).

11. Pizarro, "Revolutionary Guerrilla Groups"; Rabassa and Chalk, *Colombian Labyrinth*.

12. See note 11; Klepak, "Colombia."

13. See note 12; Kamman interview.

14. Latin America nonattribution interviews; Thomas A. Marks, *Maoist Insurgency since Vietnam* (London: Frank Cass, 1996).

15. Rabassa and Chalk, *Colombian Labyrinth*. Also see Larry Rohter, "A Colombian Guerrilla's 50-Year Fight," *New York Times*, July 19, 1999; Larry Rohter, "Colombia Rebels Reign in Ceded Area," *New York Times*, May 16, 1999; Howard LaFranchi, "Guerrilla Commander Says, 'This Is a Means,'" *Christian*

Science Monitor, July 19, 1999; Serge F. Kovaleski, "Rebel Movement on the Rise: Colombian Guerrillas Use Military Force, Not Ideology to Hold Power," *Washington Post,* February 5, 1999; Gary M. Leech, "An Interview with FARC Commander Simon Trinidad," *NACLA Report on the Americas,* September–October 2000; Clifford Krauss, "Colombia's Rebels Keep the Marxist Faith," *New York Times,* July 25, 2000; Alfred Molano, "The Evolution of the FARC: A Guerrilla Group's Long History," *NACLA Report on the Americas,* September–October 2000; "FARC: Finance Comes Full Circle for Bartering Revolutionaries," *Jane's Information Group,* January 19, 2001. This body of material is hereafter cited as newspaper reports/interviews.

16. Newspaper reports/interviews; "Survey of Colombia," *Economist,* April 21–27, 2001.

17. Newspaper reports/interviews; "Survey of Colombia."

18. Rabassa and Chalk, *Colombian Labyrinth.* Also see David Spencer, *Colombia's Paramilitaries: Criminals or Political Force?* (Carlisle Barracks, Penn.: Strategic Studies Institute, 2001); Juan Forero, "Colombian Paramilitaries Adjust Attack Strategies," *New York Times,* January 22, 2001; Juan Forero, "Rightist Chief in Colombia Shifts Focus to Politics," *New York Times,* June 7, 2001; Tod Robberson, "Militia Leader's Revelations Igniting Fear in Colombia," *Dallas Morning News,* December 17, 2001.

19. See notes 15 and 18; "Survey of Colombia."

20. See Carlos Ramos-Mrosovsky, "Colombia's Paramilitary Ceasefire: Counterinsurgency Challenges and Opportunities," *Low Intensity Conflict and Law Enforcement* (Summer 2001): 46–71.

21. Steven Metz, *The Future of Insurgency* (Carlisle Barracks, Penn.: Strategic Studies Institute, 1993), 13–15.

22. Mark S. Steinitz, "Insurgents, Terrorists, and the Drug Trade," *Washington Quarterly* (Fall 1985): 147.

23. Newspaper reports/interviews.

24. Peter A. Lupsha, "The Role of Drugs and Drug Trafficking in the Invisible Wars," in Richard Ward and Herold Smith, eds., *International Terrorism: Operational Issues* (Chicago: University of Chicago Press, 1987), 181. Also see Wm. J. Olson, "International Organized Crime: The Silent Threat to Sovereignty," *Fletcher Forum of World Affairs* (Summer–Fall 1997): 70–74.

25. Lupsha, "Role of Drugs"; Olson, "International Organized Crime"; Latin America nonattribution interviews.

26. See note 25.

27. See note 25; Peter A. Lupsha, "Towards an Etiology of Drug Trafficking and Insurgent Relations: The Phenomenon of Narco-Terrorism," *International Journal of Comparative and Applied Criminal Justice* (Fall 1989): 63.

28. Latin America nonattribution interviews.

29. Ibid.; newspaper reports/interviews.

30. Rabassa and Chalk, *Colombian Labyrinth*; Spencer, *Colombia's Paramilitaries*.

31. Latin America nonattribution interviews.

32. Ibid.

33. Ibid. Also see Stephen E. Flynn, *The Transnational Drug Challenge and the New World Order* (Washington, D.C.: Center for Strategic and International Studies, 1993); William O. Walker III, "The Foreign Narcotics Policy of the United States since 1980: An End to the War on Drugs," *International Journal of Narco-Diplomacy* (Winter 1993–94): 64.

34. Cited in Ivelaw Lloyd Griffith, *Drugs and Security in the Caribbean: Sovereignty under Siege* (University Park: Pennsylvania State University Press, 1997), 1.

35. Ibid.; see also Walker, "Foreign Narcotics Policy."

36. Latin America nonattribution interviews.

37. Ibid.

38. Max Manwaring, "U.S. Too Narrowly Focused on Drug War in Colombia," *Miami Herald*, August 15, 2001.

39. Latin America nonattribution interviews.

40. Quoted from "El Documento Oficial de Sendero," in Rogger Mercado U., *Los Partidos Politicos en el Peru* (Lima: Ediciones Latinoamericanas, 1995), 110.

41. Latin America nonattribution interviews. Also see Martha Crenshaw, ed., *Terrorism in Context* (University Park: Pennsylvania State University Press, 1995).

42. This observation was made in 1986 by former Secretary of State George P. Shultz in an address before the Low-Intensity Warfare Conference at the National Defense University on January 15, 1986, in Washington, D.C.

43. David C. Jordan, *Drug Politics: Dirty Money and Democracies* (Norman: University of Oklahoma Press, 1999), 19.

44. Latin America nonattribution interviews. Also see Ana Maria Bejarano and Eduardo Pizarro, "The Crisis of Democracy in Colombia: From 'Restricted' Democracy to 'Besieged' Democracy," unpublished manuscript, 2001.

45. Latin America nonattribution interviews.

46. Jordan, *Drug Politics*, 21.

47. Bejarano and Pizarro, "Crisis of Democracy."

48. Jordan, *Drug Politics*, 158–70, 193–94.

49. *Annual Report 1999* (Washington, D.C.: Inter-American Development Bank, 2000), 141.

50. Data taken from Mauricio Rubio, "La Justicia en Una Sociedad Violenta," in Maria Victoria Llorente and Malcolm Deas, eds., *Reconocer la Guerra para Construir la Paz* (Bogota: Ediciones Uniandes—CERED—Editorial Norma, 1999), 215.

51. Jordan, *Drug Politics*, 161.

52. Ibid.

53. Kamman interview.

54. Carl von Clausewitz, *On War*, ed. and trans. Michael Howard and Peter Paret (Princeton, N.J.: Princeton University Press, 1976), 596.

55. Latin America nonattribution interviews. The argument is also made in Ernest Evans, "Our Savage Wars of Peace," *World Affairs* (Fall 2000): 90–94.

56. Author interview with General Sir Robert Thompson, January 1986, Washington, D.C.

57. Ibid. Also David Passage, *The United States and Colombia: Untying the Gordian Knot* (Carlisle Barracks, Penn.: U.S. Army War College, 2000), 21–27.

58. Latin America nonattribution interviews.

59. Ibid.

60. Niccolò Machiavelli, *The Art of War* (New York: Da Capo Press, 1965).

61. Interview with General John R. Galvin (USA, Ret.), August 6, 1997, Boston, Mass.; interviews with Lieutenant General William G. Carter III (USA, Ret.), November 30, 1998, and March 2, 1990, Washington, D.C.; author interviews with General Anthony Zinni (USMC, commander-in-chief, U.S. Central Command), June 2, 1999, and October 6, 2000, Washington, D.C.; interviews with General Charles E. Wilhelm (USMC, Ret.), February 9, 2001, and June 22, 2001, Washington, D.C.

62. Galvin, Carter, Zinni, and Wilhelm interviews.

63. Ibid.

64. Ibid.

65. Clausewitz, *On War*, 88.

CHAPTER 14. REFLECTIONS ON THE SWORD MODEL OVER TWO DECADES

1. Samuel P. Huntington, *The Clash of Civilizations and the Remaking of World Order* (New York: Simon and Schuster,) 1996.

2. See, for example, Joint Pubs 3-0, *Operations* (Washington, D.C., 1993), and 3-07, *Military Operations Other Than War*; Army Field Manuals 100-5, *Operations* (Washington, D.C.: Headquarters, Department of the Army, 1993), and 100-20, *Military Operations in Low Intensity Conflict* (Washington, D.C.: Headquarters, Department of the Army, 1993). Both sets of documents discuss principles derived directly from the SWORD Model. For a complete discussion, see John T. Fishel, ed., *"The Savage Wars of Peace": Toward a New Paradigm of Peace Operations* (Boulder, Colo.: Westview Press, 1997), chapter 1.

3. Sun Tzu, *The Art of War*, trans. Samuel B. Griffith (New York: Oxford University Press), 1971, 79–80.

4. John T. Fishel, *Civil Military Operations in the New World* (Westport, Conn.: Praeger), 1997, 231.

5. Walter E. Kretchik, Robert F. Baumann, and John T. Fishel, *Invasion, Intervention, "Intervasion": A Concise History of the U.S. Army in Operation Uphold Democracy* (Fort Leavenworth, Kans.: U.S. Army Command and General Staff College Press, 1998), 176.

6. Department of State, Office of Research, M-13-04, Opinion Analysis (Washington, D.C.), January 29, 2004.

7. Associated Press, "Letter Appeals for al-Qaida Help," February 9, 2004.

8. Ibid.

9. This is analogous to making the senior officer with the preponderance of air assets the Joint Force Air Component commander in joint doctrine. But one should note that there are exceptions to this rule as well.

10. See Agency Coordinating Body for Afghan Relief (ACBAR) policy brief: "Provincial Reconstruction Teams and the Security Situation in Afghanistan, Kabul," July 24, 2003.

AFTERWORD: MAKING AND IMPLEMENTING POLICY BASED ON THE SWORD MODEL

1. Max G. Manwaring and Wm. J. Olson, eds., *Managing Contemporary Conflict: Pillars of Success* (Boulder, Colo.: Westview Press, 1996), p. ix.

2. Niall Ferguson, *Colossus: The Price of America's Empire* (New York: Penguin Press, 2004).

Selected Bibliography

EXPLANATORY NOTE

This list is provided as a reference for those who might wish to study further the Manwaring Paradigm and its applicability to different kinds of national security problems and threats. The literature is listed chronologically to show the manner in which use of the paradigm was expanded and found valid.

The growing body of literature also reveals the increasing number of academicians and practitioners who have endorsed the paradigm. Finally, its incorporation into approved national security doctrine, as shown by the paradigm's inclusion in U.S. armed forces manuals, further demonstrates its growing acceptance as an overarching paradigm for U.S. national security.

CHRONOLOGICAL LIST OF SELECT WORKS RELATED TO THE MANWARING PARADIGM

Books

Manwaring, Max G., ed. *Uncomfortable Wars: Toward a New Paradigm of Low Intensity Conflict*. Boulder, Colo.: Westview Press, 1991.

"Foreword," Wm. J. Olson
"Preface," Max G. Manwaring
"Introduction," Edwin G. Corr

"Uncomfortable Wars: Toward a New Paradigm," John R. Galvin

"Toward an Understanding of Insurgency Wars: The Paradigm," Max G. Manwaring

"Strategic Vision and Insurgency in El Salvador and Peru," Max G. Manwaring and John T. Fishel

"Low Intensity Conflict: The Institutional Challenge," Wm. J. Olson

"The Strategic Imperatives for the United States in Latin America," Fred F. Woerner

"Other Actions That Make a Difference: The Case of Peru," Max G. Manwaring, Courtney E. Prisk, and John T. Fishel

"The Need for Strategic Perspective: Insights from El Salvador," Max G. Manwaring and Courtney E. Prisk

"Conclusion," Edwin G. Corr

Corr, Edwin G., and Stephen Sloan, eds. *Low-Intensity Conflict: Old Threats in a New World*. Boulder, Colo.: Westview Press, 1992.

"Foreword," Wm. J. Olson

"Preface," David L. Boren

"Introduction," Stephen Sloan

"United States Government Organization and Capability to Deal with Low-Intensity Conflict," Edwin G. Corr and David C. Miller Jr.

"The Threat in the Contemporary Peace Environment: The Challenge to Change Perspectives," Max G. Manwaring

"Conflict in the Post–Cold War Era," John R. Galvin

"Thailand: The Domino That Did Not Fall," Robert F. Zimmerman

"The Guatemalan Counterinsurgency Campaign of 1982–1985: A Strategy of Going It Alone," Caesar D. Sereseres

"Ethiopia: A Successful Insurgency," James Cheek

"The Shining Path in Peru: Insurgency and the Drug Problem," David Scott Palmer

"Iran: Terrorism and Islamic Fundamentalism," Sean K. Anderson

"Afghanistan: Low-Intensity Conflict with Major Power Intervention," David C. Isby

"El Salvador: Transforming Society to Win the Peace," Edwin G. Corr and Courtney E. Prisk

"Government, Politics, and Low-Intensity Conflict," Thomas A. Grant

"Low-Intensity Conflict and the International Legal System," John Norton Moore

"Implications of Low-Intensity Conflict for United States Policy and Strategy," William J. Crowe

"Final Reflections," Stephen Sloan

Manwaring, Max G., ed. *Gray Area Phenomena: Confronting the New World Disorder.* Boulder, Colo.: Westview Press, 1993.

"Series Editor's Preface," Wm. J. Olson

"Editor's Note," Max G. Manwaring

"Introduction," Edwin G. Corr

"The New World Disorder: Governability and Development," Wm. J. Olson

"The New 'Bad Guys': Exploring the Parameters of the Violent New World Order," Scott B. MacDonald

"Beyond the Cold War: Toward a Theory of Engagement to Confront the Gray Area Phenomenon," Max G. Manwaring

"The Umbrella of Legitimacy," Max G. Manwaring and Courtney E. Prisk

"Constructing a Financial Enforcement Regime to Reallocate Assets from the 'Bad Guys' to the 'Good Guys,'" Bruce Zagaris

"Achieving the Elusive Unity of Effort," John T. Fishel

"Strategy for Conflict Control: An Object Suspended between Three Political-Military Magnets," Max G. Manwaring, Robert M. Herrick, and David G. Bradford

"Beyond the Cold War: An Overview and Lessons," David C. Miller Jr.

"Rubik's Cube, Manwaring's Paradigm for Gray Area Phenomenon, and a New Strategy for International Narcotics Control," Edwin G. Corr

Manwaring, Max G., and Wm. J. Olson, eds. *Managing Contemporary Conflict: Pillars of Success.* Boulder, Colo.: Westview Press, 1996.

"Editors' Note," Max G. Manwaring and Wm. J. Olson

"Foreword," Lawrence S. Eagleburger

"A New World, A New Challenge," Wm. J. Olson

"Back to the Future: Structuring Foreign Policy in a Post–Cold War World," David C. Miller Jr.

"Confronting the New World Disorder: A Legitimate Governance Theory of Engagement," Max G. Manwaring and Edwin G. Corr

"End-State Planning: The Somalia Case," Bruce B. G. Clarke

"Application of Theory and Principle: The Case of El Salvador," Edwin G. Corr

"New National Security Challenges," Wayne A. Downing

"Confronting the 'Hard Decisions' of Redefined Sovereignty and the Tools of Intervention in the New Security Environment," Dennis F. Caffrey

"The Search for Legitimate Partners in the New International Security Environment," David Passage

"Organizing the Operations Other Than War (OOTW) in the Post–Cold War Era," Edwin G. Corr and David C. Miller Jr.

"The Principle of Unity of Effort: A Strategy for Conflict Management," John T. Fishel

"The Management Structures for Just Cause, Desert Storm, and UNO-SOM II," John T. Fishel

"The Implications of the Organized Crime Phenomenon for U.S. National Security," Graham H. Turbiville

"Strategic Intelligence in the Coming Years: Foreign Policy and Defense Asset," Roy Godson

"Final Thoughts on Lessons Learned and Conflict Management," Max G. Manwaring

Fishel, John T. *Civil Military Operations in the New World.* Westport, Conn.: Praeger, 1997.

Fishel, John T. *The Savage Wars of Peace: Toward a New Paradigm of Peace Operations.* Boulder, Colo.: Westview Press, 1998.

"War by Other Means? The Paradigm and Its Application to Peace Operations," John T. Fishel

"Peacekeeping in Cyprus," Murray J. M. Swan

"UN Peace Operations in El Salvador: The Manwaring Paradigm in a Traditional Setting," Kimbra L. Fishel and Edwin G. Corr

"Peacekeeping on the Ecuador-Peru Border: The Military Observer Mission," Stephen C. Fee

"The UN Peace Operations in the Congo: Decolonialism and Superpower Conflict in the Guise of UN Peacekeeping," Matthew J. Vaccaro

"United Nations Operations in Cambodia: (A Second 'Decent Interval')," Joseph G. D. Babb and George W. Steuber

"Piecemeal Peacekeeping: The United Nations Protection Force in the Former Yugoslavia," John A. MacInnis

"Intervention in the Dominican Republic," Lawrence A. Yates

"Peace Enforcement in Somalia: UNOSOM II," Thomas J. Daze and John T. Fishel

"The US and the UN in Haiti: The Limits of Intervention," Thomas K. Adams

"Lessons That Should Have Been Learned: Toward a Theory of Engagement for 'The Savage Wars of Peace,'" Max G. Manwaring and Kimbra L. Fishel

"Winning the Savage Wars of Peace: What the Manwaring Paradigm Tells Us," David M. Last

Fishel, John T., Walter E. Kretchik, and Robert F. Baumann. *Invasion, Intervention, "Intervasion": A Concise History of the U.S. Army in Operation Uphold Democracy.* Fort Leavenworth, Kans.: U.S. Army Command and General Staff College Press, 1998.

Manwaring, Max G., and John T. Fishel, eds. *Toward Responsibility in the New World Disorder: Challenges and Lessons of Peace Operations.* Portland: Frank Cass, 1998.

> "An Interview with General John R. Galvin, U.S. Army (Ret.), Dean, Fletcher School of Law and Diplomacy, 6 August 1997," Max G. Manwaring
>
> "Tragedy in the Balkans: A Conflict Ended—Or Interrupted?" Michael Moodie
>
> "From Peace Making to Peace Building in Central America: The Illusion versus the Reality of Peace," Kimbra L. Fishel
>
> "The Challenge of Haiti's Future," Donald E. Schulz
>
> "Waiting for 'The Big One': Confronting Complex Humanitarian Emergencies and State Collapse in Central Africa," Walter S. Clarke
>
> "Normative Implications of 'The Savage Wars of Peace,'" John T. Fishel
>
> "Beyond the Logjam: A Doctrine for Complex Emergencies," John MacKinlay
>
> "Policing the New World Disorder: Addressing Gaps in Public Security during Peace Operations," Michael J. Dziedzic
>
> "Facing the Choice among Bad Options in Complex Humanitarian Emergencies," Dayton L. Maxwell
>
> "The 'Almost Obvious' Lessons of Peace Operations," Max G. Manwaring and Edwin G. Corr

Manwaring, Max G., and Anthony James Joes, eds. *Beyond Declaring Victory and Coming Home: The Challenges of Peace and Stability Operations.* Westport, Conn.: Praeger, 2000.

> "Foreword," William Walker
>
> "A Multiplicity of Threats, a Paucity of Options: The Global Security Environment at the End of the Twentieth Century," Richard L. Millet
>
> "Defense and Offense in Peace and Stability Operations," Max G. Manwaring and Edwin G. Corr
>
> "The Establishment of Order and the Rule of Law: Legitimacy in the Tradition of Non-Traditional Operations (NTOs)," Thomas K. Adams
>
> "Isolating the Belligerents: A Key to Success in the Post-Counterinsurgency Era," Anthony James Joes

"Sustaining Life, Relieving Suffering, and Regenerating the Economy,"
   Arthur E. Dewey
"Military Intelligence and the Problem of Legitimacy: Opening the Model,"
   Everett C. Dolman
"Beyond Jointness: Civil-Military Cooperation in Achieving the Desired
   End-State," John T. Fishel
"A Grand National Security Strategy for Legitimate Governance and Crisis
   Prevention," Robert M. Herrick
"Legitimate Civil Society and Conflict Prevention: Let's Get Serious,"
   Dayton L. Maxwell
"The Anarchic State versus the Community of Nations: The Real Cleav-
   age in International Security," Michael J. Dziedzic
"America Coping with Chaos at the Strategic Level: Facilitator for Democ-
   ratic Stability in the Post-Counterinsurgency Era," Joseph N. McBride
"Responding to the Failed State: Strategic Triage," Robert H. Dorff
"Some Final Thoughts," Edwin G. Corr and Max G. Manwaring

Manwaring, Max G., ed. ". . . To Insure Domestic Tranquility, Provide for the Common Defence . . ." Carlisle Barracks, Penn.: Strategic Studies Institute, 2000.

   "Overview," Max G. Manwaring
   "A Strategic Perspective on U.S. Homeland Defense: Problem and
      Response," John J. Hamre
   "The Army of the Constitution: The Historical Context," Gregory J. W.
      Urwin
   "The Public's Expectations of National Security," Peter D. Feaver
   "Security Expectations for Transnational Corporations," George K.
      Campbell
   "Ballistic and Cruise Missile Threats," Steven A. Cambone
   "Chemical and Biological Terrorism: Political Hype or Bona Fide
      Post–Cold War Threat?" Russell Howard
   "Infrastructure Warriors: A Threat to the U.S. Homeland by Organized
      Crime," Thomas A. Johnson
   "Threat of Civil Unrest and Insurrection," William A. Navas Jr.
   "Missile Defense," John Costello
   "Evolving Roles and Missions for the Reserve Components in Responding
      to Incidents Involving Weapons of Mass Destruction," Ellen Embrey
   "In Support of the Civil Authorities," Donald A. Haus
   "Where Domestic Security and Civil Liberties Collide," Charles J. Dunlap Jr.
   "A Strategic View of Where the Army Is: Homeland Defense and Issues
      of Civil-Military Relations," Don M. Snider, John A. Nagl, and Tony
      Pfaff

"Toward a National Security Policy and Strategy for Now and the Twenty-first Century," Edwin G. Corr and Max G. Manwaring

Manwaring, Max G., ed. *Deterrence in the Twenty-first Century.* Portland: Frank Cass, 2001.

"Editor's Preface," Max G. Manwaring

"Introduction," William J. Crowe Jr.

"Reopening the Deterrence Debate: Thinking about a Peaceful and Prosperous Tomorrow," Michael P. C. Carns

"Deterrence and the Nature of Strategy," Colin S. Gray

"Ten Reasons Why Nuclear Deterrence Could Fail: The Case for Reassessing U.S. Nuclear Policies and Plans," John M. Weinstein

"Some Possible Surprises in Our Nuclear Future," George H. Quester

"The Role of Nuclear Weapons in U.S. Deterrence Policy," Robert G. Joseph

"Deterrence and Conventional Military Forces," Gary L. Guertner

"Terrorism in the Twenty-first Century: Reassessing the Emerging Threat," Daniel S. Gressang IV

"Countering Traumatic Attacks," Richard Danzig

"Deterrence and Competitive Strategies: A New Look at an Old Concept," Robert H. Dorff, and Joseph R. Cerami

"The Challenge of Preventive Diplomacy and Deterrence in the Global Security Environment," Edwin G. Corr and Max G. Manwaring

Manwaring, Max G., Edwin G. Corr, and Robert H. Dorff, eds. *The Search for Security: A U.S. Grand Strategy for the Twenty-First Century.* Westport, Conn.: Praeger, 2003.

"Foreword," David L. Boren

"Vague Threats and Concrete Dangers: The Global Security Environment: Governance and Legitimacy," Richard L. Millett

"The Current U.S. National Security Strategy and Policy: A Brief Appraisal," Robert H. Dorff

"Managing Globalization: Lessons for Constructing a Strategic Bridge to the Future," Max G. Manwaring

"The Central Political Challenge in the Global Security Environment: Governance and Legitimacy," Edwin G. Corr and Max G. Manwaring

"The Major Economic Challenge in the Global Security Environment: Competing in an Interdependent World," Leif Rosenberger

"The Information Challenge in the Global Security Environment," Dennis M. Rempe

"The Challenge of Deterrence in the Global Security Arena: Thinking about a Peaceful and Prosperous Tomorrow," Edwin G. Corr and Max G. Manwaring

"A Grand Strategy for the United States at the Start of the New Millennium: The Broad Outlines," Edwin G. Corr and Max G. Manwaring

"Strategy, Grand Strategy, and the Search for Security," Robert H. Dorff

Journal Articles and Chapters in Edited Books Not Listed Above

Galvin, John R. "Uncomfortable Wars: Toward a New Paradigm." *Parameters* (December 1986): 2–8.

Manwaring, Max G., and John T. Fishel. "Insurgency and Counter-Insurgency: Toward a New Analytical Approach." *Small Wars and Insurgencies* (Winter 1992): 272–310.

Manwaring, Max G., and Court Prisk. "A Strategic View of Insurgencies: Insights from El Salvador." *Small Wars and Insurgencies* (Spring–Summer 1993): 53–72.

Corr, Edwin G. "Part 4, Including the Excluded in El Salvador: Prospects for Democracy and Development." In *Institutions of Development and Democracy*, ed. Peter L. Berger. San Francisco, Calif.: ICS Press, Institute for Contemporary Studies, 1993.

Manwaring, Max G. "Latin American Security and Civil-Military Relations in the New World Disorder." *Low Intensity Conflict and Law Enforcement* (Summer 1995): 29–43.

Corr, Edwin G., and John Van Doorn. "A New Strategy for International Narcotics Control." *Low Intensity Conflict and Law Enforcement* (Summer 1995): 1–28.

Olson, Wm. J., ed. "Small Wars." *Annals of the American Academy of Political and Social Science* (September 1995): special issue.

"Preface: Small Wars Considered," Wm. J. Olson

"Small Wars: Definitions and Dimensions," Roger Beaumont

"The Rule of Law in Small Wars," William V. O'Brien

"The Arms Trade, Military Assistance, and Recent Wars: Change and Continuity," Stephanie G. Neuman

"State Disintegration and Ethnic Conflict: A Framework for Analysis," Richard H. Shultz Jr.

"The Role of the United States in Small Wars," Carnes Lord

"The Balkan Tragedy," Michael Moodie

"The Turkish Imbroglio: ITS Kurds," James Brown

"The Large Small War in Angola," Christine M. Knudsen, with William I. Sartman

"Societal Transformation for Peace in El Salvador," Edwin G. Corr

"Peru's Sendero Luminoso: The Shining Path Beckons," Max G. Manwaring
"Wars without End: The Indo-Pakistani Conflict," Sumit Ganguly

Fishel, John T. "Little Wars, Small Wars, LIC, OOTW, the GAP, and Things That Go Bump in the Night." *Low Intensity Conflict and Law Enforcement* (Winter 1995): 372–98.

Krueger, Kimbra. "U.S. Military Intervention in Third World Conflict." *Low Intensity Conflict and Law Enforcement* (Winter 1995): 399–428.

Manwaring, Max G., and Edwin G. Corr. "A Political-Military Strategy for Development." *International Development Conference (IDC) Policy Bulletin*, June 1996, pp. 1–4.

Krueger, Kimbra. "The Destabilization of Republican Regimes: The Effects of Terrorism on Democratic Societies." *Low Intensity Conflict and Law Enforcement* (Autumn 1996): 253–77.

Manwaring, Max G., and John T. Fishel, eds. "Toward Responsibility in the New World Disorder." *Small Wars and Insurgencies* (Spring 1998): special issue (article titles and authors are listed as chapters under book by the same name above).

Fishel, Kimbra L., and Edwin G. Corr. "The United Nations Involvement in the Salvadoran Peace Process." *World Affairs* (Spring 1998): 202–11.

Manwaring, Max G. "Confronting the 'Savage Wars of Peace': Lessons from the U.S. Army Experience in Bosnia-Herzegovina." *Small Wars and Insurgencies* (Autumn 1998): 134–44.

Fishel, Kimbra L. "Relating Doctrine to Strategy: A Prelude to Success for Twenty-First Century Warfare." *Low Intensity Conflict and Law Enforcement* (Autumn 1999): 23–38.

Manwaring, Max G., ed. "Deterrence in the Twenty-first Century." *Small Wars and Insurgencies* (Autumn 2000): special issue (article titles and authors are listed as chapters under book by the same name below).

Evans, Ernest. "Our Savage Wars of Peace." *World Affairs* (Fall 2000): 90–94.

Fishel, Kimbra L. "Challenging the Hegemon: Al Qaeda's Elevation of Asymmetric Insurgent Warfare onto the Global Arena." In *Networks, Terrorism, and Global Insurgency*, ed. Robert J. Bunker. Taylor and Francis, 2004.

U.S. Armed Forces Field Manuals and Publications

SWORD Papers (out of print). Archived in their entirety by a private research organization, the National Security Archives, in Washington, D.C.

U.S. Army Field Manual (FM) 90-8. *Counterguerilla Operations*, Washington, D.C.: Headquarters, Department of the Army, 1986.

Manwaring, Max G., and Court Prisk. "A Strategic View of Insurgencies: Insights from El Salvador." *Mc Nair Papers*, May 1990.

U.S. Army Field Manual (FM) 100-5. *Operations.* Washington, D.C.: Headquarters, Department of the Army, 1993.

U.S. Army Field Manual (FM) 100-20. *Military Operations in Low Intensity Conflict.* Washington, D.C.: Headquarters, Department of the Army, 1990.

Joint Pub 3-0. *Operations.* Washington, D.C., 1993.

Joint Pub 3-07. *Joint Doctrine for Military Operations Other than War.* Washington, D.C.: Headquarters, Department of the Army, 16 June 1995.

U.S. Army Field Manuel Interim (FMI). *Counterinsurgency Operations.* Washington, D.C.: Headquarters, Department of the Army, October 2004.

Unpublished Papers

Krueger, Kimbra. "The National Security Strategy of the Clinton Administration: An Incorporation of Lessons Learned from Recent Military Interventions." Unpublished master's thesis, University of Oklahoma, June 1995.

Corr, Edwin G., Charito Kruvant, and Max G. Manwaring. "The Search for United States Security: A Forward Strategy for the Twenty-first Century." Unpublished paper, Project in Search of a National Security Strategy, December 2000.

INDEX

ABOUT THE AUTHORS

John T. Fishel is professor of national security policy at the Center for Hemispheric Defense Studies of the National Defense University, having assumed that position in 1997. He has specialized in Latin American affairs throughout his career, focusing on issues of national development and security policy. He has written extensively on civil military operations and peacekeeping and is the author of *Civil Military Operations in the New World* (1997) and the editor and coauthor of *"The Savage Wars of Peace": Toward a New Paradigm of Peace Operations* (1998). He is a past president of the Midwest Association for Latin American Studies (MALAS) and a former president of the North Central Council of Latin Americanists (NCCLA). Dr. Fishel served as a member of the Board of Visitors of the U.S. Army School of the Americas. While on active duty as a lieutenant colonel in the U.S. Army, he served in the United States Southern Command where he was, successively, chief of the Civic Action Branch of the Directorate of Policy, Strategy, and Plans (J5); chief of research and assessments of the Small Wars Operations Research Directorate (SWORD); chief of the Policy and Strategy Division of the J5; and deputy chief of the U.S. Forces Liaison Group. Concurrent with the latter position, he served as special assistant to the commander, U.S. Military Support Group–Panama and to the commander, U.S. Army–South.

Max G. Manwaring holds the General Douglas MacArthur Chair of Research and is professor of military strategy at the U.S. Army War College. He is a retired U.S. Army colonel and has served in various civilian and military positions, including the U.S. Army War College, the U.S. Southern Command, and the Defense Intelligence Agency. Dr. Manwaring holds a Ph.D. in political science from the University of Illinois and is a graduate of the U.S. Army War College. He is the author and coauthor of several articles, chapters, and reports dealing with political-military affairs and global and regional security concerns. He is editor or coeditor of *El Salvador at War*; *Gray Area Phenomena: Confronting the New World Disorder*; *Beyond Declaring Victory and Coming Home: The Challenges of Peace and Stability Operations*; and *The Search for Security: A U.S. Grand Strategy for the Twenty-first Century*.